◉ 汉 ◉ 语 ◉ 教 ◉ 学 ◉ 名 ◉ 家 ◉ 讲 ◉ 坛 ◉

汉语教与学必备：教什么？怎么教？简体
(上) 什么篇：语用与语法走廊

Chinese Essentials: What and How (Volume One)
What: A Functional and Grammatical Walkthrough
(Simplified Chinese Edition)

■ 傅海燕 著 ■

北京语言大学出版社
BEIJING LANGUAGE AND CULTURE UNIVERSITY PRESS

图书在版编目（CIP）数据

汉语教与学必备：教什么？怎么教？上，什么篇：
语用与语法走廊/傅海燕著. – 北京：北京语言大学出版社，2007.05（2013.07 重印）
ISBN 978-7-5619-1867-8
Ⅰ.汉…
Ⅱ.傅…
Ⅲ.汉语–对外汉语教学–教学研究
Ⅳ.H195

中国版本图书馆CIP数据核字（2007）第068226号

北美地区售书独家代理：美国希望教育基金会
Executive Agency in North America: Hope Education Foundation
www.hope-edu.org Tel:1-800-341-7983

书　　名：汉语教与学必备：教什么？怎么教？（上）
　　　　　什么篇：语用与语法走廊（简体）
责任印制：陈　辉

出版发行：北京语言大学出版社 BEIJING LANGUAGE AND CULTURE UNIVERSITY PRESS
社　　址：北京市海淀区学院路 15 号　　邮政编码：100083
网　　址：www. blcup. com
电　　话：发行部　(86 – 10)82303650/3591/3648
　　　　　海外部　(86 – 10)82303080
　　　　　编辑部　(86 – 10)82303647
　　　　　读者服务部　(86 – 10)82303653/3908
　　　　　网上订购电话　(86 – 10)82303668
　　　　　客户服务信箱　service@ blcup. com
印　　刷：北京中科印刷有限公司
经　　销：全国新华书店

版　　次：2007 年 5 月第 1 版　2013 年 7 月第 5 次印刷
开　　本：787 毫米 × 1092 毫米　1/16　印张：23. 25
字　　数：427 千字
书　　号：ISBN 978 – 7 – 5619 – 1867 – 8/H · 07086
　　　　　05500

凡有印装质量问题，本社负责调换。电话：（86–10）82303590

目录
Contents

B. 汉字 Characters 13

1. 数字与生活 Numbers in Life 22

作 者
Author

Haiyan Fu has been teaching Chinese to speakers of other languages at postsecondary institutions since 1982 and teaching high school for the last eight years. She is currently teaching all levels of Mandarin Chinese at Northside College Preparatory High School in Chicago. In 2003, she was selected to appear in the Annenburg Foundation production "Teaching Foreign Languages K-12: Putting the Standards to Practice." Fu is a trainer in the U. S. Department of Education's Teacher-to-Teacher Training Corp; a writer for Chicago Public Schools' Project MAJIC, a U. S. Department of Education-funded effort to develop K-12 curricula for Chinese and Japanese; an AP Chinese textbook reviewer for the College Board, and has been president of the Midwest Chinese Teachers Alliance since 2000. In 2006 she was elected as a board member of Chinese Language Association of Secondary-Elementary Schools.

Fu has a Master's Degree in education from Smith College, and an Ed. D. from the University of Massachusetts at Amherst, specializing in second language acquisition, instructional leadership and curriculum development. She is certified in Chinese, English, ESL, Language Arts and Bilingual Education in the State of Illinois.

傅海燕自 1982 年开始在中国及北美大学从事对外汉语教学。1999 年开始在芝加哥高中教授汉语。2003 年傅老师的课堂教学被选入 Annenburg 基金会与美国外语教学协会委托波士顿电视台录制的课堂教学示范系列，作为培训中小学外语教学师资的样板。2004 年加入美国教育部资助的芝加哥公立学校汉语日语教学大纲编写小组。2004 至 2005 年审阅伊州中文教师资格考试框架设计、内容与评分；2005 年开始为全美大学委员会审阅中文教材。自 2000 年起担任美国中西部中文教师联盟主席。2006 年被选为美国教育部教师对教师培训计划的培训员、美国中小学教师协会理事会理事。

1989 年获史密斯学院教育硕士，1996 年获麻州大学教育学院教育博士。主要研究课堂教学教法及课程设计与发展。持有美国伊州初高中的中文、英文、英文为第二外语、双语教学及语言艺术等科目执教证书。

致 谢
Acknowledgements

After 26 years of teaching Chinese to non-Chinese language speakers, I have accumulated some classroom experience that I wish to share with other teachers. However, I would never have thought about writing anything down if it was not for the encouragement and support of the following people.

My husband, Kenneth Kocanda, urged me to take on this project and helped to edit the book. Without his continuous support and countless hours of work, this book would not have been possible.

Several people gave me feedback and suggestions. The contribution of these three friends, colleagues, and partners on many projects was instrumental in this particular book. Their generosity in sharing their experiences and opinions as well as the encouragement to make this book a reality is a testimonial to their friendship and professionalism and will always be cherished.

Dr. Yu, Hongwei translated the segment of Questions and Answers and compiled the List of Measure Words and the Usage of "duo."

Jane Lu contributed to the early idea of this book and cooperated with me to begin this project.

Dr. Yvonne Lau, who has worked with me on many projects, and given me suggestions on styles of writing and discussed concrete examples of classroom practice with me.

Special gratitude goes to Golden Yuan for believing in me and giving me technical support to publish this book.

I dedicate this book to all my students and their parents, especially those who granted me permission to use their work in this book.

Acknowledgement of Permission:

Student Work (1999 to 2006 Northside College Preparatory High School)

前言
Preface

"What" and "How"
"教什么"与"怎么教"

In Chinese we call teaching — "教书," which literally means "teaching book." Traditionally, a language teacher comes to class with a textbook and student workbooks. The teacher teaches according to the book and students learn from their books. This kind of practice would be convenient if there were books fit for all classroom situations. The reality is that in the United States, Chinese as a world language in the K-12 classroom is an emerging, fast-growing and ever-changing phenomenon. Students of Chinese language are a very diverse population with regard to age, grade levels, needs, language backgrounds and learning styles. Instructional conditions vary in terms of class size, contact hours, intensity of instruction and the availability of equipment and materials, etc. Professional development for teacher preparation and training is inadequate. There is no teaching material that is one-size-fits-all. An effective classroom teacher must have an effective teaching practice to cope with these challenges. Many teachers have organized teaching and learning materials based on the needs and characteristics of students with the goal of making classroom practice more practical than just "teaching books." This is a good practice. This is true teaching: 教学 vs. 教书. This kind of practice should not be used out of desperation but out of necessity.

"Teaching"译成中文常常成了"教书"。按照字面的意思译成英文"教书"就成了"teaching book"。传统的教学方式就是老师照本宣科，学生在练习本上做功课。这样的做法本可方便课堂教学，前提是有一本教科书能满足所有课堂教学的需求。在美国，目前汉语在中小学课堂作为外国语教学虽起步不久，但发展迅速。学生的来源及情况十分复杂。学生的年龄、年级、需要、语言文化背景、学习方式方法都不同；班级人数、授课时间、教学强度、教具和教材的装备不一。教师的培训不足。没有一部教材是万金油。要想教得好，就得找出好的教学办法迎刃而上。很多老师早就开始根据学生情况，针对教学的需求，自己组织上课用的材料。这才是对路的教学：是“教学”而不是“教书”。这样的教学不应是出于不得已，而应是必需。

This series is designed to facilitate true teaching. It aims at reflecting and encouraging a break from traditional practice by combining language materials, teaching references, and instructional design into a single series for easy, quick and solid practical use.

编这套书的目的就是要辅助这样的教学。反映并鼓励这种打破传统的教学办法，把教学的素材、教学参考资料和教案设计集中在一起。使教与学的索引，参考、运用简便，省时，实际。

This series endeavors to face two essential questions for a teacher of K-12 world language:

What do I teach in a K-12 world language classroom?

How do I teach in a K-12 world language classroom?

这套书试图面对中小学（幼儿园至12年级）汉语作为外国语教学课堂教学的两个根本问题：教什么？怎么教？

Let's consider these two questions in simple and realistic terms.

我们一起用简单而现实的语言来探讨这两个问题。

"What"
“教什么”

We expect young learners of Chinese to become world citizens and lifelong learners.

作为教师，我们期望我们的学生能成为世界公民和终身学者。

Language is a tool of communication, and thus, we teach learners a new communication tool. We teach interaction and good manners. We teach to develop high proficiency in Chinese.

语言是交际的工具。我们教我们的学生新的交际工具。教他们与人交流和交流的方式方法。教他们发展交际的技能。

Language is part of culture, and represents and reflects the world views and customs held by the people of a culture. Therefore, as language teachers, we teach learners a new perspective on life experience that is different in many ways from their own. We provoke curiosity and nurture respect and love through achieving understanding in another language.

语言是文化不可分割的部分。语言代表并反映不同文化中人们的世界观和风俗习惯。在教语言的同时，我们介绍给我们的学生新的、与他们自己不同的对待人生的看法和角度。我们通过了解另一种语言引发好奇，培养尊重和爱。

Learning a foreign language is something with which most young learners have no experience. In addition to teaching a language, we teach learners how to learn something that is challenging and unfamiliar. We impart knowledge and skills so that at a young age, learners can discover a new world through studying a world language and discover their own strength in learning. We foster diligence and work ethic, and teach them develop knowledge and learning skills.

在课堂上学习外国语是学习一个对大多数幼小学生来说完全陌生的知识领域。我们教给他们怎么学具有挑战性的科目。我们传授知识和方法。让孩子们通过学习一种新的语言去学着探索新的世界，发现自己的能力和长处。我们培养勤奋和上进。我们教他们学会知识及学习方法并锻炼学习能力。

"How"
"怎么教"

A language teacher's job is to make the learning process easy, fun, and to make learning make sense to learners. We try to engage learners in this long-term, effective and fruitful endeavor.

教师的职责是将学习的过程和学习的内容化难为易，做到寓教于乐，使学习触类旁通。通过这样的教学理念与实践让学生致力于长期、有效的努力中。

Making learning easy, making it fun, and making it make sense are correlated. If something does not make sense, then it won't be fun, thus it won't be easy. If something is too hard, then it is not fun. If something is interesting, it must make sense one way or another and because it is fun it will be enjoyable and it won't feel too hard. If it feels easy the learner will be more inclined to continue.

化难为易、寓教于乐、触类旁通是相关的。不懂就没意思，就不会容易；太难就不会有趣；有意思一定是理解了妙趣所在；而有趣使你更投入从而不感到太辛苦。感觉容易就不会因畏惧而退缩。

Make it Easy. Nothing is easy. Learning a language is not an easy endeavor. But this does not mean there is no way to make the learning process easier for learners. Making learning easy by no means implies a lowering of standards. It simply means finding sensible ways to set up learners for success instead of failure.

化难为易。世上无易事。学习一门外国语绝非一件容易的事。但是这并不是说不能找出办法简化学习的过程。化难为易也不是要降低标准。化难为易是找出办法帮助学生成功。

Make it Fun. Making it fun eases the anxiety, sustains interest, and lets learners enjoy the process. It promotes the active participation of learners.

寓教于乐是为了消除紧张，保持学习兴趣，让学生在学习上感到满足与愉快。鼓励学生的积极参与。

Make it Make Sense. Making it understandable makes learning meaningful to learners. It requires the instructor to understand learners. What makes sense and what does not to these learners?

触类旁通指的是学生的理解。一方面，学习的内容要在学生理解程度以内，并能加强学生对目的语言和文化的理解，达到举一反三；另一方面，学生觉得学习的内容有意义，即与他们的生活有联系，学习的内容可以用来表达自己的思想感情。这需要教师了解学生。

Being able to speak in a foreign language is a rewarding experience, especially for a language like Chinese. Regardless of any scientific evidence, most of people have the notion that Chinese is a harder language to learn than most others. So, if a young learner speaks Chinese successfully, the sense of pride and achievement will be tremendous. This enthusiasm can translate into a passion and a motivation for more learning, even for other subject areas.

学会一门外国语是一个有回报的经历，特别是学会说汉语。不管有否科学依据，多数人觉得汉语是种很难学的语言。要是一个小孩子会说汉语，就会感到自豪，会有很大的成就感。这样的热情鼓励学习，不光是汉语还可以派生对其他学科的学习热忱。

How does a teacher achieve the above objectives? The answer is: Know your students, know your subject, and know your methodologies.

教师怎么才能做到“化难为易、寓教于乐、触类旁通”呢？答案是：懂得并了解你的学生，懂得并了解你要教什么，懂得并了解你怎么教。

This series will help you with the latter two areas.

这套书帮助你弄明白这后两项。

Integration of “What” and “How”
“教什么”与“怎么教”的结合

The “What” part of the book provides a series of building blocks. Each block is structured with a topic and connects functional language use with linguistic structures. Grammatical patterns are grouped according to functional use, and vocabulary is ordered by category and topic.

这套书的“什么篇”介绍一系列的集装板块。每一个板块都围绕一个话题将语言材料与语言功用串联在一起。也就是说，语言的语法结构是按语言的功用挑选组装在一起的。词汇是按话题和类别排列的。

The “How” part presents a progression and sequence of teaching and learning for Chinese in grades 6 ~ 12 classrooms. It demonstrates sampled thematic unit and lesson design variables and related instructional strategies, activities, and assessments to provide users with concrete "how" tips for good classroom practices and guides the user to connect "what" and "how." The unit design intends to be pragmatic, yet flexible and helpful to the users. At the same time, it respects the users' choice of methods and texts.

这套书的"怎么篇"建议中小学、主要是6 ~ 12 年级的汉语课堂教与学的进程和步骤。建议并示范以主题贯连的教学单元、教案设计，包括变量的设计；有关的教学指导建议、课堂活动和测试。并给使用者一些具体的课堂教学的小诀窍。引导使用者把"教什么"和"怎么教"——教学内容和教学方法联系起来。教学单元的设计力求具实用性、灵活性和支持性，同时尊重使用者对教材和教法的选择。

The design comes from this analogy:

这套书的设计来自这样一个比喻：

Building a house is a constructive process. When building a house, we must have basic building materials, such as bricks, a framework, a blueprint, etc. The process is initiated with a purpose, proceeds with a blueprint, and involves an architect and the work, skills, and creativity of builders.

盖一座房子是一个建造过程。盖房子要有基本的建造原料，如砖瓦泥沙等；要搭起架子来，还要有蓝图。这个全过程的展开首先需要一个明确目的，然后要图纸设计，要有建筑设计师和建筑工人的参与，贡献他们的智慧与劳动，他们的技术和创造精神。

In a language class, a teacher facilitates a creative, constructive process for learners engaging the target language. This resembles the process of building a house. The learners are builders. The teacher is an architect. The purpose of the tasks is to build learners' proficiency in the target language; the blueprints are unit designs and lesson plans — a carefully structured road map to success; the bricks are the vocabulary; the frameworks for connecting basic structures are sentence patterns.

在语言课堂上，老师协助学生参与学习目的语这样一个创造性的、建设性的过程。就像盖房子的过程一样。学生是建筑工人，老师是建筑设计师；教学的目的是发展目的语的语言能力和水平；蓝图就是精心设计的教学大纲和教案，建筑材料是词汇及使用知识，框架是语法句型和运用。

However, the construction that takes place in a language classroom requires more when compared to constructing a building. 1) The classroom construction process is a hands-on experience using more experimentation. It is an interactive and on-going process with goals of long-term progress, requiring recycling and spiraling language materials. 2) The teacher is more than an architect. A teacher is a provider, a facilitator, a tutor, a motivator, and a mentor. A teacher must provide the learners with building materials, to help to develop the skills, and to give room and opportunity for the learners' creativity. More importantly, a teacher must demonstrate, model, and nurture love for learning and ways to achieve learning. 3) The learners are special builders. The learners are in different developmental stages in terms of physical, mental, and emotional maturity. They have specific characteristics and needs in terms of cognition, motivation, learning styles, and cultural and linguistic diversity. More importantly, the learners must feel ownership in this constructive process. They are decision-makers and critical thinkers in learning as well as active and creative users of the language. The new language should become a conduit for expressing their true feelings.

然而，课堂中的建设过程比盖房更复杂。1）这个过程不仅需要第一手参与的经历，而且是一个不断尝试的过程；是一个有长远目标的、互动的、进行的过程；需要不断复习、重复，螺旋式上升性地运用语言材料。2）老师不仅仅是一个建筑工程师，还是一个供应师，不断地提供建筑的材料，帮助提高建筑的技巧，并给予机会让学生有创造发展的空间；同时老师还得展示、示范，培养学生对学习的热爱和学习的技能。3）学生是特别的建筑工人。他们处于身、心、情感发育的不同成熟阶段。他们在认知、学习动机、学习风格、语言文化背景方面的特点和需求不一。更重要的是，他们要在学习过程中有主人翁的态度和权益。他们是学习和语言运用的决策人、思考者。目的语将成为他们表达真实情感的又一渠道。

This series is an endeavor to bring "What" and "How" together in an organic way by providing "what" as building materials with basic frameworks and demonstrating "how" as blueprints. It is written with a sincere hope to provide a service to K-12 Chinese language teachers and learners everywhere.

这套书以"什么篇"提供建筑材料和框架，"怎么篇"做蓝图，两部分所反映的教学理念和思路，探索的教学设计和框架，分享的教学经验和技巧，力图将"教什么"和"怎么教"有机地结合起来。这不是一套语法理论的书，也不是一套教学法研究的书。而是为中小学汉语教学课堂提供的具体服务，是中小学汉语作为外国语教与学的参考、辅助与必备。

Fu, Haiyan, Ed. D.

傅海燕

简介

Introduction

What do we teach in our grades 6 to 12 Chinese language classrooms? How do we teach effectively? These are two important questions. “What” and “how” are integrated in the sense that “what” supports and supplements “how”, and “how” guides and implements “what”. This series intends to look at these two questions from a practical perspective classroom teacher's point of view to share some wisdom and instructional tips. For the convenience of presentation, the series divides real 6-12 Chinese classroom practice into a “What” section and a “How” section. We begin with the section on “What” and followed with the section on “How”.

在我们的6~12年级的汉语课堂上，我们到底教什么、怎么教才更有效果？这是两个大而复杂的问题。在现实的课堂上，“教什么”和“怎么教”是一个整体。“教什么”是“怎么教”的框架和实体；“怎么教”引导并贯彻“教什么”。这套书试图从一个实际的角度，一个课堂教师的视角来探讨这两个问题。为了论述方便，将6~12年级汉语课堂教学的实际分成“教什么”和“怎么教”两个部分。先讨论“教什么”再讲“怎么教”。

The section “What: A Functional and Grammatical Walkthrough” provides a series of building blocks. Each block is structured with a topic to connect functional use with linguistic structures. Grammatical patterns are grouped according to functional use, and vocabulary is ordered by category and topic. The design and organization come from the following rationales:

- First, the ultimate purpose of language is communication, thus the starting point of language teaching and learning should be meaningful and functional.
- Second, grammatical patterns and vocabulary are fundamental to the construction of meaning. They are the organic part and substance of meaningful and functional communication.
- Thirdly, 6-12 graders are neither young children nor adults. They are adolescents. They are a special group of learners. Some of their learning characteristics are expressing individual identity and ideas, looking for patterns

and thinking analytically and critically.

Effective classroom teaching and learning must reflect, incorporate and facilitate these needs and learning styles of young learners.

这套书的什么篇：语用和语法走廊，介绍一系列的集装板块。每一个板块都是围绕一个话题将语言材料与语言功用串联在一起。也就是说，语言的语法结构是按语言的功用挑选组装在一起的。词汇是按话题和分类出现的。这样的设计与组织基于以下的理念：

首先，语言的使用目的是交流。语言教学的起点应是有意义和实用的。

其二，语法句型和词汇是表达语意的基本材料，是实际交流的有机组成和实质。

第三，6~12年级的学生不是小孩子也非成人。他们是青少年。青少年是一组特殊的学习群体。表达自我与思想、搜寻概念模式、分析批判思考是他们学习的一些特点。

有效的课堂教学必须反映、包容、并支助学生的需求和学习风格。

The section aims at providing a service to 6-12 grades Chinese teachers (especially those new to the profession) with clear mapping, quick reference and supplementary materials for classroom teaching and learning.

这套书正是要为课堂教师特别是刚入行的教师服务。为课堂教与学提供清晰的路线图，一目了然地查阅资料和课堂用教材。

使用说明
Users' Guide

A teacher, no matter what methods and textbooks are used for classroom instruction, needs to take two important steps when designing a lesson plan. First, knowing what to teach: having a clear picture or framework of the content of teaching and learning and a general mapping of specifics and details of the content; Second, knowing how to teach: considering the needs and characteristics of the learners, then applying practical ideas and strategies for instruction and activities.

一个教师，不管在课堂教学时用哪种教学法、用什么教科书，在设计教案时需要两个重要的步骤：其一是知道教什么。脑子里应该对教学内容有一个清楚的概念，对教学的种种细节有一个大致的规划；其二是明白怎么教。从学生的需求和特点出发想出课堂教学与活动的办法，拿出招数来。

A learner, from time to time, needs more materials and references for intensive and extended learning.

学生呢，时不时地总是需要更多的材料和资料用来强化和扩展学习内容。

The purpose of this Section is to meet these challenges.

本书什么篇的目的就是要面对这两方面的挑战。

Focusing on the first step "what," we provide quick, easy, and practical content to be applied in the 6-12 Chinese classrooms. The content of teaching and learning is organized by topic, theme-based grammatical patterns, and categories of vocabulary.

针对"教和学什么"的问题，什么篇为6~12年级汉语课堂教学提供切实可行的教学内容。教学的内容是按题目编排的，按主题组织语法点、分类出词汇。

The second step is "how." The sample unit designs map suggested teaching scope, sequence and content organization by themes. All unit designs and teaching tips are in Chapter Two.

"怎么教和学"这部分内容均在怎么篇里。在这部分里，介绍了十个主题教学单元及教学参考建议，教与学的范围、步骤和内容都由主题连贯起来。

Intended Objectives 目标

1. To integrate content and context of language use;
2. To reveal vertical as well as horizontal connections between grammatical patterns and functions of language;
3. To make the content of teaching and learning more flexible and accessible for various and diverse classroom situations; and
4. To make reviewing, recycling and spiraling language materials for teaching and learning more convenient.

"什么篇"的设计构思的目的是:

1. 将语言使用的内涵和外延融会在一起;
2. 从而揭示语法与语用横向与纵向的联系;
3. 使教学内容更具灵活性，便利多样化的课堂教学;
4. 方便复习、重复和螺旋上升式地使用语言教学材料。

Format 编排

1. Topics are selected according to functional use of the language;
2. Teaching and learning foci and related cruxes are listed as a table of contents, and then demonstrated and explained in order under each topic;
3. Related grammatical patterns and vocabulary are listed under each topic; and
4. Cultural or other relevant notes, if any, are at the end of the topical section.

"什么篇"编排原则:

1. 题目按语用挑选;
2. 每个题目下的篇章的目录列出本章节的教学重点及相关的教学难点，依次示范与讲解;
3. 每一题目下列出相关的语法点及词汇表;
4. 有关文化或其他注释。

Application　使用

1. Teachers may use this Section to become familiar with the teaching and learning content in a context of young English speakers in 6-12 classrooms.
2. Teachers will find quick references and explanations about some of the difficulties experienced by young English speakers in 6-12 classrooms.
3. Teachers may incorporate the provided content materials to customize lesson plans or supplement other existing teaching and learning materials.
4. Teachers and learners may pinpoint the connection between grammatical patterns and functional language use.
5. Teachers may directly use or demonstrate the charts and vocabulary lists presented here.
6. Learners may expand their language use by using all the information provided.
7. Parents and administrators may get an overview of Chinese teaching and learning in 6-12 classrooms in order to provide supervision and feedback about the process.

“什么篇”的适用对象：

1. 教师可以用本章全面熟悉6～12汉语课堂教学的内容；
2. 教师可以快速查阅6～12汉语课堂教学中出现的难点的注解；
3. 教师可以用本部分中提供的教学素材根据自己的需求编排教案或用来做补充教材；
4. 教师和学生都可以对语法点和语用的联系一目了然；
5. 教师可以直接使用或在课上展示本部分中的词汇表；
6. 学生可以用本部书中的资料扩展语用范围；
7. 家长和校方行政管理人员能对汉语教学的概况有一定的了解，从而对课堂的教与学有一定的监督指导。

A

语音——汉语拼音

Phonetics
—Hanyu *Pinyin*

现行使用的汉语语音拼写系统有数个，拼音是其中之一。为什么我们教与学拼音呢？有几个实用的原因。

There are several systems in use of Chinese pronunciation. *pinyin* is one of them. Why do we teach/learn *pinyin*? There are several practical reasons:

1）使用拼音的人口最多。

2）联合国指定拼音为拼写中国城市和姓名的标准方式。

3）多数新出的字典和出版物用拼音作为汉语语音的拼注方法。

4）拼音是一种计算机输入方法。可以直接使用英文键盘。使用者不用重新背替代键码。

这对母语为英文的中文文字处理软件使用者来说，是方便快捷的。

1）*pinyin* is used by most Chinese-speaking populations.

2）The United Nations has designated *pinyin* as the standard method for spelling Chinese names and cities.

3）Most newer dictionaries and publications use *pinyin* as phonetic spelling for Chinese characters.

4）*pinyin* as an input method for computerized word processing uses a standard English keyboard. It does not require the user to memorize a new keyboard arrangement.

Thus, it is convenient for English speakers to use.

校方、家长和学生可以根据学习的目的和需求作出教学上的选择。如何有效地教语音请参照《怎么篇：组织教学》中有关问答部分和列举的教学活动。

School, parents and students should make the decision and choice based on the needs. As for how to teach writing characters effectively, please refer to its questions and answers and sample activities on teaching and learning phonetics in Section Two *Designing Teaching—How to Teach and Learn.*

本节简单介绍中小学生学拼音应知道和注意的有关使用拼音的知识，重点是语音、声调和拼读。

This chapter introduces very basic practical knowledge about *pinyin* and its use in K-12 Chinese classroom instruction. It emphasizes pronunciation, tones, and phonetic spelling.

教学重点 Content of Teaching and Learning

音节	Syllables
声母及特点	Initials and Their Features
韵母及特点	Finals and Their Features
声调	Tones
汉语语音表（见附录）	Phonetic Chart（应加 bopomofo 符号）

教学难点 Difficulties

韵母的拼写	Spelling of the Finals
声母的读法	Pronunciation of the Initials
拼读	Pronunciation of Words
声调标号	Tone Marks

教学重点

Content of Teaching and Learning

音节 Syllables

基础的汉语词语一般为单音节词，由一个声母与一个韵母结合发声。一共有差不多402个这样的音节组合。

The basic Chinese word is monosyllable which consists of a consonant and a vowel. There are about 402 such units.

声母及特点 Initials and Their Features

声母也叫Initials，因为声母发起一个音节。汉语的声母不能单独发音，必须与韵母拼读才能发音。一共有21个声母。

In the *pinyin* system, consonants are called "initials" because they usually begin with a syllable. Chinese initials cannot be pronounced without finals. There are 21 such initials.

韵母及特点 Finals and Their Features

韵母也叫Finals，因为音节以韵母结尾。一共有39个韵母。

In the *pinyin* system, finals end with syllables of sound. There are 39 such finals.

韵母的发音 Pronunciation of the Finals

读韵母要注意如下方面：

1）英语的复合元音在发音时有从一个音向另一个音的过渡；汉语不同。

2）对学生来讲几个有问题的韵母：

"ian"听起来更像"ien"但拼做"ian"。

"o"只可跟"b，p，m，f"拼，独自不能发声。

"er"只有三个声调，没有第一声；第二声如"儿"；第三声如"耳"；第四声与其他声调略不同，如"二"。

"e"不是英文的"ee"，而"i"雷同英文的"ee"，不是英文的"ai"。

跟"zh，ch，sh，r，z，c，s"相拼的"-i"不是同一个"i"。

To pronounce Chinese finals correctly, pay attention to the followings:

1) When pronouncing compound vowels in English, there is a distinct, though smooth transition from one sound to the next. In Chinese, compound finals should be uttered as one sound. No transition should be detected.

2) Learner be aware: There are a few finals which are more problematic than others to English learners:

"ian" sounds more like "ien" but is spelled as "ian";

"o" only goes with "b, p, m and f." It cannot be pronounced without a consonant.

"er" has only 3 tones. The first tone is absent. The second tone is pronounced as in "儿", The third tone is as in "耳" and the fourth tone, is a little different, as in "二".

"e" is not an "ee" sound, while "i" is an "ee" sound, not an "ai" sound as in English. " – i" is not a real "i" and is not an "ee" sound either, it only goes with "zh, ch, sh, r, z, c, s".

韵母的拼写　Spelling of the Finals

韵母按其发音特点可分成4组：

Vowels can be divided by articulation into four groups.

1）第一组韵母是独立的韵母。可自成音节，拼写不变。有：

Group I: Independent vowels. When standing alone as a word, nothing changes. e. g. :

a, ai, ao, an, ang, e, ei, en, eng, er, o, ou, ong

2）第二组韵母是以 i 开头的韵母。有：

Group II：Any vowel started with an "i"

i, ia, iao, ian, iang, ie, in, ing, iu（iou）, iong

3）第三组韵母是以 u 开头的韵母。有：

Group III：Any vowel started with an "u"

u, ua, uai, uan, uang, ueng, ui（uei）, un（uen）, uo

4）第四组韵母是以 ü 开头的韵母。有：

Group IV：Any vowel started with a "ü"

ü, üe, üan, ün

第二、三、四组的韵母在自成音节时，拼写都有变化。请参看教学难点一"韵母的拼写"。

All Groups II to VI vowels, as stand-alone syllables, need spelling changes. Please refer to Difficulty One "难点一 韵母的拼写" below.

声调 Tones

声调是构成词语意义不可缺少的一部分。

英语是一种有语调的语言：句尾的调高表示语气，由此表明话语的情绪即意思。

汉语是一种有声调的语言：声调有区别语义的作用。汉语普通话有 4 个基本声调和一个轻声。

Tones are an important part of the meaning of words.

English is an intonation language. The pitch at the end of a sentence indicates mood. For example, pitch typically rises at the end of a question.

Chinese is a tone language. The tone of each sound differentiates meaning. In Common Speech（普通话 *Putonghua*）, there are four tones plus a neutral tone.

汉语语音表 Phonetic Chart（应加 bopomofo 符号）

（见附录）

教与学提示　Tips for Teaching/Learning *Pinyin*

中小学生学习拼音应在有语义的上下文中进行。首先明确一些概念："音"和"词"的区别："音"是发声；"词"是有语义的声音。

Learn phonetics in meaningful contexts. First, some definitions: The difference between "sound" and "words": Sounds—noise and words—sounds with meaning.

汉语的单音节词/字有三个相辅相成的组成部分：形，声，义。

三者缺一不可。对中小学生来说，学说话，哪怕是一个字一个字地、一个词一个词地、一个句一个句地说，也比分开来学发音、声调和拼读更有实际意义。在学说话的过程中学会正确地发音、正确的声调、正确地使用词语、正确地拼读和书写。

In Chinese, a monosyllable word/character has three componants: Shape—appearance; Pronunciation—sound, tone, symbol/spelling and Meaning (s).

They are inseparable. Therefore it will make more sense to K-12 learners when teaching phonetics, we deal with these elements/aspects at once. Besides learning all the sounds, spellings and phonetic rules, we learn how to say them for meaningful purposes. That is to say, when learning words, we learn how to pronounce them correctly and fluently and we learn how to spell and write them correctly.

如何有效地教语音，请参照《怎么篇：组织教学》中有关问答部分和列举的教学活动。

For teaching pronunciation effectively, please refer to Volume Two *How: Designing Teaching*. It also contains questions and answers and sample activities on teaching and learning phonetics.

教学难点

Difficulties

难点一 韵母的拼写 Spelling of the Finals

韵母按其发音特点可分成4组。

There are four groups of vowels according to the articulation：

第一组韵母是独立的韵母。可自成音节，拼写不变。

Group Ⅰ：Independent vowels. When standing alone as a word，nothing changes.

a，ai，ao，an，ang，e，ei，en，eng，er，o，ou，ong

第二组韵母是以i开头的韵母。

Group Ⅱ：Any vowel starts with an “i”.

i，ia，iao，ian，iang，ie，in，ing，iu（iou），iong

这组韵母在自成音节时，拼写有变化：

When standing alone as a word，two situations occur：

a. 当韵母有复合元音出现时，“i” 由 “y” 替代。

“i” will be changed to “y” when the final consists of more than one vowel.

羊　yáng　sheep

b. 当韵母只有一个元音 “i” 时，前加 “y”。

a “y” will be added at the front when the final has only one vowel.

一　yī　one

第三组韵母是以u开头的韵母。

Group Ⅲ：Any vowel starts with an “u”.

u，ua，uai，uan，uang，ueng，ui，un，uo

这组韵母在自成音节时，拼写有变化：

When standing alone as a word, two situations occur:

a. 当韵母有复合元音出现时，“u” 由 “w” 替代。

“u” will be changed to “w” when the final consists of more than one vowel.

完 wán finish

b. 当韵母只有一个元音 “u” 时，前加 “w”。

a “w” will be added at the front when the final has only one vowel.

五 wǔ five

第四组韵母是以 ü 开头的韵母。

Group IV: Any vowel starts with a “ü”.

ü, üe, üan, ün

这组韵母在自成音节时，拼写有变化。在韵母前加 “y”。

When standing alone as a word, spelling changes and a “y” will be added at the front.

语 yǔ language

其他应注意 Spelling Exceptions

第一组，没问题。Group I: Trouble free.

第二组，“iou” 与声母拼时，写成 “iu”:

Group II: “iou” when spelled with a consonant, appears as “iu” as in:

六 liù six

在自成音节时，拼写成 “you”:

When standing alone as a word, it becomes “you,” as in:

有 yǒu have

第三组，“uei” 和 “uen”

“uei” 与声母拼时，写成 “ui”:

“uei” when spelled with a consonant, appears as “ui” as in:

会 huì know how

在自成音节时，拼写成“wei”：

When standing alone as a word, it becomes “wei” as in:

为　　wèi　　be

“uen”与声母拼时，写成“un”：

“uen,” when spelled with a consonant, appears as “un” as in:

混　　hùn　　mix

在自成音节时，拼写成“wen”：

When standing alone as a word, it becomes “wen” as in:

问　　wèn　　ask

第四组的韵母只可以跟5个声母拼：“j, q, x, n, l”。

Group IV: This group goes with only five initials: “j, q, x, n and l”.

跟“j, q, x”拼时，去掉韵母上面的两个小点。

When spelled with “j”, “q” and “x”, they drop the two dots on top of the vowel, as in:

句　jù　sentence　　群　qún　group　　学　xué　learning

跟“n, l”拼时，保持两个小点 ü：

When spelled with “n” and “l”, they keep the two dots on top of the vowel, as in:

女　nǚ　woman　　绿　lǜ　green

难点二　声母的读法 Pronunciation of Initials

汉语的声母本身不发音，只有在跟韵母结合时才发音。由于拼音用英文的字母做书写符号，请注意发音上的不同。幼小的学生如果同时学习英文的拼读，更要在教学中强调区分。

Initials in Chinese cannot be pronounced without the help of vowels. The *pinyin* system utilizes Western alphabets for spelling. The learner should be aware of the differences in pronunciation. For K-3 students, if learning *pinyin* at the same time with English spelling, differentiation is needed.

难点三 拼读 Pronunciation of Words

在语流中，拼读时有变声变调的情况。

Some words, when in combination with others, change tone.

变调 Changing of the Tones

1）两个三声相遇，第一个三声变成二声。

When a third tone meets with another third tone the first third tone changes into a second tone.

ˇ + ˇ = ˊ + ˇ
你 好 = 你 好

2）“不 not, no” 是第四声。当 “不” 后面跟了四声词时变成二声。

When “不 not, no” of being fourth tone is followed by another fourth tone “不” changes into a second tone.

ˋ ˋ = ˊ ˋ
不对 = 不 对

3）“一” 是一声。但若 “一” 后跟了一声或三声词时变成四声。

When “一 one” of first tone is followed by another first tone or third tone “一” changes into a fourth tone.

ˉ ˉ = ˋ ˉ　　ˉ ˇ = ˋ ˇ
一 些 = 一 些　　一 点 = 一 点

“一” 后跟了四声词时变二声。

When “yi” of first tone is followed by another fourth tone “yi” changes into a second tone.

ˉ ˋ = ˊ ˋ
一 件 = 一 件

难点四　声调标号 Tone Marks

在哪儿标声调号？Where do we put the tone marks?

在元音“ɑ e o i/u”上。先后的优先顺序也是如此。

Tone marks are put on vowels. But if the vowel contains more than one of the above letters, in general, the priority order goes like this:

ɑ e o i/u.

In other words, in a situation like:

“ɑi”, the tone mark should be on the “ɑ”;

“ei”, on the “e”;

“ou”, on the “o”;

“iu”, on the “u”;

“ui”, on the “i”.

B

汉字 Characters

汉字是汉语的文字表达符号。学习汉字包括认读和书写。记忆和书写汉字是英语为母语背景的学生学习上的一个难点。

本节针对幼儿园至十二年级学生学习上的难点，简单介绍学习汉字所应具有的知识。其中包括：汉字的使用，汉字的形成与汉字的书写和汉字文字处理软件的使用。如何有效地教汉字，请参照《怎么篇：组织教学》中有关问答部分和列举的教学活动。

Chinese characters are the basic symbols of the Chinese written system. Learning Chinese characters includes the recognition and production of texts using characters. Memorizing and writing characters present challenges to English-speaking learners.

This chapter introduces the basic knowledge of learning characters keeping the needs of K-12 learners in mind. The basic knowledge includes the use of Chinese characters, the composition and writing of Chinese character, and the use of Chinese word processors. As for how to teach writing characters effectively, please refer to the question and answer and sample activities on teaching and learning characters in chapters in Volume Two *How*: *Designing Teaching*.

教学重点 Content of Teaching and Learning

汉字的使用	The Use of Chinese Characters
汉字的书写形成	Chinese Characters and Composition
书写汉字	Writing Characters
用计算机写汉字	Computerized Writing

教学难点 Difficulties

记忆汉字	Memorizing Chinese Characters

教学重点

Content of Teaching and Learning

汉字的使用 The Use of Chinese Characters

汉字有两个书写版本：繁体和简体。有的地区、有的人用繁体字；有的地区、有的人用简体字。古代的文献用繁体字，现代很多地区和大多数人在日常生活中用简体字。K-12 的学生应知道、接受和尊重这一语言文字使用的历史与现状。校方、家长和学生可以根据学习的目的和需求作出教学上的选择。

现在的计算机技术可以使两种字体在转换时易如反掌。同时为不同需要的学生提供两个版本也不是一个大的技术问题。

There are often two systems of Chinese characters: traditional and simplified. Some Chinese-speaking regions and people use traditional characters and others use the simplified versions. Ancient historical documents and texts were written in traditional characters. In modern times, many regions and the majority of Chinese users employ the simplified version of characters. K-12 learners should be aware of this and accept and respect the history and reality of this aspect of Chinese. As for which version to study, school, parents and students should make the decision based on the needs of the students.

Computer technology, namely the word processor, has simplified use of both versions along with the easy conversion of texts from one system to the other. Making texts available in both or either version according to student requests should not be a big technical problem.

汉字的书写形成 Chinese Characters and Composition

一般对中小学生简单介绍三个类型的汉字。（参考摘录书目：胡双宝《汉字史话》中华书局 1980）

We usually introduce three kinds of characters to K-12 learners. (Reference: Hu, Shuangbao《汉字史话》中华书局 1980)

象形字 Pictographs

象形字来源于古代人对自然事物、事件及景物形象的图画描绘。这样的字一般为独体字。这样的字虽不多，但是形象能引起学生的兴趣，吸引学生的注意力。

Pictographs originated from ancient drawings of nature, objects, and events. Most pictographs have only single element. Although they are not in great numbers, introducing this kind of characters can stimulate student's interest and attention to learning.

会意字 Ideographs

会意字是象形字的引申，常由两个象形字组合而成，把两个或更多的形象放在一起力图表达一个新的或抽象的意思。可以在学习象形字的基础上学习。

Ideographs are mostly the combination of two pictographs. Two or more images together express a new or abstract meaning. We should use pictographs as the basis for introducing ideographs.

形声字 Pictophonetics

我们今天用的多数的汉字是形声字。形声字也是合体字。一般由两部分组成：一部分表意思，一部分表读音。由于长时间的进化演变，表义的部分可能已失去原来的意思，表音的部分并不规律。切忌"望文生义"造成理解错误，或"望字生音"念错字。

The great majority of the characters we use today fall into this category. A pictophonetic character has two parts: A picto part indicates meaning and a phonetic part indicates sound. Due to centuries of evolution, changes in meaning and pronunciation occurred. Many characters have lost their original meanings and, usually, the sound indicators of characters are not regular or accurate. Be aware of this in actual use.

书写汉字 Writing Characters

书写汉字主要是谈手写与用计算机写。如何有效地教汉字，请参照《怎么篇：组织教学》中有关问答部分和列举的教学活动。

Writing characters refers to producing characters by hand and creating texts with a computer. As for how to teach writing characters effectively, please refer to the question and answer and sample activities on teaching and learning characters chapters in Volume Two *How*: *Designing Teaching*.

手写汉字 Writing by Hand

手写汉字可以用至少三个方法来提高书写记忆的能力。一个是利用对偏旁部首的记忆和提示，一个是理顺笔画熟练笔顺，还有一个是通过书法艺术。

There are at least three methods to help with memorizing characters. First, relies on radicals for hints; the second is to practise through correct stroke orders, and the third is to use calligraphy.

偏旁部首 Radicals

（参考摘录书目：胡双宝《汉字史话》中华书局 1980）

偏旁部首被称为义符，其本身曾有一定的意义。每个偏旁部首都能有数个至多个组合。偏旁部首不仅可以用来查新字。从记忆的角度讲，重复出现的符号容易记得牢。新出现的字中如有已知会写的部件容易记住。另外，偏旁部首自有定义对一些新字的字义有提示作用。按偏旁部首或已知的独体字来学写新字容易帮助记忆。

Radicals are pictographs used in character dictionary indices. (Reference: Hu, Shuangbao《汉字史话》中华书局 1980) From the view point of memory, symbols that appear repeatedly have a better chance to be remembered. If a new character has a familiar radical, it will be easier to learn. Also, radicals were originally pictographs. They have their own orginal meanings. They often provide hints to the meanings or nature of the characters they are used in.

笔画笔顺　Stroke Orders

老一辈的人学汉字都十分强调正确的笔画和笔顺。理顺笔画熟练笔顺，熟能生巧，顺理成章，不失为帮助记忆的好办法之一。帮助学生养成书写的好习惯。但不可认定这是唯一的办法，过分偏颇而顾此失彼，使幼小学生失去写字的兴趣。多鼓励少批评。

Older generations of Chinese learners learned writing characters with prescribed stroke orders. Practising the right way of writing helps the students to make progress and achieve fluency. Younger learners should be encouraged to foster good writing habits. However, no one way is the only way. Gaining encouragement and learning through successful experience is the key. It is important to constantly give young students positive reinforcement rather than a negative one.

书法艺术　Art of Calligraphy

书法是一门艺术。练习书法不仅是学习文化的一部分，也可以帮助中小学生加强对汉字的记忆理解。同时对书法艺术的学习与欣赏还能帮助学生增加对汉字书写的热情，激发其更大的学习动力。

Calligraphy is an art form. Practising Chinese calligraphy is not only an integral part of learning the Chinese culture, but will also be helpful in remembering and understanding characters. Learning and appreciating Chinese calligraphy will inspire and motivate young students to write and practise characters.

用计算机写汉字　Computerized Writing

用计算机写汉字的好处

用计算机写汉字是件好事情。首先，文章可以随意编排。重整段落，修改内容，转换字体都不在话下。可用的字体数不胜数。还有，用文字处理软件可以念文章、翻译文章，并能帮助和极大地支持初学者阅读和编写中文文章。

The Benifits:

Using a word processor to create Chinese texts is a great thing. First, texts can be easily manipulated and the transfer of passages or the revision of texts is no longer a major issue. Conversion back and forth between traditional and simplified versions requires only a few mouse clicks and choices of fonts are numerous. Second, with a word processor, a beginning learner can access and create texts in Chinese with tremendous assistance and support. For example, written texts can be read by the computers for listening or be translated from one language to another.

用计算机写汉字的三个可能的麻烦

A. "ü"在哪儿?

这是一个技术问题。用拼音输入时的方便在于可以直接使用英文键盘。但是英文键盘没有"ü"。不同的中文文字处理软件有不同的解决办法:例如,微软用"V"键,其他的一些用"uu"替代。

B. 为什么写的汉字常不对?

这个问题大得多。语言转换汉字不能达到绝对的准确。汉语的每个语音都会有很多相应的汉字。计算机文字处理的能力不尽人意。打字时得不断选字、改字,以保证准确性。这又费精力又费时间。对初学者来说很具挑战性,得特别留心。尤其是在 AP 中文测试这样的应试当中,速度和准确性缺一不可。

C. 对手写汉字有什么影响呢?

用计算机写汉字方便,若更多的时间和精力放在这,渐渐地对手写汉字会有副作用。人们不用动脑记忆也不用动手书写了。更别提练书法了。

有利有弊。扬长避短才难能可贵。

The Drawbacks:

There are three important issues related to using a Chinese word processor.

A. Where is "ü"?

This is a little technical problem. The *pinyin* input method seems to be a preferable one due to the fact that it utilises an English keyboard. An English keyboard can satisfy all of the letters except "ü." Different word processors find different solutions. For example:

Key designates " ~ " for this feature; Microsoft word employs "v," others may use “uu.”

B. How does one get the characters right?

This is a bigger problem. Typing characters on a computer by phonetic spelling is still not as convenient as one would like it to be: Each sound/spelling is associated with multiple characters. With almost no exception, word processors require inputer to identify and choose the correct characters. This operation can be time-consuming and tedious. The learner must be aware and be careful when creating texts so as to choose the correct character matching the given *pinyin*. Also, for testing situations like the online AP Chinese test, practicing typing with speed and accuracy is a must.

C. What happens to writing by hand?

This is a by-product. Some concerns have already been raised that as more time and effort are put into using word processors to create text in Chinese, writing by hand as a skill and a means of memorization of characters has been negatively affected. Not to mention the negative impact on calligraphy as an art.

There are obvious advantages and disadvantages in Chinese computing. Taking advantages of the positives and trying to avoid the negatives are rare and commendable.

教学难点

Difficulties

记忆汉字 Memorizing Chinese Characters

记忆汉字可能是多数学生的难点。虽然记住和正确书写汉字不容易，但是学习的趣处正在于其挑战性。千万不能把学认学写汉字变成一件头疼的事，总是有挫败感。还是要通过成功的经验鼓励学生的学习兴趣，帮助学生找到有效的方法和知识记住更多的汉字。

如何有效地教与学汉字，请参照《怎么篇：组织教学》中有关问答部分和列举的教学活动。

Memorizing characters is a difficult job for most learners. Challenging as it is, learners should be encouraged to find practical ways to expand their knowledge and memory of more characters. Doesn't the fun part of learning come from its challenge? The key is to inspire learning through successful learning experiences not through failure.

As for how to teach writing characters effectively, please refer to the question and answer and sample activities on teaching and learning characters in chapters in Volume Two *How*: *Designing Teaching*.

1

数字与生活

Numbers in Life

数字是日常生活中经常用到的。不管多大的孩子学习汉语，从一开始就可以学习数字。为什么要学数字呢？涉及数字的话题有很多。

最简单的有：数数儿，数东西/人，做算术；稍复杂一点的有：谈年龄、号码，如：电话号码、门牌号码、公共汽车号，等等；再难一点的还有：钱、日历；更难的还有：大数目、数学计算，等等。

请参考以下的内容，按教与学的需求，选择使用。

"Numbers" is a topic used daily. Beginning students of Chinese, regardless of age, may learn numbers from the very beginning. Why do we learn numbers? Many basic topics in life require numbers.

The simplest situations are: counting, numbering objects/people, doing basic arithmetic. More complicated topics include: talking about age, or numbers such as telephone number, street number, bus number, and so on. More sophisticated topics are: money, calendar. Larger numbers and mathematical calculations are even more difficult.

Select from the content listed below according to teaching and learning needs. Customize them as needed.

教学重点 Content of Teaching and Learning

数字/数目	Number, Amount, Quantity, Digit
数学用语	Mathematical Terms
名量词	Measure Words for Noun (Nominal Measure Word)
钱	Cash, Money
年龄	Age
电话号码	Telephone Number
日历	Calendar

教学难点 Difficulties

年龄　　Age

"一" vs. "幺"

"二" vs. "两"

换算	Conversion of Big Numbers from English to Chinese
对数字的听力理解	Listening Comprehension of Numbers
名量词	Measure Word for Noun (Nominal Measure Word)
“多”的使用	Use of “多”

词汇表 Glossary

数目表	Number
数学用语表	Mathematical Terms
常用量词表	List of Commonly Used Measure Words

教学重点

Content of Teaching and Learning

数字/数目　Numeral, Number, Amount, Quantity, Digit

基本数字　Basic 10 Numbers

yī	èr	sān	sì	wǔ	liù	qī	bā	jiǔ	shí
一	二	三	四	五	六	七	八	九	十

大数目　Large Numbers

shí	èrshí	sānshí	sìshí	wǔshí	liùshí	qīshí	bāshí	jiǔshí
十	二十	三十	四十	五十	六十	七十	八十	九十

yìbǎi
一百 ……

yìqiān
一千 ……

	qiān	bǎi	shí	gè
Basic Units:	千	百	十	个
	1,	0	0	0

中文数目每4位数为一新单元。英文用的阿拉伯数字是3位进制。常用数字单位:

For Chinese numbers, every four digits consist of a unit. While in English it is three. The commonly used units are as follows:

zhào	yì	wàn	gè
兆	亿	万	个
千百十兆	千百十亿	千百十万	千百十个

换算的关键　Critical Units for Conversion

10, 000	ten thousand	一万
100, 000	a hundred thousand	十万

1，000，000	a million	一百万
100，000，000	a hundred million	一亿
1，000，000，000	a billion	十亿

e. g. ：

2，031	二千〇三十一
12，345	一万 二千三百四十五
356，005	三十五万 六千〇五
4，507，889	四百五十万 七千八百八十九
80，008，000	八千万 八千
900，675，000	九亿 〇六十七万 五千
1，300，000，000	十三亿

Jiānádà de rénkǒu yuē wéi (approximately)： liǎngqiān qībǎi wàn
加拿大 的 人口 约 为 两千 七百 万

Měiguó de rénkǒu yuē wéi sān yì
美国 的 人口 约 为： 三 亿

Zhōngguó de rénkǒu yuē wéi shísān yì
中国 的 人口 约 为： 十三 亿

数学用语 Mathematical Terms

整数 zhěngshù {math} integer，whole number，round number

- 正数 zhèngshù {math} positive number
- 负数 fùshù {math} negative number
- 零 líng zero

小数 xiǎoshù {math} decimal

1.75 yì diǎn qī wǔ
一 点 七 五

0.25 líng diǎn èr wǔ
〇 点 二 五

分数 fēnshù {math} fraction

1/2	èr fēn zhī yī 二 分 之 一
2/3	sān fēn zhī èr 三 分 之 二
3/4	sì fēn zhī sān 四 分 之 三
1/16	shíliù fēn zhī yī 十六 分 之 一
50%	bǎifēnzhī wǔshí 百分之 五十
75%	bǎifēnzhī qīshíwǔ 百分之 七十 五

算术 suànshù arithmetic

加	jiā	"+"	add
	1+1=2	yī jiā yī děngyú èr 一加 一 等于 二	
减	jiǎn	"−"	subtract
	4−2=2	sì jiǎnqù èr děngyú èr 四 减去 二 等于 二	
乘	chéng	"×"	multiply
	2×2=4	èr chéngyǐ èr děngyú sì 二 乘以 二 等于 四	
除	chú	"÷"	divide
	6÷3=2	liù chúyǐ sān děngyú èr 六 除以 三 等于 二	
等于	děngyú	"="	be equivalent to
以	yǐ	by	
进位	jìnwèi	{math} carry	

数学 shùwué mathematics (as a subject)

代数	dàishù	algebra
几何	jǐhé	geometry

三角	sānjiǎo	trigonometry
函数	hánshù	{math} function
统计	tǒngjì	statistics

名量词 Measure Words for Noun (Nominal Measure Word)

汉语的名词和数词之间必须用量词。

When describing an amount/quantity of objects, a measure word is needed to connect the number with the noun.

量词的使用 Rules of Using Measure Words

1）数词加量词修饰名词

When a number is used to quantify a noun, a measure word is needed:

+ Measure Word + Noun

liǎng	ge	rén	
两	个	人	two persons

2）"这""那""哪"加量词修饰名词

When "this/these", "that /those" or "which" is used to designate a noun, a measure word is needed:

"这/那/哪" + Measure Word + Noun

nà	ge	rén	
那	个	人	that person

钱 Cash, Money

中国钱

人民币 rénmínbì RMB (unit of currency in the PRC)

	Written	Colloquial
yuan unit	元 yuán	块 kuài
Ten cent unit (one – tenth of a yuan)	角 jiǎo	毛 máo

Cent unit (one – tenth of a jiao) 分 fēn

"二" is a problematic number in terms of money:

èr (liǎng) yuán èr jiǎo 二 (两) 元 二 角	liǎng kuài èr (máo) 两 块 二 (毛)
èrshí yuán èr jiǎo èr fēn 二十 元 二 角 二 分	èrshí kuài èr máo èr (fēn) 二十 块 二 毛 二(分)
èrbǎi èrshí èr yuán èr jiǎo 二百 二十 二 元 二 角	èrbǎi èrshí èr kuài èr 二百 二十 二 块 二

美国钱 American Money

美金 měijīn/美元 měiyuán US dollar, American dollar

Dollar unit 美元 měiyuán

Cent unit 美分 měifēn

其他 Other

欧元 ōuyuán Euro

换算 huànsuàn Convert; Conversion (from one system of calculation to another)

Yì měiyuán děngyú bā yuán rénmínbì
一 美元 等于 八 元 人民币。
One U. S. dollar equals eight RMB Yuan.

钱的使用 Other Expressions Related to Use of Money

价钱	jiàqián	Price	零钱	língqián	Small change
花钱	huā qián	Spend money	用钱	yòng qián	Spend money
付钱	fù qián	Pay	找钱	zhǎo qián	Give change

一共 yígòng Altogether, Total

多少钱 duōshao qián How much

一共多少钱? How much is it in total?

钱的所有 How Much Money Do You Have?

"块" kuài is a measure word for Chinese currency.

"钱" qián is the noun.

Wǒ yǒu liǎng kuài qián
我 有 两 块 钱。I have two dollars.

问句 Questions & Answers

1）数目小于十，用"几" If the number is less than 10, use "几".

Nǐ yǒu jǐ kuài qián
你 有 几 块 钱？
How much money do you have?

Wǒ yǒu liǎng kuài qián
我 有 两 块 钱。
I have two dollars.

2）数目大于十，用"多少"

If the number is more than 10, use "多少".

Nǐmen yǒu duōshao qián
你们 有 多少 钱？
How much money do you have?

Wǒmen yǒu èrshí kuài qián
我们 有 二十 块 钱。
We have twenty dollars.

年龄 Age (of a person, animal, plant)

1）谈年龄，用"岁"。

When talking about one's age, use "岁 suì years of age".

2）问年龄，用"多大?"

To ask about one's age, use "多大?". （"大" and "小" are used to describe people's age, not size.）

Jīnnián nǐ duō dà
今年 你 多 大？How old are you this year?

Wǒ (shì) shísì suì
我 (是) 十四 岁。I am 14.

电话号码 Telephone Number

(See chapter 2: Self Introduction for more details)

电话号码用个位数字。

To say a telephone number, use single digit.

Wǒ de diànhuà shì (qī qī sān) èr sān líng wǔ liù qī bā
我 的 电话 是 (七 七 三) 二 三 〇 五 六 七 八。

日历 Calendar

(See chapter 6: Time for more details)

中文日期的排列顺序总是从大到小。

When discussing calendar units, longer (time) concepts go before smaller ones.

年 nián year

月 yuè month

日 rì day

èr líng líng liù nián bā yuè sānshí rì
二 〇 〇 六 年 八 月 三十 日

教学难点

Difficulties

难点一 年龄 Age

对不同年龄的人问年龄要用不同的说法以示敬重。

For different age group, a different question may be more appropriate:

For little children:

你几岁（suì）？

For young people or people of your own age group:

你多大？

For senior citizens:

Nín duō dà suìshu　/Nín duō dà niánjì
您　多　大　岁数？/您　多　大　年纪？

难点二　“一” vs. “幺”

数数儿的时候，排顺序的时候，用“一”：

“一” is used for counting:

一二三……（numeral）

第一，第二，第三……（ordinal number）

连续读单个数字的组合时，用“幺”或“一”。

“幺” can be used for reading digital numbers in sequence.

e. g.: telephone number or room number.

Room “105” can be read as

“一〇五”或“幺〇五”.

Telephone:（312）1456781:

“三一二一四五六七八一”，或者“三幺二幺四五六七八幺”

难点三　“二” vs. “两”

数数儿的时候，排顺序的时候，用“二”。

“二” is used for counting.

一二三……（numeral）

第一，第二，第三……（ordinal number）

“两”作为起始数用在量词前。

“两”, as an initial number for 2, has to be used if a measure word follows it (but only as a whole number, not a fraction) .

	2 people	两个人
	2 o'clock	两点（钟）
	2 dollars	两块钱
but:	2.20 dollars	两块二
	2.02 dollars	两块○二
	2:22pm	下午两点二十二（分）

难点四　换算 Conversion of Big Numbers from English to Chinese

英文数目的进制分隔是每3个数字出现一个新的单位：

English numbers (Arabic numbers) have 3 digits per unit:

1, 000, 000, 000.

(billions, millions, thousands, 000)

中文是四个。换算时有5点要注意：

Chinese numbers have 4 digits per unit. Five points need to be emphasized:

1) Unit: Every four digits begin a new unit.

2) When to read unit word:

Do not say the unit word until all digits in the unit are mentioned.

1/23, 45/6, 789 一亿二千三百四十五万六千七百八十九

3) When to read “0”:

When “0” is at the beginning of the unit.

1/0001/0001　　一亿○一万○一

When “0” is in the middle of the unit.

1/0101/1011　　一亿○一千○一万一千○一十一

Not when it is at the very end of the number.

1/00, 00/0, 000　　一亿

1/10，00/1，110　　一亿一千万（○）一千一百一十

10/10，00/1，100　　十亿一千万（○）一千一百

4）“10” in sequence can be read “一十”：

111：一百一十一

5）The most important/difficult conversions are：（Remember！）

10，000	10 thousand	一万
100，000	100 thousand	十万
1，000，000	a million	一百万
10，000，000	10 million	一千万
100，000，000	100 million	一亿
1，000，000，000	a billion	十亿

难点五　对数字的听力理解 Listening Comprehension of Numbers

数字的听力理解比较难，需要多练习。

It is always hard to listen to and comprehend numbers. It will require constant practice.

难点六　名量词 Measure Words for Noun（Nominal Measwre Word）

名量词的使用　Rules of Using Measure Words for Noun

1）数字加名词时，必须使用量词：

When a number is used to quantify a noun，a measure word is needed：

+ Measure Word + Noun

liǎng	ge	rén	
两	个	人	two persons

2）“这/那/哪”指示名词时，应使用量词：

When “this/these”，“that /those” or “which” is used to designate a noun，a measure word is needed：

“这/那/哪” + Measure Word + Noun

nà ge rén
那 个 人 that person

3）“几”询问小于10的量，放在量词前：

For numbers between 1 and 10, Chinese uses “几” before a measure word for questions:

jǐ ge
几 个 For amount

jǐ suì
几 岁 For age

jǐ yuán
几 元 For money

jǐ diǎn
几 点 For time

jǐ jīn
几 斤 For weight

4）“多少”询问大于10的量，放在量词前：

For numbers bigger than 10, Chinese uses “多少” before a measure word for question:

duōshao gè
多少 个 For amount

duōshao suì
多少 岁 For age

duōshao yuán
多少 元 For money

duōshao jīn
多少 斤 For weight

名量词的其他用法 Other Functions of Measure Words for Noun

1）量词重叠表示“每”，无例外：

Measure words can also be duplicated meaning “every one”:

gègè: Tāmen gègè dōu hěn bàng
个个：他们 个个 都 很 棒 。
Everyone of them is wonderful.

2）数词与量词重叠做状语表示顺序：

Numerals and measure words can be duplicated, showing the order of actions:

yí ge yí ge de: yí ge yí ge de chī
一 个 一 个 地：一 个 一 个 地 吃
Eat one by one.

yì bǐ yì bǐ de: qǐng yì bǐ yì bǐ de xiě
一 笔 一 笔 地：请 一 笔 一 笔 地 写
Please write it stroke by stroke.

难点七　“多”的使用 Use of “多”

1）“多”和“少”作为形容词在描述时，不可脱离副词单用。

“多” and “少” are adjectives that cannot be used by themselves when describing something. They require adverbs in company to form descriptions.

wrong	correct
我有多朋友。	我有很多朋友。

2）“多”作为副词，与一个形容词结合表示疑问。

“多” as an adverb together with an adjective can forma question:

Duō cháng
多　长？　For length

Duō cū
多　粗？　For thickness

Duō kuān
多　宽？　For width

Duō jiǔ
多　久？　For time

Duō gāo
多　高？　For height

Duō yuǎn
多　远？　For distance

Duō dà
多　大？　For age, area, capacity and volume

3）“多”作为副词，与一个形容词结合表示感叹。

The same structure as above can also be used to show exclamations:

Duō gāo a
多　高　啊！　How high (tall)!

Duō dà a
多　大　啊！　How big!

Duō yuǎn a
多　远　啊！　How far away!

词汇表

Glossary

常用量词表 List of Commonly Used Measure Words

(Some measure words in Chinese can find their equivalents in English while a lot others do not.)

把 bǎ For things with a handle or for things that can be grasped (like a chair)

一把

椅子	yǐzi	chair
刀子	dāozi	pocket knife
雨伞	yǔsǎn	umbrella

杯 bēi Glass, cup of liquid

一杯

水	shuǐ	water
酒	jiǔ	alcoholic beverage, wine
果汁	guǒzhī	fruit juice, syrup

本 běn Copy of books

一本

书	shū	book
字典	zìdiǎn	Chinese character dictionary
词典	cídiǎn	dictionary
杂志	zázhì	(news, etc.) magazine
课本	kèběn	textbook
画报	huàbào	pictorial

场 chǎng　For recreation or sporting events, performances and speeches

一场

球赛	qiúsài	ball game
电影	diànyǐng	movie, motion picture
话剧	huàjù	modern drama
音乐会	yīnyuèhuì	concert, musical recital
演说	yǎnshuō	speech
辩论	biànlùn	debate, argue

顶 dǐng　Top (of the head, a thing)

一顶

帽子	màozi	cap, hat

段 duàn　Section, part, period of time

一段

路	lù	road, path
树枝	shùzhī	branch, twig
文章	wénzhāng	article, essay
音乐	yīnyuè	music
时间	shíjiān	time
故事	gùshi	story, plot (like of a novel)

副 fù　For a set of things

一副

眼镜	yǎnjìng	eyeglasses
鞋带	xiédài	shoelace
耳环	ěrhuán	earring

个 gè　General classifier

一个

人	rén	person

学校	xuéxiào	school
东西	dōngxi	thing, object
故事	gùshi	story, plot (like of a novel)

件 jiàn　For an item of clothing, luggage, or an incident

一件

东西	dōngxi	thing, object
事	shì	affair, matter, thing, incident, event
行李	xíngli	baggage, luggage
衣服	yīfu	clothes, clothing
家具	jiājù	furniture

节 jié　Length or sections

一节

课	kè	lesson, class
车厢	chēxiāng	compartment (of a train)
绳子	shéngzi	rope, string, cord
音乐	yīnyuè	music

句 jù　For sentences or lines of verse

一句

话	huà	sentence (spoken or written)
诗	shī	poetry, poem, verse

棵 kē　For plants

一棵

花	huā	flower
草	cǎo	grass
树	shù	tree
庄稼	zhuāngjia	crop (mostly grain or cereal crop)

颗 kē　For small and round things (like bean, pearl)

一颗

豆子	dòuzi	beans，peas，legumes
珍珠	zhēnzhū	pearl
心	xīn	heart

块 kuài　For lump or chunk of things，things in shape of a flat sheet or the colloquial term for money

一块

蛋糕	dàngāo	cake
巧克力	qiǎokèlì	chocolate
糖	táng	candy，sweets
地	dì	land，floor
钱	qián	cash，money

辆 liàng　For vehicles

一辆

汽车	qìchē	motor vehicle，automobile，car
坦克	tǎnkè	tank（the military vehicle）
摩托车	mótuōchē	motorbike，motorcycle
自行车	zìxíngchē	bicycle
卡车	kǎchē	truck

门 mén　For academic subjects

一门

课	kè	lesson，class
科学	kēxué	science
学问	xuéwèn	knowledge，scholarship
技术	jìshù	skill，technique，technology

篇 piān　For articles，journals or pages

一篇

文章	wénzhāng	article, essay
讲义	jiǎngyì	lecture notes
日记	rìjì	diary, journal

瓶 píng　Bottle, vase, jar

一瓶

水	shuǐ	water
牛奶	niúnǎi	milk (from a cow)
酒	jiǔ	alcoholic beverage

首 shǒu　For songs, poems

一首

诗	shī	poetry, poem, verse
歌	gē	song

双 shuāng　Set of two

一双

鞋	xié	shoes
筷子	kuàizi	chopsticks

艘 sōu　For ships or large vessels

一艘

船	chuán	boat, ship, vessel
快艇	kuàitǐng	speedboat, motor launch

所 suǒ　For schools, hospitals and houses

一所

学校	xuéxiào	school
医院	yīyuàn	hospital
房子	fángzi	house, building

条 tiáo　For long and usually soft objects, some animals or items of news

一条

裤子	kùzi	pants, trousers
裙子	qúnzi	skirt
围巾	wéijīn	scarf, muffler
领带	lǐngdài	necktie
河	hé	river
鱼	yú	fish
狗	gǒu	dog
新闻	xīnwén	news
消息	xiāoxi	news, tidings

听 tīng　Tin, can (from the English "tin")

一听

可口可乐	Kěkǒukělè	Coca-cola
雪碧	Xuěbì	Sprit
七喜	Qīxǐ	Seven Up
啤酒	píjiǔ	beer

位 wèi　Formal classifier for people

一位

老师	lǎoshī	teacher
先生	xiānsheng	Mister, sir
小姐	xiǎojie	young (unmarried) lady

张 zhāng　For flat things like a sheet of paper, a table, etc.

一张

纸	zhǐ	paper
报纸	bàozhǐ	newspaper
票	piào	ticket
地图	dìtú	map

画	huà	painting, drawing
照片	zhàopiàn	photograph
桌子	zhuōzi	table, desk
床	chuáng	bed, couch, bench

支 zhī　For long, narrow and stiff object

一支

笔	bǐ	pen
香烟	xiāngyān	cigarette
枪	qiāng	gun, rifle

枝 zhī　Branch

一枝

花	huā	flower
玫瑰	méigui	rose

只 zhī　For one of a pair of things, especially body parts, or small animals

一只

眼睛	yǎnjing	eye
脚	jiǎo	foot
手	shǒu	hand
耳朵	ěrduo	ear
鞋	xié	shoe
袜子	wàzi	sock
猫	māo	cat
老鼠	lǎoshu	rat, mouse
鸟	niǎo	bird
鸡	jī	chicken
手套	shǒutào	glove, mitten

座 zuò　For large and fixed structures (like mountains, bridges)

一座

山	shān	mountain
桥	qiáo	bridge
大楼	dàlóu	multi-storied building

Note

有些名词可用数个不同的量词。

Some nouns can be quantified by several different measure words.

a dog：

yì zhī gǒu　yì tiáo gǒu
一 只 狗　一 条 狗

a boat/ship：

yì zhī chuán　yì tiáo chuán　yì sōu chuán
一 只 船　一 条 船　一 艘 船

（*Measure Word List – Compiled by Yu Hongwei*）

2

自我介绍 Self Introduction

自我介绍是人际交流的第一步。这一话题涉及的内容可有：问候、介绍姓名、年龄、家庭住址和电话等。

在每一个小话题里我们都将提示相关的句式的结构和用法以及难点。请根据需求加减使用。

Self introduction is the initial step of an interpersonal communication. This topic covers greetings, an introduction to names, age, home addresses, telephone numbers, etc.

In each sub-topic, we provide related grammatical structures and explain functional usages as well as grammatical difficulties . Please make your selections for teaching and learning as needed.

教学重点 Content of Teaching and Learning

问好	Greetings
介绍姓名	Introducing Names
介绍年龄	Introducing Age
介绍电话号码	Introducing Telephone Numbers
介绍家庭住址	Introducing Home Addresses
称谓	Titles

教学难点 Difficulties

形容词谓语句	Adjective as Predicate
“不”的变调	Tone Sandhi for “不”
汉语的“Yes/No”	Yes and No in Chinese
“姓”与“名”的位置	Positions of “姓” and “名”
“姓”与“叫”的使用	Practical Uses of “姓” and “叫”
“姓” and “名” vs. “是”	
请教尊姓大名	Formal and Informal Ways of Inquiring Names

文化联系 Cultural Relations

其他问候方式	Other ways of Greeting
请教尊姓大名	Respectful Ways of Asking about Names
姓名的排行	Order of Naming the Children
男孩名和女孩名	Meanings of Chinese Names：Boys Vs. Girls
介绍年龄	Introduing Age
称谓	Titles

词汇表 Glossary

常用（人与物）代词表	List of Commonly Used Pronouns for People/Animals and Objects

教学重点

Content of Teaching and Learning

问好 Greetings

In Chinese, we use the following patterns to say "Hi!":

句型 Sentence Patterns

	Subject	+ Adjective	
	Nǐ	hǎo	
A：	你	好！	Hi!
	Nǐ	hǎo	
B：	你	好！	Hi!

提问与回答 Questions and Answers

	Subject	+ (Adverb)	+ Adjective	
	Nǐ		hǎo	ma
A：	你		好	吗？
	How are you doing?			
	Wǒ	hěn	hǎo	
B：	我	很	好。	
	I am very well.			
	Nǐ		máng bu máng	
A：	你		忙 不 忙？	
	Are you busy?			
	Wǒ	bú tài	máng	
B：	我	不 太	忙。	
	Not really.			

否定形式 Negative："不"

A：	Nǐ	máng ma	
	你	忙 吗？	
	Are you busy?		

B: Wǒ bù máng
我 不 忙。

I am not busy.

Note

1）汉语的形容词可以直接做谓语描述情形，不用动词的帮助。

In Chinese, adjectives can be directly used without the help of verbs to describe a situation.

2）否定形式“不”直接放在形容词前。

The negator“不” goes right in front of the adjective.

3）有两种“肯定/否定”的问句。（请参阅 Chapter：Questions.）

There are two major ways to ask a“yes/no” question. (For more detail, see Chapter 14：Questions.)

a. Add a“吗” at the end of the sentence.

Nǐ hǎo ma
你 好 吗？

b. Use positive/negative form of an adjective.

Nǐ máng bu máng
你 忙 不 忙 ？

文化联系 Cultural Relations

日常生活中还有以下问候方式：

In daily life you may ask about a person's action as a form of greeting：

in the morning：

Zǎo
早 ！Good morning! (meaning：You got up early)

during the day：

Chīle ma
吃了 吗？Have you eaten?

Qù nǎr
去 哪儿？Where are you going?

Mángzhe na
忙着 哪！/？You are busy！/Are you busy？
You're working hard！/Are you working hard？
You don't really expect a serious answer.

介绍姓名 Introducing Names

In Chinese：

介绍姓 Introducing one's last name：

Wǒ xìng Wáng
我 姓 王 。My Last name is Wang.

介绍名 Introducing one's first name/full name：

Wǒ jiào Xiǎomíng
我 叫 小明 。(Introducing first name)

Wǒ jiào Wáng Xiǎomíng
我 叫 王 小明 。(Introducing full name)

也可以说 Also you may say：

Wǒ de míngzi jiào Wáng Xiǎomíng
我 的 名字 叫 王 小明 。

(Introducing full name)

问姓名 Inquiring Names

英文的"What is your name?"既问姓又问名。中文要用两个不同的问题。

In English, we use "What is your name?" to ask for one's first or full name. In Chinese, we must use different verbs to ask for one's first or full name.

(last name)

Nǐ xìng shénme
你 姓 什么 ？

(first name/full name)

Nǐ jiào shénme
你 叫 什么 ？

Nǐ jiào shénme míngzi
你 叫 什么 名字？
Nǐ de míngzi jiào shénme
你 的 名字 叫 什么？

若问中文或英文名字：

To ask about one's name specifically in Chinese or in English：

Nǐ de Zhōngwén míngzi jiào shénme
你 的 中文 名字 叫 什么？
What is your Chinese name?

Nǐ de Yīngwén míngzi jiào shénme
你 的 英文 名字 叫 什么？
What is you English name?

文化联系 Cultural Relations

请教尊姓大名 Respecful Ways of Asking about Name

可以介绍另外两种更礼貌的或在正式场合请教姓名的方式。

We may also ask adult names with respect or at a formal occasion by using：

Qǐng wèn nín jiào shénme
请 问，您 叫 什么？May I ask，what your name is?
Nín guì xìng
您 贵 姓？ May I have your honorable last name?

姓名的排行/男孩名和女孩名

Order of Naming the Children/Meanings of Chinese Names：Boys vs. Girls

这两个题目都可以作为文化学习来讨论。

在此扼要说明的是，中文的名字一般由两个或三个字组成：姓（也有少数双姓的），双字（或单字）的名。不少家庭的名字有传统的排行。形式不同。家里同一代人的名字常用一种形式。

传统上，名字多选用褒义的词语。一些有阳刚气的字词被选来做男孩名，而女孩名多为表美好的字与词。现代的名字则五花八门，不一定强调男女之分。

Both topics can be used for cultural discussions.

Generally speaking, Chinese names used to have two or three characters. However, there are exceptions. Chinese families would have part of their first names chosen by their ancestors to distinguish different generations. So siblings of the same generation in the extended family were easily identified.

Traditionally, words with positive meanings are chosen for names. Some words are specifically chosen for boy names, and some are favored for girls. However, modern names can be gender mutual.

介绍年龄 Introducing Age

介绍年龄用“岁”。

To introduce age, we use a number plus “岁.” No verb is needed.

Wǒ (shì) shíwǔ suì
我 （是） 十五 岁。 I am 15.

Tā jīn nián jiǔ suì
他 今 年 九 岁。 He is nine this year.

根据长幼用不同方法问年龄。

To ask about one’s age is more complicated. It depends on the age of the person.

1）10 岁以下的：

For people younger than 10 years of age:

Nǐ (jīn nián) jǐ suì
你（今 年） 几 岁？

2）10 岁以上的：

For people who are older than 10:

Nǐ (jīn nián) duō dà
你（今 年） 多 大？

3）长者/长辈：

For people who are adults (to show respect):

Nín duō dà suìshu　　Nǐ duō dà niánjì
您　多　大　岁数？/ 你　多　大　年纪？

文化联系　Cultural Relations

介绍年龄是汉语里一个经常的话题。这与西方文化习惯不同。

In Chinese, age is an often used ice-breaker in conversation. Students should be aware of the cultural differences between the East and the West.

介绍电话号码　Introducing Telephone Numbers

电话号码要读单个数码。Telephone numbers are read digit by digit.

(312) 7738209：(三幺二) 七七三八二〇九

(For the use of "一" and "幺", see the details in Chapterl: Numbers in Life.)

问电话号码　Inquiring a Telephone Number

问电话号码的标准形式是：Use either of the following standard formats:

Qǐng wèn nín de diànhuà (hàomǎ) shì shénme
请　问，您　的　电话　(号码)　是　什么　？　or
Nǐ de diànhuà shì duōshao (hào)
你　的　电话　是　多少　(号)？
What is your telephone number?

实际上：　For practical use, we simply say:

(Qǐng) gěi wǒ nǐ de diànhuà (hàomǎ)
(请)　给　我　你　的　电话　(号码)。
Qǐng bǎ diànhuà (hàomǎ) gěi wǒ
请　把　电话　(号码)　给　我。
(Please) give me your telephone number.

介绍家庭住址　Introducing Home Addresses

有三个句子可用来介绍你的家庭住址：

In Chinese, there are three structures that may be used to introduce your home addresses: (They have the same meaning.)

Wǒ jiā zài Zhījiāgē
我 家 在 芝加哥。
Wǒ zài Zhījiāgē zhù
我 在 芝加哥 住。
Wǒ zhù zài Zhījiāgē
我 住 在 芝加哥。

} I live/My family lives in Chicago.

介绍具体的地址 Introducing a street address

1）英文先说门牌号码，后说街名。

In English, we say the street number first, then the street name.

e.g.: 1050 S. Clark Street

2）汉语先说街名，后说门牌号码。（由大至小）

In Chinese, all addresses go from larger concepts to smaller ones.

nán jiē hào
e.g.: Clark 南 街 1050 号

问家庭住址 Inquiring Locations/Home Addresses

In Chinese, there are, again, three structures that may be used to inquire your home addresses: (They have the same meaning.)

Nǐ jiā zhù nǎr Nǐ jiā zài nǎr
你 家 住 哪儿？/你 家 在 哪儿？
Nǐ zài nǎr zhù
你 在 哪儿 住？
Nǐ jiā zhù zài shénme dìfang
你 家 住 在 什么 地方？

} Where do you /does your family live?

完整回答 Complete Answer

Wǒ (jiā) zhù zài Zhījiāgē nán jiē hào
我（家）住 在 芝加哥 Clark 南 街 1050 号。

称谓 Titles

1）英文，头衔在姓前。

In English, the title goes before the family name: Mr. Smith

中文，姓在头衔前。

In Chinese, the title goes after the family name: 王先生

2）英文的称谓/头衔简单。

In English, title use is not complex.

For male: Mr.

For female: Mrs. /Miss. /Ms.

中文的称谓复杂。

In Chinese, titles reflect political conditions and social status.

For male: 先生

For female: 太太（夫人）/小姐/女士

文化联系 Cultural Relations

A. 不同的地方/区域流行不同的称法。例如天津人习惯称熟人“张哥”“李姐”等；台湾人习惯用“先生”“太太”。

There are many Chinese-speaking regions in the world. A title can be regionally specific. For example, people from Tianjin like to address one another by using family terms, such as “张哥—brother” and “李姐—sister”; people from Taiwan have the habit to use “先生—Mr., 太太—Mrs.”

B. 中国大陆的妇女婚后多不改姓夫姓。不能轻易认为一个王女士就是王太太。用“女士”安全些。

Women from mainland China mostly do not change their maiden names after marriage. Therefore it is incorrect to assume that a Ms. Wang is a “王太太”. In formal situations, it is advisable (safer) to speak to a woman as “女士”, rather than other titles.

C. 通常“先生”也指丈夫，“太太”指某人之妻。例如：“我先生”“我太太”，“你先生”“你太太”。

People often use “先生” to refer to one's husband and “太太” to one's wife, e. g. “我先生—my husband”, “我太太—my wife”; “你先生—your husband”, “你太太—your wife”.

D. 不少人喜欢被人冠以学术头衔和职位头衔。例如“王大夫”“李处长”等。

People formally prefer academic/job titles to other titles, for example, “王大夫 Dr. Wang”, “李处长 Director Li.”

E. 长期以来，“同志”是在中国大陆一个普遍又普通的称谓。现在“同志”一般在工作单位或年纪大的人中间使用。

For a long time “同志” had been a term to address everyone in PRC. But now “同志” is used in the work units or among aged people.

F. 熟人之间或非正式场合，中国人喜欢用如下的称谓：

Among acquaintances or in informal situations, Chinese people sometimes use the following prefixes:

For young people: “小 xiǎo little” + last name, e. g. “小王，小李……”

– A term of endearment used in front of people's names

For older people: “老 lǎo old” + last name, e. g. “老王，老李……”

– A prefix to names to indicate affection, respect or familiarity

For tall and big people: “大 dà big” + last name, e. g. “大王，大李……”

– A prefix to names to indicate endearment

G. 用家庭亲属的称谓称呼他人或陌生人也是一种常用的礼貌方式。

As a common practice, it is courteous to address strangers on street according to age by using terms for family members or relatives, e. g.

For a man about your father's age: “叔叔” – Uncle

For a woman about your mother's age: “阿姨” – Aunt

For a man of your grandfather's age: “老大爷，老爷爷” – Grandpa

For a woman of your grandmother's age: “老大妈，老奶奶” – Grandma

For people more or less of your own age:

“大哥，大姐，小弟弟，小妹妹” – Brother/Sister

For little children: “小朋友”, etc. – Little friends

教学难点

Difficulties

难点一 形容词谓语句 Adjective as Predicate

英文形容和描述时要用动词"to be"。汉语直接用形容词。

In Chinese, we use adjectives directly to describe (without use of a verb).

Subject + Adjective

你 好。

他 不 好。

When translating from English to Chinese, the learner must avoid using "是".

难点二 "不"的变调 Tone Sandhi for "不"

常用词有常有的麻烦。"不"后跟四声的单音节词时，变二声。

When "不 bù not; no" is followed by a 4th tone, it changes to 2nd tone.

难点三 汉语的"Yes"/"No" Yes and No in Chinese

英文的肯定是 Yes，否定是 No。

In English, "Yes" means yes, and "No" means no!

中文没有一对一的表达方式。接受就肯定，否则否定。

In Chinese, there are no exact, equivalent expressions. To agree or to accept uses the positive form of an expression; otherwise uses the negative form.

A：你去不去？（Are you going?）

B：去，你呢？（Yes. And you?）

A：不去。（No.）

或用“对/好”表示赞同。Or use “对/好” to agree.

英文的 Yes 是表示说话人自己的肯定意见。No 是表示说话人自己的否定意见。不是同意不同意别人的意见。

Also, once again, generally, in English, “yes” means yes and “no” means no as far as actions are concerned, e. g. :

A：Are you going? B：Yes, I am going.

A：Aren't you going? B：Yes, I am going.

or：A：Are you going? B：No, I am not going.

A：Aren't you going? B：No, I am not going.

汉语的点头肯定是同意或接受别人的意见；摇头否定是不同意或不接受别人的意见。

While, in Chinese, depending on the question, we can answer positively to agree with or accept the other speaker's words by nodding our heads, or not by shaking our heads, e. g. :

A：你去吗？(Speaker uses the positive：Are you going?)

B：去，我去。(Agree：Yes, I am.)

or：B：不，我不去。(Disagree：No, I am not.)

A：你不去吗？(Speaker uses the negative：Aren't you going?)

B：不，我去。(Disagree：No, I am.)

or：B：对，我不去。(Agree：Yes, I am not)

难点四 姓与名的位置 Positions of “姓” and “名”

在口语中，英文先表名后表姓。

In English：Surname/family name is usually stated after the given name.

e. g. : John Smith

John (given name) Smith (family name)

中文总是先表姓后表名。

In Chinese：Surname/last name is always stated first.

e. g. : Yao, Ming 姚明

Yao (family name)　Ming (given name)

难点五　"姓"与"叫"的使用 Practical Uses of "姓" and "叫"

"姓"只介绍姓。

"叫"介绍名或全名。

"姓" introduces family name only.

"叫" introduces either a given name or full name.

难点六　"姓" and "名" vs. "是"

英文介绍姓名时说："My name is Jane Smith."

In English, we say "My name is Jane Smith."

中文用"姓"介绍姓，"叫"介绍名。说：我姓王，我叫王小明。当然也可以说："我是王小明。"用来认证自己是那个人。有细微的差别。

In Chinese: "姓" and "叫" are verbs which introduce names. We say: 我姓王，我叫王小明。

However, one can says "我是王小明。" to identify oneself. Please pay attention to the subtleness of usages.

难点七　请教尊姓大名

Formal and Informal Ways of Inquiring Names

1) 正式场合，用"您"表示礼貌与尊重。

Formal way of inquiry: Use "您" to show respect.

您姓什么？

2) 非正式场合，用"你"。

Informal way of inquiry: Use "你".

你姓什么？

3）郑重请教尊姓大名时，问：

Very formal way to inquire one's last name (in this case, first name is avoided):

Qǐng wèn, nín guì xìng
请 问，您 贵 姓？

词汇表

Glossary

常用（人与物）代词表

List of Commonly Used Pronouns for People/Animal and Objects

人称代词 Personal Pronoun

我	wǒ	I
你	nǐ	you
他	tā	he
她	tā	she
我们	wǒmen	we
你们	nǐmen	you
他们	tāmen	they (including both genders)
她们	tāmen	they (feminine)

非人称代词 Other Pronoun

它	tā	it (third person singular, neutral)

指示代词 Demonstrative Pronoun

这	zhè/ "zhèi"	this
那	nà/nèi	that

每　　　měi　　　each, every

疑问代词　Interrogative Pronoun

(See Chapter 14: Questions)

Note

汉语的名词没有数的概念。"们 men"是一个后缀，只用来表人称代词的复数。很少的名词在极少的情况下可以用"们"表复数，如：人们/人们 rénmen。这与英文不同。

Chinese, in general, has no plural forms for nouns. "们 men" is a suffix added to the above personal pronouns to indicate plurality. It is occasionally added to nouns indicating people, e. g.: 人们/人们 rénmen people. It does not apply to other nouns/situations.

3

家人 Family Members

这一节的话题是谈家庭、家人和亲属关系。除了词汇以外，重点是动词“有”及量词的使用。家庭关系和称谓是文化的传统、观念和习俗的一部分。在语言的使用上有很多反映。并且也可以引出不少对文化的讨论。请酌情参考使用有关部分。

This chapter is about family, family members and relatives. Besides vocabulary, the major grammatical points are "to have" as predicate and the use of measure words. Family relations and titles are part of the cultural tradition, cultural values and practices in Chinese-speaking regions. Language usage significantly reflects culture in this regard. This topic can provoke many discussions about culture. Select the relevant content for teaching and learning.

教学重点 Content of Teaching and Learning

家人	Family Members
有/没有	Have /Not to Have
量词	Measure Words
问答	Questions and Answers

教学难点 Difficulties

兄弟姐妹排行	Order of Your Siblings
非嫡系兄弟姐妹	Half/Step Siblings
亲戚	Relatives
不/没有	Negatives
名量词	Measure Words for Noun (Nominal Measure Words)

文化联系 Cultural Relations

中国家庭	Chinese Family

词 汇 表 Glossary

家人与关系	Family Members and Relationships
亲戚	Relatives

教学重点

Content of Teaching and Learning

家人 jiārén Family Members

家庭成员 Family Members

Immediate Family:

爸爸	bàba	papa, daddy
妈妈	māma	mother, mom
哥哥	gēge	elder brother
弟弟	dìdi	younger brother
姐姐	jiějie	elder sister
妹妹	mèimei	younger sister

Grandparents:

Paternal:

爷爷	yéye	grandfather
	formal:	祖父 zǔfù
奶奶	nǎinai	grandmother
	formal:	祖母 zǔmǔ

Maternal:

姥爷	lǎoye	grandfather
	formal:	外公 wàigōng/外祖父 wàizǔfù
姥姥	lǎolao	grandmother
	formal:	外婆 wàipó/ 外祖母 wàizǔmǔ

家庭关系 Family Relationships

父母	fùmǔ	father and mother, parents

Biological Parents:

生父	shēngfù	birth father
生母	shēngmǔ	birth mother

Step Parents：

继父	jìfù	stepfather
继母	jìmǔ	stepmother
孩子	háizi	child，children
男孩子	nán háizi	boy
女孩子	nǚ háizi	girl
儿子	érzi	son
女儿	nǚ'ér	daughter
独生子	dúshēngzǐ	only son
独生女	dúshēngnǚ	only daughter

Siblings：

兄弟姐妹	xiōngdì jiěmèi	siblings
双胞胎	shuāngbāotāi	twins

Spouse：

丈夫	zhàngfu	husband（legal）
妻子	qīzi	wife（legal）
先生	xiānsheng	husband（Mr.）
太太	tàitai	（夫人 fūrén wife）（Mrs.）

亲戚 qīnqi Relatives

Paternal

伯父	bófù	uncle（father's elder brother）
伯母	bómǔ	aunt（wife of father's elder brother）
叔叔	shūshu	uncle（father's younger brother）
婶	shěn	aunt（wife of father's younger brother）
姑姑	gūgu	aunt（father's sister）
姑父	gūfù	uncle（husband of father's sister）

Maternal:

舅舅	jiùjiu	uncle (mother's elder or younger brother)
舅妈	jiùmā	aunt (wife of mother's brother)
姨	yí	mother's sister; wife's sister
姨父	yífù	uncle (husband of mother's sister)

表亲 biǎoqīn Cousin; Relationship between Cousins

(First cousins: Call them brothers and sisters according to age.)

paternal 堂 táng (with the same family name)

堂哥 堂姐

堂弟 堂妹

maternal 表 biǎo (with different family name)

表哥 表姐

表弟 表妹

(Second cousins: Call your parents' cousins uncles and aunts.)

堂叔 表舅

堂姑 表姨

其他亲属关系 qítā qīnshǔ guānxi

Other Relationships among Relatives (by blood or marriage)

孙子	sūnzi	grandson
孙女	sūnnü	granddaughter
外孙	wàisūn	grandson (daughter's son)
外孙女	wàisūnnü	granddaughter (daughter's daughter)
侄子	zhízi	nephew (brother's son)
侄女	zhínü	niece (brother's daughter)
外甥	wàisheng	nephew (sister's son)
外甥女	wàishengnǚ	niece (sister's daughter)

公公	gōnggong	father-in-law（husband's father）
婆婆	pópo	mother-in-law（husband's mother）
岳父	yuèfù	father-in-law（wife's father）
岳母	yuèmǔ	mother-in-law（wife's mother）
女婿	nǚxu	son-in-law
儿媳	érxí	daughter-in-law

有/没有 yǒu/méiyǒu Have/Not to Have

功用 Function：表所有 To specify prossession

句型 Sentence Patterns：

Subject +	Verb +	(# ge) +	object.
Wǒ	yǒu		dìdi
我	有		弟弟。
Wǒ	méiyǒu		mèimei
我	没有		妹妹 。

否定形式 Negative Form: （没有 méiyǒu not have）

Never say "不有".

量词 Measure Words

量词连接数词与名词。

When numbering objects, a measure word is needed to connect the number with the noun.

Wǒ yǒu liǎng ge dìdi

我 有 两 个 弟弟。

问答 Questions & Answers

If a number is less than 10, use "几 jǐ how many".

Nǐ bàba māma yǒu jǐ ge háizi
你 爸爸 妈妈 有 几个 孩子?
Tāmen yǒu liǎng ge érzi hé yí ge nǚ'ér
他们 有 两 个 儿子 和 一 个 女儿。

If a number is greater than 10, use "多少 duōshao how many".

Nǐmen bān yǒu duōshao xuésheng
你们 班 有 多少 学生 ?
Wǒmen bān yǒu shí'èr ge xuésheng
我们 班 有 十二 个 学生 。

教学难点

Difficulties

难点一 兄弟姐妹排行 Order of Your Siblings

中英对比 Compare English and Chinese:

1）中文的"brother"分哥哥和弟弟；"sister"分姐姐和妹妹。

In English, we refer all our male siblings as "brothers" and all our female siblings as "sister".

In Chinese, we call older male siblings as "哥哥" and younger ones "弟弟", older female siblings as "姐姐", and younger female siblings as "妹妹".

2）中文可按年龄的大小分。

In Chinese, we also number our siblings or relatives in order by age: "大哥""二哥""三哥""四哥"，"大表姐""二表姐""三表姐""四表姐"等。

难点二 非嫡系兄弟姐妹 Half/Step Siblings

按中国的文化，在一个家庭里，不管有无血缘关系，按年龄大小互称兄弟姐妹。

In English, we refer to half/step siblings directly as "step brothers/sisters" or "half brothers/sisters."

In Chinese, we normally don't differentiate half/step siblings from other siblings.

If needed, half siblings may be called:

tóng fù yì mǔ tóng mǔ yì fù de xiōngdì jiěmèi
同 父 异 母/同 母 异 父 的 兄弟 姐妹

难点三 亲戚 Relatives

中文没有"second cousin"这个概念。父母的"cousin"是你的堂（叔/姑/舅/姨）或表（叔/姑/舅/姨）。

In English, parents' cousins are second cousins.

In Chinese, we refer to our parents' cousins as our parental/maternal uncles and aunts.

paternal	maternal
堂（叔/姑/舅/姨）	表（叔/姑/舅/姨）

文化联系 Cultural Relations

出于礼貌，非亲属之间也可以用亲属称谓互相称呼。

To be polite, usually, we refer to other people in terms of relatives, e. g.

For older adults: "爷爷，奶奶";

For adults closer in age to parents: "叔叔，阿姨";

For people of our own age: "哥哥，姐姐", etc.

难点四 不/没有 Negatives

1）"有"的否定是"没有"。

The negative form for “有” is “没有”.

Never say “不有”. This cannot be overly emphasized.

“不”和“没”的不同

Both “不” and “没” are negatives. However, they have different emphases:

a. “不”否定日常重复的行为动作。

“不” denies the occurrence of a habitual/repeated action.

我每天都不吃早饭。

I don't eat breakfast. (everyday/without exception)

b. “不”否定意愿。

“不” also denies the willingness of an action.

昨天他怎么说都不来（不肯/不愿意）。

He would not come (no matter what, he was unwilling.)

c. “没”否定一件特定事件/行为的发生。

“没” simply denies the completion of a specific action.

我每天都吃早饭，可是今天没吃。

I eat breakfast daily but did not this morning (missed one meal.)

难点五　名量词 Measure Words for Noun (Nominal Measure Words)

请参阅数字节中的量词注释和量词表。

This is an important grammatical point. Please see the List of Commonly Used Measure Words for beginning learners Chapter 1: Numbers in Life.

文化联系

Cultural Relations

中国家庭　Chinese Family

这里有很多话题可谈。中国传统的居住习惯如有“四代同堂”等。传统的中国人家庭观念包括“尊老爱幼”“孝敬父母”等，以及现代中国的“独生子女”一代。

There are many cultural traditions, values, and practices under this topic to learn about. We may begin with phrases like “四代同堂”, “尊老爱幼”, “孝敬父母”, and “独生子女”.

4

国家/人/语言

Country/People/Language

谈论国家、人和语言不仅是自我介绍的一部分，也是学习地理、文化、社会风情等有关的内容。可考虑酌情编入不同的教学单元。

本节教学重点之一是词汇。故词汇放在首要位置。汉语的国名、国人和语言的联系明确，容易学习记忆。美国作为一个多元民族、多元文化的国家，学生的家庭背景情况不一，在提供词汇时，不要保守，让学生各得其所。

其他句型和语法点是这个话题的必需，请参考使用。新老师务请审阅教学难点以防患于未然。

Speaking about countries, people, and languages is part of self introduction. It is also an opportunity to study geography, culture, and other customs. Combine it with any topic according to the class instructional needs.

This chapter takes advantage of clear and easy connections between vocabularies of country, people and language. It emphasizes learning vocabulary. It puts vocabulary in the forefront. The USA is a country of immigrants with multicultural and multi-lingual backgrounds. Provide the necessary vocabulary to all students for convenient use.

The sentences patterns and instructional difficulties are musts for this topic. Make sure to be thoroughly familiar with them for proper classroom instruction and explanation.

教学重点 Content of Teaching and Learning

谈国籍与语言	Speaking about Citizenship and Language
谈地点	Speaking about Locations
简单问句	Simple Questions
复杂问句	Complex Questions

教学难点 Difficulties

“Chinese”	Function of “哪”
“是” vs. “在”	“也” vs. “和”
“Latin” vs. “Spanish”	“And” vs. “和”

"在" vs. "在住" vs. "住在"
"说" vs. "告诉"
"Where are you from?"
"也" vs. "还"
"都不" vs. "不都"
"都" vs. "All"

文化联系 Cultural Relations

我们都是美国人 We are all Americans
汉语/中文/华文 Chinese Language

词汇表 Glossary

国家/人 Country/People
语言 Language
有关地理词 Related Geographical Terms

教学重点

Content of Teaching and Learning

谈国籍与语言 Speaking about Citizenship and Language

功用 Function：Identifying People and Language

句型 Sentence Patterns：

是 shì to be

Tā shì Zhōngguórén
他 是 中国人 。
He is a Chinese.

Wǒ shì Měiguórén
我 是 美国人 。
I am an American.

Wǒmen shì Zhōngguórén yě shì Měiguórén
我 们 是 中国人 ，也 是 美国人 。
We are Chinese and American.

说 shuō to speak

Zhōngguórén shuō Zhōngwén
中国人 说 中文 。
Chinese people speak Chinese.

Měiguórén shuō Yīngyǔ
美国人 说 英语 。
American people speak English.

其他句型：副词和连词

也 yě also，too；还 hái still，yet，also，as well；
都 dōu all；和 hé and，with

Wǒmen shuō Hànyǔ yě shuō Yīngyǔ
我们 说 汉语 ，也 说 英语 。
We speak Chinese and English，too.

Tāmen yě shuō Yīngyǔ bù dōu shuō Hànyǔ
他们 也 说 英语 ，不 都 说 汉语 。

They also speak English but not all of them speak Chinese.

Tā shuō Yīngyǔ yě shuō Fǎyǔ hái huì shuō yìdiǎnr Hànyǔ
他 说 英语，也 说 法语，还 会 说 一点儿 汉语。
He speaks English, French, also a little Chinese.

Wǒ de péngyou shì Mòxīgērén hé Měiguórén
我 的 朋友 是 墨西哥人 和 美国人 。
My freinds are Mexican and American.

Tā shuō Xībānyáyǔ hé Fǎyǔ
他 说 西班牙语 和 法语。
He speaks Spanish and French.

谈地点 Speaking about Locations

功用 Function: Identifying Locations

句型 Sentence Patterns:

是 shì to be

Wǒ shì Zhōngguórén
我 是 中国人。
I am a Chinese.

Tā shì Fǎguórén
他 是 法国人 。
He is a French.

在 zài to be at

Zhōngguó zài Yàzhōu
中国 在 亚洲。
China is located in Asia.

Fǎguó zài Ōuzhōu
法国 在 欧洲 。
France is located in Europe.

简单问句 Simple Questions

Nǐ shì nǎ (guó) rén
你 是 哪 （国） 人？ Where are you from?

Wǒ shì Zhōngguórén
我 是 中国人 。 I am a Chinese.

Zhōngguó zài nǎr
中国 在 哪儿？ Where is China?
Zhōngguó zài Yàzhōu
中国 在 亚洲 China is located in Asia.

Nǐ shuō shénme yǔ
你 说 什么 语？ What language do you speak?
Wǒ shuō Hànyǔ
我 说 汉语 。 I speak Chinese.

Tā ne
他 呢？ What about him?
Tā shuō Yīngyǔ yě shuō Xībānyáyǔ
他 说 英语 ，也 说 西班牙语 。He speaks English and Spanish.

复杂问句 Complex Questions

wèn dá fùzá jù zhíjiē yǐnyǔ yǔ jiànjiē yǐnyǔ
问 答：（复杂 句：直接 引语 与 间接 引语）

Direct quote：

Wǒ wèn tā (Nǐ) shì nǎ (li) rén
我 问 他“（你） 是 哪（里） 人？”
Tā shuō Wǒ shì Měiguórén
他 说 ：“我 是 美国人 。”
I asked him, “Where are you from?” He said, “I am an American.”

Indirect quote：

Wǒ wèn tā Nǐ shì nǎ (guó) rén
我 问 他：你 是 哪 （国） 人？
Tā shuō tā shì Měiguórén
他 说 他 是 美国人 。
I asked him where he is from. He said he is an American.

Direct quote：

Wǒ wèn tā nǐ shì nǎr rén
我 问 他：“你 是 哪儿 人？”

Tā gàosu wǒ　Wǒ shì Měiguórén
他　告诉　我："我　是　美国人　。"

I asked him, "where are you from?" He told me, "I am an American."

Indirect quote:

Wǒ wèn tā　(nǐ) shì nǎ (guó) rén
我　问　他:(你) 是　哪　(国)　人?

Tā gàosu wǒ tā shì Měiguórén
他　告诉　我 他 是　美国人　。

I asked him where he is from. He told me that he is an American.

Look at the following examples to summarize your own rules:

亚洲:

越南	Yuènán	Vietnam	
	越南人		越南语
泰国	Tàiguó	Thailand	
	泰国人		泰国语
韩国	Hánguó	(South) Korea	
	韩国人		韩国语

欧洲:

波兰	Bōlán	Poland	
	波兰人		波兰语
意大利	Yìdàlì	Italy	
	意大利人		意大利语

教学难点

Difficulties

难点一　"Chinese"

怎么翻译"Chinese"这个词?这个词的英文意思一个是名词,指中国人和中国语言;一个是形容词,指跟中国有关的或从中国来的。这是初学者、特别是中小学生容易搞乱的。

In English, the word "Chinese" can be used two ways:

1) As a noun to refer to a person of Chinese origin or the Chinese language.

2) As an adjective to modify a noun: a Chinese movie or a Chinese restaurant.

Learners sometimes say, "汉语饭馆" instead of "中国饭馆"。

The correct usages need to be emphasized.

难点二 "是" vs. "在"

初学者，特别是中小学生常把"是"和"在"放在一个句子里。区别的办法是：

"是"——to be 是用来定义、鉴别身份的。

"在"——to be at 是用来明确地点与时间的。

Learners, often, use "是" and "在" in the same sentence, which is wrong in Chinese.

"是" is "to be". The function of this word is to identify what is what and who is whom.

"在" is "to be at". (If translate "在" as "to be at" it helps English speakers.) The function of this word is to identify the location.

Even though English the following sentences are more or less the same in meaning, they do not have the same structure:

"I am a student at Chicago High School."

"I attend school at Chicago High (I go to Chicago High)."

"是" and "在" have different grammatical functions. See below:

Subject + Location + Verb + Object

Wǒ shì Zhījiāgē Zhōngxué de xuésheng
我 是 芝加哥 中学 的 学生 。
I am a Chicago High School student.

Wǒ zài Zhījiāgē Zhōngxué shàngxué
我 在 芝加哥 中学 上学 。
I attend school at Chicago High School.

难点三 "Latin" vs. "Spanish"

Be prepared to address the following:

Very rarely, some children are confused about "Latin", "Latinos", "Spanish".

A simple answer:

The language most Latinos speak is called Spanish.

Latin is a classical written language.

难点四 "在" vs. "在住" vs. "住在"

I live/My family lives in Chicago.

Wǒ jiā zài Zhījiāgē
我 家 在 芝加哥。("在" as a verb)

Wǒ jiā zài Zhījiāgē zhù
我 家 在 芝加哥 住。("在" as a proposition)

Wǒ jiā zhù zài Zhījiāgē
我 家 住 在 芝加哥。("在" as resultative complement)

难点五 "说" vs. "告诉"

"说" is "to speak/say". It takes a direct or indirect quote. For example:

Tā shuō Wǒ shì xuésheng
他 说:"我 是 学生。"(A)

Tā shuō tā shì xuésheng
他 说 他 是 学生。(B)

"告诉" is "to tell". It takes direct and indirect object and quote. For example:

Tā gàosu wǒ Wǒ shì xuésheng
他 告诉 我:"我 是 学生。"(C)

Tā gàosu wǒ tā shì xuésheng
他 告诉 我 他 是 学生 。(D)

In (A) and (C) the quotes (with quotation marks " ...") are direct quotes.

In (B) and (D) the quotes (without quotation marks) are indirect quotes.

In (C) and (D), "我" is the indirect object, the quotes (direct and indirect) are the direct objects.

难点六 "Where are you from?"

"Where are you from?" 这句话很难翻译成中文。特别是在美国这样一个多民族的移民国家里，情况太复杂了，一言难问清。我们建议说：

This question is hard to translate into Chinese, if you ask this in the US, a country of immigrants. In order not to alienate anyone, the possible solutions we suggest are:

Nǐ jiā zǔ shàng shì nǎr rén
你（家/祖 上 ancestors, forefathers）是 哪儿 人？

Nǐ jiā zǔ shàng shì nǎ guó rén
你（家/祖 上 ）是 哪 国 人？

下面的两句有政治敏感的嫌疑，不太合适。

It could be politically sensitive and inappropriate to say:

Nǐ (jiā) shì cóng nǎr lái de
你（家）是 从 哪儿 来 的？

Nǐ shì nǎ guó rén
你 是 哪 国 人？

难点七 Function of "哪"

哪儿 nǎ (r) where

Zài nǎr
在 哪儿？

Qù nǎr
去 哪儿？
Cóng nǎr dào nǎr qù
从 哪儿 到 哪儿 去？

哪 nǎ/něi which, what

Nǐ zài nǎ ge xuéxiào shàngxué
你 在 哪 个 学校 上学 ？
Nǐ zài shénme xuéxiào shàngxué
（你 在 什么 学校 上学 ？）
Nǐ shì nǎ ge dìfang de rén
你 是 哪 个 地方 的 人？
Nǐ shì shénme dìfang de rén
（你 是 什么 地方 的 人？）

难点八 “也”vs.“和”

“也”和“和”也是学生常用错的。

Often, learners think “也” and “和” are both like the English “and/also”. The differences must be emphasized, and can be simply emphasized like this:

“也” connects two verbal phrases:

Wǒ shuō Yīngyǔ yě shuō Hànyǔ
我 说 英语，也 说 汉语 。
Tā yǒu gēge yě yǒu dìdi
他 有 哥哥，也 有 弟弟。

“和” connects two noun phrases:

Wǒ shuō Yīngyǔ hé Hànyǔ
我 说 英语 和 汉语 。
Tā yǒu gēge hé dìdi
他 有 哥哥 和 弟弟。

难点九 “And” vs. “和”

英语的“And”可以连接句子，“和”不能。请比较。

Often, learners assume “And ” and “和” have the same grammatical functions in both English and Chinese. However, they do not. “And ” can connect words, phrases, clauses, and sentences. “和” can connect words or phrases, but cannot connect clauses/sentences.

(words) He and I

tā hé wǒ
他 和 我

(phrases) Watch movie and play on the computer

kàn diànyǐng hé wán diànnǎo
看 电影 和 玩 电脑

(clauses) I watched a movie at home and also watched one at school.

Wǒ zài jiā kànle yí gè diànyǐng zài xuéxiào kànle yí ge
我 在 家 看了 一 个 电影 ，在 学校 看了 一 个
diànyǐng hé
电影 。(No “和”)

(sentences) I have two brothers. And he has no brother.

Wǒ yǒu liǎng ge gēge Tā méiyǒu gēge hé
我 有 两 个 哥哥。他 没有 哥哥。(No “和”)

Note

It can never be over-emphasized that “和” cannot connect sentences.

难点十 “也” vs. “还”

“也” and “还” both can be translated into “also” and “too”.

“也” and “还” both are used to connect verbal phrases.

However, what “也” connects usually has equal weight, while “还” also means “still”, it has a notation of “in addition to”.

Wǒmen shuō Yīngyǔ yě shuō Hànyǔ
我们 说 英语，也 说 汉语。
Tā shuō Yīngyǔ Hànyǔ hái shuō yìdiǎn Fǎyǔ
他 说 英语、汉语、还 说 一点 法语。

难点十一 “都不” vs. “不都”

The first word controls the following one:

“都不” means “all not”; “不都” means “not all”

他们都不是中国人。

They are all not Chinese/ None of them is Chinese.

他们不都是中国人。

They are not all Chinese/Not all of them are Chinese.

难点十二 “都” vs. “All”

“都”在汉语里是一个副词，只能放在动词的前面。“All”是无所不在的。

“都” in Chinese is an adverb. It can only be put before a verb to modify the verb. “都” can never be put before a noun or at the beginning of a sentence while the English “all” can.

都 dōu all (“All” at the beginning of a sentence)

我们都是学生。(“都” before the verb) All of us are students.

所有 suǒyǒu all (“All” before a noun)

我们认识所有的人。

(You cannot say “都人” because “人” is not a verb.)

Unless, you say: 这儿的人我们都认识。We know all the people.

Other words meaning “All”:

全 quán 1) complete, total, whole, entire, all

2）completely，totally，entirely

全家	quán jiā	entire family
全国	quán guó	whole country，entire nation，nationwide
全年	quán nián	annual，yearly
全天	quán tiān	entire day
我们全都是中学生。		We are all high school students.
他们全都没有中文书。		None of them has a Chinese book.

整 zhěng whole，complete，entire

整天	zhěng tiān	all day，whole day，all day long
整年	zhěng nián	all year，whole year，all year long
整个国家	zhěnggè guójiā	whole nation

文化联系

Cultural Relations

我们都是美国人 We are all Americans

In Chinese，there are two ways to specify the ethnicity/origin of a U. S. citizen. For Chinese Americans：

1）华裔（Huá yì）美国人

华裔，refers to the Chinese origin or Chinese descent of citizens of countries other than China. “华” refers to China/Chinese. “裔 ” means origin/descent，especially the citizens of countries other than the countries of origin.

2）美籍华人（Měi jí Huárén）American Citizen of Chinese descent. “籍” means “citizenship/registry”. As such，there can be other Americans：

Japanese-American： 日裔（Rì yì）美国人（Měiguórén）/美籍（Měi jí）日本人（Rìběnrén）

	Fǎ yì Měiguórén　Měi jí Fǎguórén
French-American:	法 裔 美国人 / 美 籍 法国人
	Fēi yì Měiguórén　Měi jí Fēizhōurén
African-American:	非 裔 美国人 / 美 籍 非洲人
	Lādīng yì Měiguórén　Měi jí Lādīngrén
Latin-American:	拉 丁 裔 美国人 / 美 籍 拉丁人

汉语/中文/华文　Chinese Language

我们学的是"汉语/中文/华文"，也叫"普通话"或"国语"。中国有很多种方言，例如：广东人说广东话。

The Chinese we are learning is "普通话 pǔtōnghuà", common spoken language, standard spoken Chinese, modern standard Chinese (based on the Beijing dialect, also known as Mandarin or Guoyu).

Many Chinese and Chinese Americans speak different dialects. For example:

Guǎngdōngrén shuō Guǎngdōnghuà
广东人 说 广东话 。

or:

Shànghǎirén shuō Shànghǎihuà
上海人 说 上海话 。

Tiānjīnrén shuō Tiānjīnhuà
天津人 说 天津话 。

词汇表

Glossary

国家/人　guójiā/rén　Country/People

	国家 (Nation, Country):		人 (People):	
China	中国	Zhōngguó	中国人	Zhōngguórén
The United States of America	美国	Měiguó	美国人	Měiguórén
The United Kingdom	英国	Yīngguó	英国人	Yīngguórén

France	法国	Fǎguó	法国人	Fǎguórén
Germany	德国	Déguó	德国人	Déguórén
Japan	日本	Rìběn	日本人	Rìběnrén
Mexico	墨西哥	Mòxīgē	墨西哥人	Móxīgērén
Puerto Rico	波多黎各	Bōduōlígè	波多黎各人	Bōduōlígèrén
Poland	波兰	Bōlán	波兰人	Bōlánrén
Canada	加拿大	Jiānádà	加拿大人	Jiānádàrén
Russia	俄罗斯	Éluósī	俄罗斯人	Éluósīrén
The Philippines	菲律宾	Fēilǜbīn	菲律宾人	Fēilǜbīnrén
(South) Korea	韩国	Hánguó	韩国人	Hánguórén
(North) Korea	朝鲜	Cháoxiǎn	朝鲜人	Cháoxiǎnrén
Thailand	泰国	Tàiguó	泰国人	Tàiguórén
India	印度	Yìndù	印度人	Yìndùrén
Pakistan	巴基斯坦	Bājīsītǎn	巴基斯坦人	Bājīsītǎnrén

语言 yǔyán Language

	yǔ 语 Spoken Language		wén 文 Written Language	
Chinese	汉语	Hànyǔ	中文	Zhōngwén
English	英语	Yīngyǔ	英文	Yīngwén
French	法语	Fǎyǔ	法文	Fǎwén
German	德语	Déyǔ	德文	Déwén
Japanese	日语	Rìyǔ	日文	Rìwén
Spanish	西班牙语	Xībānyáyǔ	西班牙文	Xībānyáwén
Latin	拉丁语	Lādīngyǔ	拉丁文	Lādīngwén

有关地理词 Related Geographical Terms

地球 dìqiú earth, globe

大洲 dàzhōu continent

亚洲 Yàzhōu Asia

非洲	Fēizhōu	Africa		
欧洲	Ōuzhōu	Europe		
美洲	Měizhōu	America		
	北美州	Běiměizhōu	North America	
	中美洲	Zhōngměizhōu	Central America	
	南美洲	Nánměizhōu	South America	
	拉丁美洲	Lādīngměizhōu	Latin America	
大洋洲	Dàyángzhōu	Oceania		
南极洲	Nānjízhōu	Antarctic		
北极	běijí	North Pole, Arctic Pole		

大洋	dàyáng	Ocean	
	太平洋	Tàipíngyáng	Pacific Ocean
	大西洋	Dàxīyáng	Atlantic Ocean
	印度洋	Yìndùyáng	Indian Ocean
	北冰洋	Běibīngyáng	Arctic Ocean

中国	Zhōngguó	China
首都	shǒudū	Capital, capital city
省	shěng	Province
城市	chéngshì	Big city
农村	nóngcūn	Village, countryside
北京	Běijīng	Beijing (capital, PRC)
上海	Shànghǎi	Shanghai (municipality, PRC)
天津	Tiānjīn	Tianjin (municipalcity, PRC)
重庆	chóngqìng	Chongqing (municipal city, PRC)
香港	Xiānggǎng	Hong Kong (SAR)
澳门	Àomén	Macao, Aomen (SAR)
广东	Guǎngdōng	Guangdong (Province)

台湾	Táiwān	Taiwan (Province)	
台北	Táiběi	Taipei (Provincial capital, Taiwan)	
大河	dàhé	Great river	
	黄河	Huáng Hé	Huang he River, Yellow River
	长江	Cháng Jiāng	Changjiang, Yangtse River
名山	míngshān	Famous mountains	
	泰山	Tài Shān	Mount Tai (in Shandong Province)
	华山	Huà Shān	Mount Hua (in Shaanxi Province)
	阿里山	Ālǐ Shān	Mount Ali (in Taiwan Province)
古迹	gǔjì	Historic sites	
	长城	Chángchéng	Great Wall of China
	故宫	Gùgōng	Imperial Palace

5

工作与职业

Work and Occupation

工作与职业的话题牵扯两方面的词汇：工作/职业和工作地点。本节着重讨论学习这两方面的询问、表述和连贯表达。

这个话题也与文化社会的因素有很多联系。汉语的学习可与学生的家庭背景与社区文化相结合扩展讨论学习。

Work and occupation is a topic involving two kinds of vocabularies: work/occupation and the workplace. This chapter stresses the facilitation of inquiry, the statement of each aspect and the combination of the two.

This topic also has connections with cultural and social vocabularies. Language learning creates an opportunity for further discussion about students' families and community backgrounds.

教学重点 Content of Teaching and Learning

工作与职业	Work and Occupation
询问/表述职业	Asking and Speaking about Occupation
工作地点	Workplace
询问/表述工作地点	Asking and Speaking about Workplace

教学难点 Difficulties

“做” vs. “是”	
地点在句中的位置	Position of Location Word in a Sentence

文化联系 Cultural Relations

工作与职业	Work and Occupation

词汇表 Glossary

职业	Occupations
工作地点	Workplace
跟学习相关的词汇	Words Related to Study

教学重点

Content of Teaching and Learning

工作与职业 Work and Occupation

职业 Occupations

老师	lǎoshī	Teacher
律师	lǜshī	Lawyer, attorney
工程师	gōngchéngshī	Engineer
医生	yīshēng (大夫 dàifu)	Doctor, physician
护士	hùshi	Nurse (in a hospital)
经理	jīnglǐ	Manage, director
职员	zhíyuán	Employee, office worker, staff member
商人	shāngrén	Merchant, businessman, trader
演员	yǎnyuán	Performer, actor, actress
艺术家	yìshùjiā	Artist
警察	jǐngchá	Police officer
消防队员	xiāofáng duìyuán	Fireman, fire fighter
售货员	shòuhuòyuán	Shop assistant, salesperson
秘书	mìshū	Secretary
保安员	bǎo'ānyuán	Security guard
工人	gōngrén	Worker
学生	xuésheng	Student, pupil

大学生	dàxuéshēng	University student, college student
中学生	zhōngxuéshēng	Middle-school student
小学生	xiǎoxuéshēng	Elementary school student

询问/表述职业 Asking and Speaking about Occupation

句型 Sentence Patterns：

工作 gōngzuò work，occupation，job

做 zuò act as，work，do

Zuò shénme gōngzuò
做 什么 工作 ？

是 shì am，is，are . . .

Shì lǎoshī
是 老师 。

工作地点 Workplace

公司	gōngsī	Company，corporation，firm
医院	yīyuàn	Hospital
商店	shāngdiàn	Shop，store
书店	shūdiàn	Bookstore
饭馆	fànguǎn	Restaurant
餐馆	cānguǎn	Restaurant
饭店	fàndiàn	Hotel，restaurant
咖啡馆	kāfēiguǎn	Coffee shop
酒吧	jiǔbā	Bar（especially Western-style），pub
图书馆	túshūguǎn	Library
警察局	jǐngchájú	Police station
派出所	pàichūsuǒ	Police substation
银行	yínháng	Bank
幼儿园	yòu'éryuán	Kindergarten，nursery school
剧院	jùyuàn	Theater，theater club
政府机构	zhèngfǔ jīgòu	Government institution

学校	xuéxiào	School	
	大学	dàxué	University, college
	中学	zhōngxué	Middle school, high school
	小学	xiǎoxué	Elementary school, primary school

询问/表述工作地点 Asking and Speaking about Workplace

句型 Sentence Patterns:

地方 dìfang place, location

Zài shénme dìfang gōngzuò
(在 什么 地方 工作 ?)

Zài nǎr gōngzuò
在 哪儿 工作 ?

Zài gōngsī gōngzuò
在 公司 工作 。

文化联系

Cultural Relations

这个话题可与现实生活紧密联系，也可作文化对比。但公立学校学生的家庭背景各不相同，这个话题会有敏感区。一方面鼓励学生与生活实际联系，另一方面不应让学生感到不舒服。

Applying this topic is a good opportunity to make real-life connections and cultural comparisons. However, be aware, in K-12 schools, especially public schools, students come from all social-economical backgrounds. This topic, potentially, may be sensitive to some students. The teacher needs to encourage the use of language in real-life situations, while avoiding situations that may cause discomfort.

教学难点

Difficulties

难点一 “做” vs. “是”

Asking about a person's profession uses the verb “做”, but the answer uses the verb “是”.

句型 Sentence Patterns

Subject	+ Place	+ Verb	+ Object.
Nǐ bàba 你 爸爸		zuò 做	shénme gōngzuò 什么 工作 ?
Wǒ bàba 我 爸爸		shì 是	lǎoshī 老师。
Nǐ bàba 你 爸爸	zài nǎr 在 哪儿	gōngzuò 工作 ?	
Tā 他	zài zhōngxué 在 中学	gōngzuò 工作 。	

难点二 地点在句中的位置

Position of Location Word in a Sentence

Location word is always placed before the action verb. A name of a place can be used as the location of an action or as a modifier of a noun. (Learners often confuse the two in use.)

句型 Sentence Patterns:

Subject	+ Place	+ Verb	+ Object.

A.
Tā shì Zhījiāgē Dàxué de xuésheng
他 是 芝加哥 大学 的 学生 。

He is a student in the University of Chicago.

(A: U of C defines the student as part of the identification.)

B.
Tā zài Zhījiāgē Dàxué shàng xué
他 在 芝加哥 大学 上 学。

He studies at the University of Chicago.

(B: U of C is the location where action happens.)

Combination:

Subject	+ Adverb	+ Verb	+ Object
Nǐ 你		zuò 做	shénme 什么 ?
Wǒ 我		shì 是	dàxuéshēng 大学生 。
Nǐ 你	zài nǎr 在 哪儿	shàng xué 上 学 ?	
Wǒ 我	zài Díbǎo Dàxué 在 迪堡 大学	shàng xué 上 学。	
Wǒ 我		shì 是	Díbǎo Dàxué de xuésheng 迪堡 大学 的 学生 。
Nǐ bàba 你 爸爸		zuò 做	shénme 什么 ?
Wǒ bàba 我 爸爸		shì 是	jīnglǐ 经理。
Tā 他	zài nǎr 在 哪儿	gōngzuò 工作 ?	
Tā zài 他 在	shāngdiàn 商店	gōngzuò 工作 。	
Tā 他		shì 是	shāngdiàn de jīnglǐ 商店 的 经理。

Tā	bú	shì	fànguǎn de jīnglǐ
他	不	是	饭馆 的 经理。
Tā māma		zuò	shénme
他 妈妈		做	什么 ？
Tā		shì	dàifu
她		是	大夫。
Tā	zài nǎr	gōngzuò	
她	在 哪儿	工作 ？	
Tā	zài dàxué yīyuàn	gōngzuò	
她	在 大学 医院	工作 。	
Tā		shì	nàge yīyuàn de dàifu
她		是	那个 医院 的 大夫。

词汇表

Glossary

跟学习相关的词汇 Words Related to Study

学	Learn, study		
	学习	xuéxí	Study, learn
	上学	shàng xué	Go to school, attend school
学校	xuéxiào	School	
	大学	dàxué	University, college
	中学	zhōngxué	Middle school, high school
	小学	xiǎoxué	Elementary school, primary school
学生	xuésheng	Student, pupil	
	大学生	dàxuéshēng	University student; college student
	中学生	zhōngxuéshēng	Middle-school student
	小学生	xiǎoxuéshēng	(Elementary) school child; pupil

Dàxuéshēng shàng dàxué
大学生 上 大学。
Dàxuéshēng zài dàxué xuéxí
大学生 在 大学 学习。
Zhōngxuéshēng shàng zhōngxué
中学生 上 中学。
Zhōngxuéshēng zài zhōngxué xuéxí
中学生 在 中学 学习。
Xiǎoxuéshēng shàng xiǎoxué
小学生 上 小学。
Xiǎoxuéshēng zài xiǎoxué xuéxí
小学生 在 小学 学习。
Wǒmen zhù zài Zhījiāgē Wǒmen dōu shì xuésheng zài Zhījiāgē
我们 住 在 芝加哥。我们 都 是 学生，在 芝加哥
shàng xué
上 学。

Wǒ gēge shì dàxuéshēng
我 哥哥 是 大学生。
Wǒ gēge xuéxí Hànyǔ
我 哥哥 学习 汉语。
Wǒ gēge zài Díbǎo Dàxué xuéxí Hànyǔ
我 哥哥 在 迪堡 大学 学习 汉语。
Wǒ gēge de Hànyǔ lǎoshī shì Wáng lǎoshī
我 哥哥 的 汉语 老师 是 王 老师。
Nǐmen shì zhōngxuéshēng
你们 是 中学生
Nǐmen yě xuéxí Hànyǔ
你们 也 学习 汉语。
Nǐmen zài Lādīng Zhōngxué xuéxí Hànyǔ
你们 在 拉丁 中学 学习 汉语。
Nǐmen de Hànyǔ lǎoshī bú shì Wáng lǎoshī
你们 的 汉语 老师 不是 王 老师。
Tāmen shì xiǎoxuéshēng
他们 是 小学生。

Tāmen yě dōu xuéxí Hànyǔ
他们 也 都 学习 汉语 。

Tāmen zài Bài'ěr Xiǎoxué xuéxí Hànyǔ
他们 在 拜尔 小学 学习 汉语 。

Tāmen de Hànyǔ lǎoshī yě bú shì Wáng lǎoshī
他们 的 汉语 老师 也 不 是 王 老师 。

Zhè shì wǒmen de Hànyǔ lǎoshī Tā xìng Wáng
这 是 我们 的 汉语 老师，他 姓 王 。

Wáng lǎoshī bú shì Měiguórén Tā shì Zhōngguórén yě shì
王 老师 不 是 美国人 。他 是 中国人 ，也 是
Jiānádàrén
加拿大人 。

Tā shuō Yīngyǔ Fǎyǔ hé Hànyǔ
他 说 英语 、法语 和 汉语 。

Tā fùmǔ de jiā zài Běijīng Tā zhù zài Zhījiāgē
他 父母 的 家 在 北京 。他 住 在 芝加哥 。

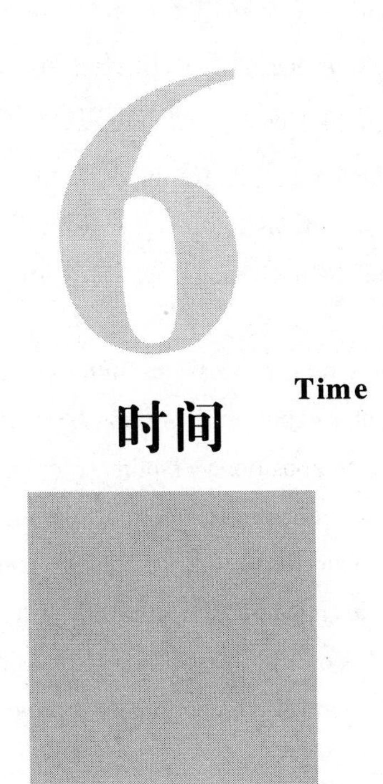

6 时间 Time

时间是非常重要的概念。在日常生活中我们谈论时间，谈论行为发生的时间，特别是汉语的动词本身没有时态，时间词因此更为关键。

本节按时间词的语用功能将时间词分为两类：时间点与时间段。并介绍简单常用时间词、其他时间词的组成、时间词在句中的位置、与时间有关的问句形式。

时间的表达与两个成分休戚相关。第一，时间的表达不仅与行为动作有紧密联系，而且有时是通过行为动作表达的。其二，很多时间词是通过数字表达的。学了数字再学时间，两者可以在教学上相辅相成。

Time is an important concept. In our daily life, we talk about time itself as well as its relationship to actions and events. Chinese verbs have no tenses, and thus do not reflect time themselves. Time expressions, therefore, become more critical in language use.

This chapter divides time expressions into two categories according to pragmatic functions: moment in time and periods of time. It also introduces simple daily time expressions, compositions of other time expressions, position of time expressions in sentences, and question forms relating to time.

Time expressions relate to two other language elements: verbs and numbers. Firstly, time indicates the moment and duration of actions, while actions can be used to indicate time. Secondly, many time expressions have a numeric component. This points to the natural connections and possible sequence of instruction.

教学重点 Content of Teaching and Learning

时间点	Point in time—Moment
日历	Calendar
一天	A Day
钟点	O'clock
过去/现在/未来	Past/Present/Future
动词组指示时间	Actions Indicating Time
时间段	Period of time—Duration
度量	Measurements

对比	Compare
句型与提问	Sentence Patterns and Questions
时间点句型	Point in Time
时间段句型	Time Duration

教学难点 Difficulties

时间点在句中的位置	Position of Time Phrase in the Sentence
行为指示时间	Actions Indicate Time
时间点做名词定语	Point in Time as Attributive
“Year” vs. “年”	
上？下？	Last and Next
时间点与时间段	Point in Time vs. Period of Time

教学重点

Content of Teaching and Learning

时间点 Point in Time —Moment

使用规则 Rules:

1）时间的表达总是从大概念到小概念。

Time expressions always proceed from the larger concept to the smaller one.

2）时间点在动词前。

Time expressions (moment of time) are always put before verbs.

日历 rìlì calendar

年 nián year

yī jiǔ jiǔ jiǔ nián
一 九 九 九 年

èr líng líng líng nián èr líng líng líng nián
二 零 零 零 年（二 ○ ○ ○ 年）

In English, we say, "the year nineteen ninety-nine or the year two thousand" or "ninety-nine" refering to the year.

In Chinese, we read each digit and always use the word "年 nián" at the end:

一九九九年 yī jiǔ jiǔ jiǔ nián or 九九年 jiǔ jiǔ nián

月 yuè month

In English, each month has a name.

In Chinese, the months are numbered in sequence starting from January.

yīyuè	èryuè	sānyuè	sìyuè	wǔyuè	liùyuè
一月，	二月，	三月，	四月，	五月，	六月，
January	February	March	April	May	June
qīyuè	bāyuè	jiǔyuè	shíyuè	shíyīyuè	shí'èryuè
七月，	八月，	九月，	十月，	十一月，	十二月

July August September October November December

日 rì Day of the month (formal)

èr yuè yī rì
二 月 一 日

号 hào Day of the month (informal)

shí'èr yuè èrshíyī hào
十二 月 二十一 号

星期 xīngqī week

礼拜 lǐbài Week (colloquial expression)

周 zhōu Week (written expression)

星期一	礼拜一	周一
星期二	礼拜二	周二
星期三	礼拜三	周三
星期四	礼拜四	周四
星期五	礼拜五	周五
星期六	礼拜六	周六
星期日（星期天）	礼拜日（礼拜天）	
周末	zhōumò	Weekend
周日	zhōurì	Weekday

一天 yì tiān A day

早上	zǎoshang	Early morning
上午	shàngwǔ	Morning
中午	zhōngwǔ	Noon, midday
下午	xiàwǔ	Afternoon
晚上	wǎnshang	Evening, night
半夜	bànyè	Midnight

前半夜 qiánbànyè The first half of the night

后半夜 hòubànyè After midnight

钟点 zhōngdiǎn O'clock

点钟 diǎnzhōng Hour, o'clock（Also See 1：Numbers in Life Chapter）

yì diǎn liǎng diǎn
一 点 两 点

For two o'clock, always say "两点." Never say "二点".

半 bàn Half, semi-（点钟）

（According to the rule #1, "half" is smaller than " a whole hour" therefore：）

liǎng diǎn bàn
2:30 两 点 半

刻 kè Quarter of an hour

liǎng diǎn yí kè liǎng diǎn sān kè
2:15 两 点 一 刻 2:45 两 点 三 刻

分 fēn Minute（of time）

liǎng diǎn wǔ fēn liǎng diǎn shí fēn
2:05 两 点 五 分 2:10 两 点 十 分

However, in expressions more than 10 minutes, "fen" can be omitted：

liǎng diǎn shíwǔ(fēn)
2:15 两 点 十五（分）

差 chà Lack, be short of

Whatever is lacking, comes before mentioning of the whole clock.

chà wǔ fēn sān diǎn chà yí kè sān diǎn
2:55 差 五 分 三 点 2:45 差 一 刻 三 点

According to the patterns above, there are at least three ways to say 2:45

liǎng diǎn sìshíwǔ（fēn）
2:45 两 点 四十五（分）

liǎng diǎn sān kè
两 点 三 刻
chà yí kè sān diǎn
差 一刻 三 点

Think: What are the other possible ways to say it? Can other times be told in similar ways?

Variations of telling the time:

	liǎng diǎn wǔ fēn	liǎng diǎn líng wǔ(fēn)
2:05	两 点 五 分	两 点 〇 五(分)
	liǎng diǎn shíwǔ (fēn)	liǎng diǎn yí kè
2:15	两 点 十五 (分)	两 点 一刻
	liǎng diǎn sānshí (fēn)	liǎng diǎn bàn
2:30	两 点 三十 (分)	两 点 半
	liǎng diǎn sìshíwǔ (fēn)	
2:45	两 点 四十五 (分)	
	chà yí kè sān diǎn	chà shíwǔ fēn sān diǎn
	差 一刻 三 点	差 十五 分 三 点
	liǎng diǎn wǔshíwǔ (fēn)	chà wǔ fēn sān diǎn
2:55	两 点 五十五 (分)	差 五 分 三 点

其他时间词 Other Related Expressions

世纪	shìjì	century:
	19 世纪	21 世纪
	19 Century	21 Century
年代	niándài	decade (e. g. the 1980s)
	60 年代	80 年代
	the 60s	the 80s
每	měi	each, every
	每年	每天
	every year	every day
清晨	qīngchén	early morning
半夜	bànyè	midnight, in the middle of the night
秒	miǎo	second
有时候	yǒu shíhou	sometimes, at times, occasionally

过去/现在/未来 Past/ Present/ Future

Past	Present	Future
qiánnián qùnián 前年 去年 year before last last year	jīnnián 今年 this year	míngnián hòunián 明年 后年 next year year after next
qiántiān zuótiān 前天 昨天 day before yesterday yesterday	jīntiān 今天 today	míngtiān hòutiān 明天 后天 tomorrow day after tomorrow
shàng ge yuè 上 个 月 last month	zhège yuè 这个 月 this month	xià ge yuè 下 个 月 next month
shàng ge xīngqī 上 个 星期 last week	zhège xīngqī 这个 星期 this week	xià ge xīngqī 下 个 星期 next week

其他 Other Expressions

过去 guòqù in the past

从前 cóngqián in the past

现在 xiànzài now, at the present time

目前 mùqián at present

将来 jiānglái (in the) future

未来 wèilái coming (of time), future

míngnián wǔ yuè
明年 五 月 Next May

qùnián bā yuè
去年 八 月 Last August

jīntiān zǎoshang
今天 早上 This morning

zuótiān zhōngwǔ
昨天 中午 Yesterday noon

qī yuè sān hào shàngwǔ
七 月 三 号 上午 The morning of July 3

xīngqīliù wǎnshang
星期六 晚上 Saturday night

shàng xīngqīsì zǎoshang jiǔ diǎn yí kè
上 星期四 早上 九 点 一 刻

Last Thursday at 9：15 am (in the morning)

xià xīngqītiān xiàwǔ sān diǎn bàn
下 星期天 下午 三 点 半

3：30 pm (in the afternoon) next Sunday

动词组指示时间 Actions Indicating Time

用动作行为指示时间有三个词组。请注意中英文的不同。

There are three patterns help to form time expressions with actions:
(Pay attention to the structural differences in English and Chinese.)

1) During an action (while ..., When ...) action 的时候 shíhou

during class: shàng kè de shíhou
上 课 的 时候

while watching a movie: kàn diànyǐng de shíhou
看 电影 的 时候

T (V +的时候) +Main Action in Sentence.

吃饭的时候，我看书。
While eating, I read books. / I read books while eating.

2) Before an action action 以前 yǐqián

before class: shàng kè yǐqián
上 课 以前

before watching a movie: kàn diànyǐng yǐqián
看 电影 以前

T (V +以前) +Main Action in Sentence.

吃饭以前，我学习汉语。
Before eating, I study Chinese. / I study Chinese before eating.

3) After an action action 以后 yǐhòu

after class shàng kè yǐhòu
上 课 以后

after watching a movie: kàn diànyǐng yǐhòu
看 电影 以后

T (V +以后) +Main Action in Sentence.

吃饭以后，我看电视。

After eating, I watch TV. / I watch TV after eating.

时间段 Period of Time—Duration

度量 Measurements

(whole number) + measure word + more (or less) than the whole measurement

1）“年”，“天”，“分”，“刻”，“秒” are used as measurements：

一年　　一年半/一年多

两天　　两天半/两天多

五分钟　　五分多钟

一刻钟　　一刻多钟

三秒钟　　三秒半

2）“个 ” is used to measure other specified lengths of time：

The time periods to be measured are：“世纪”，“月”，“星期”，“早上”，“小时/钟头”，等.

两个月

半个月

一个多月

一个半月

一个星期　　一个多星期

一个早上

两个小时/两个钟头

半个小时/半个钟头

两个半小时（钟头）

两个多小时（钟头）

3）“从……到” pattern is used to specify a starting point to an ending point of a duration.

从一月到六月　From January to June

从八点到九点　From eight o'clock to nine o'clock

对比　Compare

时间点　Point in Time	**时间段**　Period of Time
2000 年	一年 半年 一年多 一年半
二月	两个月 半个月 一个多月 一个半月
星期一	一个星期 一个多星期
今天 明天 昨天	一天 半天 一天多
早上，晚上， 上午，中午，下午，	一个早上
两点 两点半	两个小时，两个钟头 半个钟头 两个半小时 两个多小时
两点一刻 两点十五分	一刻钟 十五分钟 一秒钟 一会儿 半天

一月	从一月到六月
八点	从八点到九点

句型与提问 Sentence Patterns and Questions

时间点句型 Sentence Patterns: Point in Time

Remember: From large to small

èr líng líng liù nián sānyuè èrshièr rì xīngqīsān shàngwǔ shíyī
二 〇 〇 六 年 三月 二十二 日 星期三 上午 十一
diǎn èrshíwǔ fēn
点 二十五 分

Remember: The point in time comes before the action:

Subject Time	+	Verb + Object

Wǒmen měitiān zǎoshang qī diǎn wǔshíwǔ fēnshàng dì yī jié kè
我们 每天 早上 七 点 五十五 分 上 第 一 节 课。
We everyday morning at 7: 55 have the first period of class.

or

Time	+	Subject + Verb + Object

Měitiān zǎoshang qī diǎn wǔshíwǔ fēnwǒmenshàng dì yī jié kè
每天 早上 七 点 五十五 分 我们 上 第 一 节 课。
Every morning at 7: 55, we have the first period of class.

问题 Questions:

General time: 什么时候？

Specific time: 几点？

Year, date: 哪年？几月几日（号）？

Point in time phrases are always before the verbs.

Subject	+	Time	+	Verb	+	Object

Nǐ shénme shíhou shàng kè
你 什么 时候 上 课？
When do you have class?

Nǐ jǐ diǎn xià kè
你 几 点 下 课?
At what time do you end class?

时间段句型 Sentence Patterns: Time Duration

Subject + Verb + Object + Verb + Duration

	Subject		Verb	Object	Verb	Duration	
	Tā	(cháng)	kàn	shū	kàn	liǎng ge zhōngtóu	
habitual:	他	(常)	看	书	看	两 个 钟头	。
	He (often) reads (books) for two hours.						
	Tā		kàn	shū	kànle	liǎng ge zhōngtóu	
done:	他		看	书	看了	两 个 钟头	。
	He read (books) for two hours.						
	Tā		kàn	shū	kànle	liǎng ge zhōngtóu	le
doing:	他		看	书	看了	两 个 钟头	了。
	He has been reading (books) for two hours.						
	Tā		kàn	shū	yào kàn	liǎng ge zhōngtóu	
Plan:	他		看	书	要 看	两 个 钟头	。
	He is going to read (books) for two hours.						

问题 Questions

Duō cháng shíjiān Duō jiǔ
多 长 时间?/多 久?
For how long?

Nǐ měi tiān kàn shū (yào) kàn duō cháng shíjiān (habitual)
你 每 天 看 书 (要) 看 多 长 时间?
How long do you read everyday?

Nǐ jīntiān kàn shū yào kàn duō cháng shíjiān
你 今天 看 书 要 看 多 长 时间?(plan)
How long are you going to read today?

Nǐ kàn shū kànle duō cháng shíjiān
你 看 书 看了 多 长 时间?(done)
How long did you read?

Nǐ kàn shū kànle duō cháng shíjiān le
你 看 书 看了 多 长 时间 了?(up to now)
How long have you been reading?

Nǐ chángcháng kàn shū kàn duō jiǔ
你 常常 看 书 看 多 久?(habitual)
How long do you usually read?

Nǐ jīntiān kàn shū yào kàn duō jiǔ
你 今天 看 书 要 看 多 久？(plan)
How long are you going to read today?

Nǐ kàn shū kànle duō jiǔ
你 看 书 看了 多 久？(done)
How long did you read?

Nǐ kàn shū kànle duō jiǔ le
你 看 书 看了 多 久 了？(up to now)
How long have you been reading?

教学难点

Difficulties

难点一　时间点在句中的位置

Position of Time Phrase in the Sentence

在句首：before or after the subject（but always before the verb）

我每天八点上课。

每天八点我都上课。

难点二　行为指示时间 Actions Indicating Time

让学生困惑的地方有两个：时间词本身、时间词在句中的位置。

This is most confusing to English speakers for two resaons：the time phrase itself, the time phrase in a sentence.

1）时间词本身 The time phrase itself：（See Chapter 18：Noun Phrases.）

In English, "during, before, after" are adverbs which go before verbs.

In Chinese, "时候，以前，以后" are nouns which go after verbs.

During an action（While ..., When ...）　action 的时候（shíhou）

During class：	上课的时候
While watching a movie：	看电影的时候

Before an action action 以前 (yǐqián)

Before class: 上课以前

Before watching a movie: 看电影以前

After an action action 以后 (yǐhòu)

After class 上课以后

After watching a movie: 看电影以后

2) 时间词在句中的位置 The time phrase in the sentence:

英文的时间状语可以在动词前或后。

In English, the time phrase may go either before or after the main action:

Before (I attended) class I read.

I read before (I attended) class.

中文的时间状语只可以在动词前。

In Chinese, the time phrase must go before the main action.

上课以前我看书。

Tip: Two "Reversals" of words order may be needed.

One Reversal:

When translating "Before class I read.", reverse the phrase itself:

Before class: 上课以前

Two Reversals:

When translating " I read before class".

Firstly reverse the time and action:

before class, then read

Secondly, reverse the word order within the time phrase itself as above.

上课以前我看书。

难点三 时间点做名词定语 Point of Time as Attributive

The point in time can be used to define a noun such as "7 o'clock movie", e. g. :

我想看七点的电影。

他要坐八点的火车。

难点四 “Year” vs. “年”

There are two differences in English and Chinese in reading a year:

1）Numbers vs. digits

In English, a year is usually read every two digits:

the year 1991 is read: Nineteen Ninety-One

or as a whole number in case of the years of 2000:

the year 2006 is read: Two Thousand and Six

In Chinese, a year is read by each individual digit:

the year 1991 is read: yi, jiu, jiu, yi 一九九一年

Note: “九十一年” means ninety-one years.

2）“年” must be used

In English, when reading a year, the word “year” is not needed.

In Chinese, when reading a year, the word “年” must be used.

一九九一年 or simply 九一年

难点五 上？下？Last and Next

这恐怕是时间词里最难的。

This is most complicated in conversion from English to Chinese.

常犯的错误 Most frequent mistakes are:

1）Using “This and That”

“这个”“那个” when referring to “今年，今天”.

This year: 今年

Today: 今天

2）Overly generalized use of “last”:

Last year: 去年

Yesterday: 昨天

3）Reversed use of “上” and “下”：

Somehow it is hard for some English speakers to think

Last 上 （past）

Next 下 （future）

4）“Last September” is in which year？

In English，“last September” is the September that has most recently passed. It could be last year's or this year's.

In Chinese，months are put in the context of a year：

今年九月 the September of this year，

去年九月 the September of last year.

The same principle applies to “next”.

明年九月 the September of next year

Seasons are just like months. They should be put in the context of a year.

难点六 时间点与时间段 Point of Time vs. Period of Time

在句中的位置 Positions in a Sentence：

时间点在动词前

Point in Time（Moment of Time）is before the action.

时间段在动词后

Period of Time（Time Duration）is used after the action.

时间词的构成 Formation of time expressions（See Time Lists and the Comparison List）

时间点不用量词

Point in Time（Time Moment）uses no measure word.

时间段用量词

Period of Time（Time Duration）uses a measure word（though some measure words are time expressions themselves）.

7 行为与事件

Actions & Events

叙述行为与事件需要动词。本节把动词另列一节是为了提供教与学扩展的需要，同时方便与其他话题组合。

本节出现的动词一是最常用的；二是按功用分类的；三是以词组形式排列的。其他的教学重点与难点分析都与动词的使用有关。

Describing and recounting actions and events require verbs. The subject of action verbs and verb phrases is provided as a whole section for convenience of expanded teaching and learning. So they may be combined with other topics.

The verbs in this chapter are commonly used. They are categorized by function, and they appear in phrases. Also listed are grammatical points and explanations that relate to the use of verbs.

教学重点 Content of Teaching and Learning

常用动词与动词词组　　Commonly Used Verbs and Verbal Phrases

教学难点 Difficulties

动词的分类　　Category of Verbs

汉语形容词的动词性　　Adjectives as Verbs

动词作时间词　　Actions Indicating Time

状语与动作的关系（对比英语）　　Relationship between Adverbial and Action (Comparing with English)

英语中的“看”　　“看” in English

汉语中的“To know”　　“to know” in Chinese

汉语中的“To visit”　　“to visit” in Chinese

补充语法点 Supplementary Notes

双宾语　　Double Object

文化联系 Cultural Relations

借：“A borrower or a lender be?”

教学重点

Content of Teaching and Learning

常用动词与动词词组 Commonly Used Verbs and Verbal Phrases

Coming and Going:

Verb	Verbal Phrase		
上	shàng	go up, get on	
	上学	shàng xué	go to school, attend school
	上课	shàng kè	go to class, attend class
	上班	shàng bān	go to work, go on duty
	上厕所	shàng cèsuǒ	go to the toilet, use the toilet
	上车	shàng chē	get into or board a vehicle
	上街	shàng jiē	go out into the streets (shopping)
	上网	shàng wǎng	{IT} get on line, get on the Internet
下	xià	go down, get off	
	下课	xià kè	get out of class
	下班	xià bān	come off duty, go off work
	下棋	xià qí	play chess (or similar board games)
	下车	xià chē	alight (from a vehicle), de-board
放	fàng	release, set free, let go, put down	
	放学	fàng xué	dismiss students from school
	放假	fàng jià	have (or grant) vacation or holiday
	放屁	fàng pì	fart; {abusive} talk nonsense
来	lái	come	
	来上学	lái shàngxué	come to school
去	qù	go, go away, leave, depart	
	去上学	qù shàngxué	go to school

回	huí	return, go back	
	回家	huí jiā	return home
	回国	huí guó	return to one's native country
	回学校	huí xuéxiào	go back to school
走	zǒu	walk, travel on foot	
	走路	zǒu lù	walk, travel on foot
坐	zuò	sit; seat, place; travel by, go by (car, airplane, etc.)	
	坐车	zuò chē	go by train (bus or car)

Daily Life

起	qǐ	rise, stand up	
	起床	qǐ chuáng	get out of bed (in the morning)
睡	shuì	sleep, go to sleep	
	睡觉	shuì jiào	sleep, go to sleep
吃	chī	eat	
	吃饭	chī fàn	eat a meal
	吃早饭	chī zǎofàn	have breakfast
	吃中饭(午饭)	chī zhōngfàn (wǔfàn)	have lunch
	吃晚饭	chī wǎnfàn	have supper (dinner)
	吃中国菜	chī Zhōngguócài	eat Chinese food
	吃墨西哥菜	chī Mòxīgēcài	eat Mexican food
	吃水果	chī shuǐguǒ	eat fruit (s)
喝	hē	drink	
	喝水	hē shuǐ	drink water or tea
	喝茶	hē chá	have tea, drink tea
	喝可口可乐	hē Kěkǒukělè	drink Coca-cola
	喝咖啡	hē kāfēi	drink coffee
	喝牛奶	hē niúnǎi	drink (cow's) milk
	喝酒	hē jiǔ	drink alcoholic beverages

	喝啤酒	hē píjiǔ	drink beer
	喝橘子水（汁）	hē júzishuǐ(zhī)	drink orange juice
	喝果汁	hē guǒzhī	drink fruit juice (syrup)
看	kàn	look, see, read, watch, visit, call on (friends, etc.)	
	看书	kàn shū	read a book
	看电视	kàn diànshì	watch television/TV
	看电影	kàn diànyǐng	watch a movie/motion picture
	看球赛	kàn qiúsài	watch a ball game
	看朋友	kàn péngyou	visit friend
	看病	kàn bìng	see a doctor
听	tīng	hear, listen	
	听音乐	tīng yīnyuè	listen to music
	听歌	tīng gē	listen to songs
说	shuō	say, speak	
	说汉语	shuō Hànyǔ	speak Chinese (spoken language)
	说话	shuō huà	speak, talk, chat
打	dǎ	strike, hit, beat, play	
	打电话	dǎ diànhuà	make a phone call
	打球	dǎ qiú	play a ball game
	打乒乓球	dǎ pīngpāngqiú	play ping-pong
	打橄榄球	dǎ gǎnlǎnqiú	play rugby/American football
	打棒球	dǎ bàngqiú	play baseball
	打篮球	dǎ lánqiú	play basketball
	打排球	dǎ páiqiú	play volleyball
	打网球	dǎ wǎngqiú	play tennis
	打羽毛球	dǎ yǔmáoqiú	play badminton
	打高尔夫球	dǎ gāo'ěrfūqiú	play golf
	打保龄球	dǎ bǎolíngqiú	play Bowling
玩	wán	play, have fun, relax	

	玩电脑	wán diànnǎo	play on the computer
	玩电动	wán diàndòng	play computer games
	玩球	wán qiú	play a ball
用	yòng	use	
	用计算机	yòng jìsuànjī	use a computer
	用笔	yòng bǐ	use a pen (writing tools)
	用汉语	yòng Hànyǔ	use Chinese
骑	qí	ride	
	骑马	qí mǎ	ride a horse
	骑车	qí chē	ride a bicycle
	骑自行车	qí zìxíngchē	ride a bicycle
	骑摩托车	qí mótuōchē	ride a motorcycle
开	kāi	open up, turn on (a light), operate (a machine)	
	开门	kāi mén	open a door, open for business
	开灯	kāi dēng	turn on a light
	开车	kāi chē	start/drive a vehicle(car, train, etc.)
	开会	kāi huì	hold a meeting, attend a meeting
滑	huá	slip, slide	
	滑冰	huá bīng	skateing, ice-skating
	滑旱冰	huá hànbīng	roller-skate
	滑雪	huá xuě	ski
	滑板	huá bǎn	skateboard
游	yóu	swim, float	
	游泳	yóu yǒng	swim
	游水	yóu shuǐ	swim
唱	chàng	sing	
	唱歌	chàng gē	sing, sing a song
跳	tiào	jump, leap	
	跳舞	tiào wǔ	dance

	跳高	tiào gāo	high jump
	跳远	tiào yuǎn	broad jump, long jump
	跳水	tiào shuǐ	dive (into water)
跑	pǎo	run	
	跑步	pǎo bù	run, jogging
写	xiě	write, compose, portray, depict, draw, paint	
	写字	xiě zì	write, practise calligraphy
	写信	xiě xìn	write a letter
	写文章	xiě wénzhāng	write an article
作(做)	zuò	do, make, be, serve as	
	做饭	zuò fàn	cook, prepare a meal (especially rice)
	做作业	zuò zuòyè	do one's (school) assignment
	做功课	zuò gōngkè	do schoolwork/homework
买	mǎi	buy, purchase	
	买东西	mǎi dōngxi	buy things
卖	mài	sell	
	卖东西	mài dōngxi	sell things
逛	guàng	take a stroll, stroll roam	
	逛商店	guàng shāngdiàn	go window-shopping

Two-word Verbs

学习	xuéxí	study, learn
	学习英语	study Englsih
	学习汉语	learn Chinese
练习	liànxí	practise, drill; exercise
	练习口语	practice oral speeches
复习	fùxí	review (lessons, etc.)
	复习语法	review grammar

预习	yùxí	prepare/preview a lesson (of a student)
	预习生词	preview new words
准备	zhǔnbèi	prepare, get ready
	准备上课	prepare to go to class
打算	dǎsuan	plan, intend; plan, intention
计划	jìhuà	plan, program; plan
休息	xiūxi	rest, take a break, relax
	休息休息	need a good rest
锻炼	duànliàn	work out; exercise
	锻炼身体	do exercise
参加	cānjiā	join, participate in, take part in
	参加课外活动	participate in extracurricular activities
参观	cānguān	visit (e. g. as an observer, tourist, etc.)
访问	fǎngwèn	visit, call on
游览	yóulǎn	sight-see, tour
知道	zhīdao	know, understand, realize
认识	rènshi	know, understand, recognize
理解	lǐjiě	comprehend, understand
了解	liǎojiě	understand, comprehend, discover, find out about
同情	tóngqíng	sympathize with, have sympathy for

教学难点

Difficulties

难点一　动词的分类 Category of Verbs

Verb "是 shì to be"

"是" in Chinese has a more limited function than "to be" in English.

1）It is used to identify what is what and who is whom. Negative form is "不是".

她是学生，她不是老师。

She is a student. She is not a teacher.

这是书，不是本子。

This is a book not a notebook.

这本书是我的，不是你的。

This book is mine, not yours.

2）It is used to identify time, location, and manner of a specific action.

他真的来了吗？是什么时候来的？是怎么来的？

Has he really come? When did he come? How did he get here?

Important Note: Unlike in English, it cannot be used to describe a person/situation.

Verb "有 yǒu to Have"

"有" basically has three functions in Chinese. Negative form is "没有".

1）Possession:

我有一个弟弟，没有妹妹。

I have a little brother, I don't have a little sister.

2）"There is/are ..."

书架上只有几本书，没有报纸。

There are only a few books on the bookshelf, there are no newspapers.

3）Comparison/estimation:

他只有五英尺一英寸，还没有我高。

He is only 5′1″, not as tall as I am.

行为动词 Action Verbs

1）英文的很多动词在中文是动词性词组，用的时候得注意。

Many action verbs in English are verbal phrases in Chinese.

Sleep －睡觉 shuìjiào "睡" is a verb; "觉" is a noun

You can say：睡个好觉 have a good sleep

When you ask about (evaluate) the action, you ask,“睡得好不好?”

2）有些动词不是动词性词组，是双音节动词。

There are also two-word verbs.

Study －学习 xuéxí “学” is a verb ；“习” is also a verb.

情态动词/助动词

Model Verbs/Auxiliary Verbs（See Model Verbs List）

Model verbs/auxiliary verbs emphasize mood/desire/capability/obligation/possibility of an action.

See Chapter 8 for more details.

难点二 汉语形容词的动词性 Adjectives as Verbs

汉语的形容词可以直接做谓语，直接形容对象和情况，不需要动词。

In Chinese, adjectives are used to describe people and situations directly as predicate.

我很好。I am fine.

直接用形容词还有比较的意思。

However, when an adjective is used by itself, it has the implication of comparing.

我好。(我比他好。)

难点三 动词做时间词 Actions Indicating Time

行为动词还可以指定时间。

Action verbs (verbal phrases) are used to indicate time.

Usually with the help of “...的时候”, “...以前”, “...以后” to form time expressions.

（For more detailed explanation，see Chapter 6：Time.）

难点四 状语与动作的关系（对比英语）Relationship between Adverbial and Action（Comparing with English）

表时间、地点和行为方式的状语在英文句中的位置灵活，可在动词前或后。

Adverbial phrases include phrases that indicate time，location，and manner of an action.

In English，adverbial phrases are placed flexibly within a sentence. They may go before or after the verbs.

（Time）	I come to school everyday at 7：30 am.
	Everyday at 7：30 am.，I come to school.
（Place）	I come to school from my house.
	From my house，I come to school.
（Manner）	I come to school by bus with my friends.
	With my friends，I come to school by bus.

表时间、地点和行为方式的状语在中文句中的位置固定，只可在动词前。

In Chinese，all adverbial phrases indicating time，location，and the conditions of an action must come before the verb in a sentence.

（Time）	我每天早上七点半去上学。
（Place）	我从我家来学校上学。
（Manner）	我跟我的朋友坐公共汽车来上学。

难点五 英语中的“看”“看”in Enghish

没有一对一的翻译。

Remember：there is no exact one to one equavelant of words in any two languages. Some words in a language refer to one thing in another language or one word may have many meanings in another language.

中文的“看”译成英文有不少定义。

The verb “看” refers to many functions of the eyes in English:

read/watch/see/observe/look/visit/view, even viewpoint, etc.

看书	kàn shū	read a book
看电影	kàn diànyǐng	watch/see a movie
看那儿	kàn nàr	look at that/there
看朋友	kàn péngyou	visit/go see friends
你怎么看?		What do you think about it? /How do you see it? / What is your opinion?

“看”, when pronounced “kān”, means to “look after, take care of, keep under surveillance, keep an eye on, detain, etc.”

难点六 汉语中的“to know” “To know” in Chinese

英文的“to know”译成中文含义也很多。

Another commonly used word in English that has many different functions in Chinese is “to know”. When learners try to translate from English to Chinese, confusions may rise.

1) When “to know” is related to “to know/ to understand ”, there are a few expressions to show nuances in functional use:

知道	zhīdao	emphasizes knowing information, knowledge
认识	rènshi	emphasizes knowing through recognition
会	huì	emphasizes knowing how, being able to do somthing through a learned skill

2) When “to know” is related to comprehension and understanding, there are several expressions to show nuances in functional use:

懂得	dǒngde	emphasizes comprehension of meaning, method, etc.
明白	míngbai	emphasizes comprehending with clarity and sensibility

理解	lǐjiě	emphasizes comprehending with rational thinking and depth
了解	liǎojiě	emphasizes comprehension of detailed information
同情	tóngqíng	emphasizes comprehension with compassion/sympathy

难点七 汉语中的"to visit" "To visit" in Chinese

"to visit"也是一个麻烦。There are many kinds of visiting in Chinese:

访问	fǎngwèn	(formal) visit, call on
参观	cānguān	visit (e. g. as an observer, tourist, etc.)
游览	yóulǎn	sight-see, tour
旅游	lǚyóu	travel, be a tourist
看	kàn	(informal) visit, call on (friends, etc.)
去玩	qù wán	go to play, visit a place to have fun/to relax

补充语法点

Supplementary Notes

双宾语 Double Object

A few verbs take two objects: Direct object and indirect object.

有的动词后跟两个宾语：直接宾语和间接宾语。

请你给我一本书。Please give me a book.

In this sentence, "我" is an indirect object of the action. and "一本书" is the direct object of the action.

Rarely, this will cause confusions. However, in the situations of using the Chinese verb "借", we need caution.

在一般情况下，直接宾语和间接宾语的使用不是一个问题。但用

“借”时，要注意。

借：“A borrower or a lender be?”

借　　jiè　　borrow，lend

As you can see，“借” is both to borrow and to lend. Thus theoretically，the sentence below can be confusing.

“借”既可借出也可借进。不明确，语义容易混淆。

Tā jièle wǒ liǎng kuài qián
他 借了 我 两 块 钱 。

It could mean：

他借给了我两块钱。He lent me two dollars.

他跟我借了两块钱。or 他借了我的两块钱。

He borrowed two dollars from me（of mine）.

By the way，the opposite word is “还 huán return，repay”.

文化联系　Cultural Relations（for your learning pleasure）

A famous quote from Shakespeare's “Hamlet”：

“Never a lender nor a borrower be.”

不要借给别人钱，也不要借别人的钱。

8

爱好/选择/责任

Hobby/
Preference/
Obligation

谈爱好也要谈选择和责任。这些表达可能和愿望的话题都离不开使用能愿动词/助动词。

本节为方便话题的展开介绍常用的能愿动词及例句。希望词汇表方便教与学的选择，并通过例句给出一些能愿动词使用的情景。

教学的难点着重强调英语学生可能遇到的困难。

Talking about hobbies also relates to choices, possibilities, responsibilities and obligations. In all these topics, modal verbs (auxiliary verbs) are indispensable.

This chapter provides a modal verbs list and usage examples. The list aims to make expanded teaching and learning convenient, and the sample sentences provide examples with situational usages.

The explanation stresses the cruxes that English speaking students might encounter.

教学重点 Content of Teaching and Learning

能愿动词/助动词表 List of Modal Verbs (Auxiliary Verbs)

能愿动词的使用:例句与比较 Use of Modal Verbs: Example & Comparison

教学难点 Difficulties

"想" vs. "要"

"想" and "要" vs. "喜欢"

"想" vs. "Want"

"Ask" in Chinese

"Can" in Chinese

"会" vs. "能" vs. "可以"

"不用" vs. "甭" & "不要" vs. "别"

Negative for "得" and "不得不"

教学重点

Content of Teaching and Learning

能愿动词/助动词表 List of Modal Verbs (Auxiliary Verbs)

想	xiǎng	Intend, want to, would like to (as verb: think, long for, recall with fondness, miss)
要	yào	Want; will (as verb: demand; as adjective: important)
别	bié	Don't (as verb: depart, leave, separate) (other usages: other, another, different)
不用	búyòng	Need not, no use to; dispense with
会	huì	Know how, be able to (for prediction: be likely to)
能	néng	Capable of; be possible
可以	kěyǐ	Be permitted to; may, can (as adjective: not bad, pretty good)
应该	yīnggāi	Should, ought to, must
必须	bìxū	Be obliged to, have to
得	děi	Must, have to
不得不	bùdébù	Cannot but, cannot help but be obliged to, have no alternative
(一定)要	(yídìng) yào	Must, (surely) have to

能愿动词的使用：例句与比较

Use of Modal Verbs: Examples & Comparison

想 xiǎng want

positive: Wǒ xiǎng gēn péngyou qù kàn diànyǐng
我 想 跟 朋友 去 看 电影 。
I want to go to see a movie with my friends.

negative: Wǒ bù xiǎng jīntiān wǎnshang qù kàn diànyǐng
我 不 想 今天 晚上 去 看 电影 。
I don't want to go to see a movie tonight.

question: Nǐ xiǎng bu xiǎng zài jiā kàn diànshì
你 想 不 想 在 家 看 电视 ?
Do you want to watch TV at home?

要 yào want

positive: Wǒ yào gēn tāmen yìqǐ qù Zhōngguó
我 要 跟 他们 一起 去 中国 。
I want to go with them to China.

negative: Wǒ bù xiǎng gēn tāmen qù Zhōngguó
我 不 想 跟 他们 去 中国 。
I don't want to go with them to China.

question: Nǐ xiǎng bu xiǎng gēn tāmen qù Zhōngguó
你 想 不 想 跟 他们 去 中国 ?
Do you want to go with them to China?

会 huì know how (of a learned skill)

Wǒ huì shuō Yīngyǔ yě huì shuō Déyǔ kěshì wǒ shuō de bú tài hǎo
我 会 说 英语，也 会 说 德语，可是 我 说 得 不 太 好。
I know how to speak English and I also know how to speak German but I don't speak well.

Zhège háizi tài xiǎo hái bú huì zǒu lù kěshì tā huì jiào bàba māma
这个 孩子 太 小，还 不 会 走 路，可是 他 会 叫 "爸爸、妈妈"。
This child is too young, and has not yet learned to walk, but he knows how to say "daddy and mommy".

能 néng able to, capable of (from a subjective view point)

Wǒmen huì shuō yìdiǎn Hànyǔ yě néng xiě hěn duō Hànzì kěshì bù
我们 会 说 一点 汉语，也 能 写 很 多 汉字，可是 不
néng kàn Zhōngwén bào
能 看 中文 报。
We know how to speak a little Chinese and we also are capable of writing many characters, but we are not proficient enough to read Chinese newspapers.

Jīntiān wǎnshang tā bù néng kàn diànshì yīnwèi tā yǒu hěn duō
今天 晚上 他 不 能 看 电视，因为 他 有 很 多
gōngkè yào zuò
功课 要 做。
He is not able to watch TV tonight because he has too much homework.

Nàge dìfang tài yuǎn méiyǒu chē bù néng qù
那个 地方 太 远，没有 车 不 能 去。
That place is too far away and you won't be able to go there without a car.

可以 kěyǐ may, to be permitted, to be allowed (from an objective view point)

Shàng kè de shíhou bù kěyǐ wán diànnǎo
上 课 的 时候 不 可以 玩 电脑。
Playing computer is not allowed during class.

Chī zhōngfàn de shíhou kěyǐ qù túshūguǎn kàn shū
吃 中饭 的 时候 可以 去 图书馆 看 书。
It is allowed to go to read in the library during lunch.

Yàoshi nǐ yǒu qián jiù kěyǐ mǎi méiyǒu qián jiù bù néng mǎi
要是 你 有 钱 就 可以 买，没有 钱 就 不 能 买。
If you have money, you can buy it; without money, you can't.

应该 yīnggāi should, ought to, must (suggest/ the right thing to do)

Wǒ (yīng) gāi zǒu le
我 (应) 该 走 了。
I must (should) go now.

Nǐ bù (yīng) gāi lái
你 不 (应) 该 来。
You should not have come.

必须 bìxū be obliged to, have to (obligated, be required/demanded to)

Xuésheng bìxū měitiān xuéxí
学生 必须 每天 学习。
A student must study everyday.

Míngtiān nǐ bìxū lái
明天 你 必须 来。
You must come tomorrow.

得 děi must, have to (no choice)

Wǒ jīntiān bù néng dǎ qiú wǒ děi zuò gōngkè
我 今天 不 能 打 球,我 得 做 功课 。
I cannot play ball today, I have to do homework.

Yào xiǎng dǎ de hǎo měitiān dōu děi liànxí
要 想 打 得 好,每天 都 得 练习。
If you want to play well, you have to practice everyday.

不得不 bùdébù cannot help but be obliged to, unwilling but have no alternative

Wǒ bù xiǎng qù kěshì bùdébù qù
我 不 想 去,可是 不得不 去。
I don't want to go but have no choice.

(一定) 要 yídìng yào must, surely have to (give order/demand)

Nǐmen yídìng yào zǎo diǎnr lái
你们 一定 要 早 点儿 来。
Make sure you come early.

教学难点

Difficulties

难点一 "想" vs. "要"

"想"和"要"都可以译成"want"/"intend to do",但是确切的意思和在句中的用法都不同。请比较。

"想" and "要", as modal verbs, both mean "want/intend to do". However, the differences are：

1）In meaning：要 is more determined than 想.

2）In structure：

要, meaning want, can be followed by either an object or a verbal phrase.

As a verb 我要这个。(a direct object)

As a modal verb 我要跟他们一起去中国。(a verbal phrase)

想 can only be followed by a verbal phrase.

As a modal verb 我想跟朋友去看电影。(a verbal phrase)

When "想" is followed directly by an object, it means "miss".

As a verb 我想我妈妈。 (an object) I miss my mom.

3）Negative：The negative form of 要 VP is 不想 VP.

As a verb 我不要那个。(a direct object)

As a modal verb 我不想跟他们去中国。(a verbal phrase)

难点二 "想" and "要" vs. "喜欢"

"想"、"要"容易和"喜欢"混淆。学生要说"想""要"却用"喜欢"。这跟英文的"would like"有"want"/"intend to do"的意思有关。

Learners often confuse "想" and "要" with "喜欢". Often when a learner means to say "想" or "要", he/she uses "喜欢." "想" and "要", as model verbs, mean "intend, want", but in English they may also be translated as "would like". "喜欢" may also refers to preferences but it is "like", meaning "to be fond of", which is different from "would like".

Compare：

Would you like (to have) some tea?

Nǐ xiǎng (yào) hē diǎnr chá ma
你 想 (要) 喝 点儿 茶 吗？

Do you like tea?

Nǐ xǐhuan hē chá ma
你 喜欢 喝 茶 吗？

难点三 "想" vs. "Want"

中文的"想"有数个用法

"想" has more usages:

(As a modal verb) intend, want to, would like to

Wǒ xiǎng qù Zhōngguó
我 想 去 中国 。
I want to go to China.

(As a verb) think

Wǒ xiǎng méiyǒu wèntí
我 想 没有 问题。
I don't think there is any probelm.

(As a verb) long for, recall with fondness, miss

Wǒ xiǎng Běijīng wǒ xiǎng wǒ māma
我 想 北京，我 想 我 妈妈 。
I miss Beijing, I miss my mom.

"想"后跟兼语句

In English, we may "want" someone to do something directly.

But in Chinese, you have to have another verb after "想" to convey the same meaning:

I want you to come with us.

Wǒ xiǎng qǐng nǐ gēn wǒmen yìqǐ qù
我 想 请 你 跟 我们 一起 去。

My mom does not want me to go.

Wǒ mā bù (xiǎng) ràng wǒ qù
我 妈 不 （想） 让 我 去。

Wanting someone to do something in Chinese implies "letting/allowing/making" someone do it.

For that effect, "请/让/叫" are needed after "想". (See the Chapter 22: Giving Instrutions.)

难点四 "Ask" in Chinese

英文的"Ask"可以提问也可以请求别人做事。汉语不同，"问"只能提问，请别人做事要用兼语句。请看对比。

In English, you may use the word "Ask" for two things:

Ask a question:

May I ask you a question?

Can I ask you what that is?

Ask someone to do something:

Could I ask you to do this for me?

He asked me to give him this book.

In Chinese, the above two functions of "ask" must be conveyed differently:

Ask a question (direct/indirect question): use "问 wèn ask, inquire"

Tā wèn wǒ yí ge xiǎo wèntí
他 问 我 一 个 小 问题。
He asked me a little question.

Tā wèn wǒ Nǐ jiào shénme míngzi
他 问 我："你 叫 什么 名字？"
He asked me, "What is your name?"

To ask someone to do something, use one of the following three expressions:

请 qǐng ask/request/invite (somebody to do something politely)

Jīntiān tā qǐng wǒ chī wǎnfàn
今天 他 请 我 吃 晚饭。
Today, he invites me to dinner.

让 ràng let/allow/have/make (somebody do something)

Lǎoshī ràng wǒmen yí gè zì xiě wǔ biàn
老师 让 我们 一 个 字 写 五 遍。
Our teacher asked us to write each character five times.

叫 jiào call on/order/make (somebody do something)

Wǒ māma jiào nǐ zài wǒ jiā chī wǎnfàn
我 妈妈 叫 你 在 我 家 吃 晚饭。
My mom asked you to have dinner at our house.

难点五　“Can” in Chinese

英文的“Can”是一个常用词，也是一个麻烦。因为汉语没有确切的对应。请对比。

A. “Can” is a simple word in English, but in Chinese, there are subtle nuances. The differences in meaning are emphasized below:

English	Chinese
can: know how (a learned skill)	会
can: capacity, capable of, proficient	能
can: capacity, allowed to conditionally	可以

还有，“Can”可以直接评估行为能否与状况。在汉语不行，会不会与做得好与否是两个概念，得用两个不同的句子表达。

B. “Can” may be used to evaluate an action:

I can swim very well.

But in Chinese, the meaning of the above sentence has to be conveyed in two:

我会游泳。　(know how)

我（游泳）游得很好。　(how well)

(See Complement of Degree in Chapter 9.)

Never say:

我会游泳游得好。　(×)

难点六　“会” vs. “能” vs. “可以”

注意“会”“能”“可以”的差别。

“会”, “能” and “可以” may overlap in meaning. But to use them appropriately, we must recognize that they emphasize different aspects of one's ability.

会　know how (a learned skill)

能　capacity, capable of, proficient (subjective)

可以　capacity, allowed to conditionally (objective)

难点七 “不用”vs.“甭”&“不要”vs.“别”

“不用”：speak faster and faster，and you get“甭”.

“不要”：speak faster and faster，and you get“别”.

难点八 Negative for“得”and“不得不”

“得”和“不得不”的否定都是“不用”。请比较。

The negative of“得”and“不得不”is“不用”.

(positive)
Wǒ jīntiān děi zuò hǎo duō gōngkè
我 今天 得 做 好 多 功课 。
I have to do a lot of homework today.

(negative)
Wǒ jīntiān bú yòng zuò gōngkè
我 今天 不 用 做 功课 。
I don't have to do homework today.

(positive)
Wǒ jīntiān bùdébù zuò hǎoxiē gōngkè
我 今天 不得不 做 好些 功课 。
I have no choice but to do a lot of homework.

(negative)
Wǒ jīntiān bú yòng zuò nàxiē gōngkè
我 今天 不 用 做 那些 功课 。
I don't need to do that homework.

9

Evaluating Actions

评议行为

评议行为是表述一个主观的看法，不是描述一个客观的事实，所用的句型一般带程度补语。主观的看法可以有感情的成分在内，用不同的副词和形容词来表示强调。

本节介绍评议行为时程度补语的使用、所涉及的副词和形容词，并指出和注释中英文对副词和形容词使用的一些不同点。

Evaluating, judging or commenting on actions and events is stating opinions from personal or suggestive point of views. It is not about giving a factual report. It requires sentences with complement of degree that employ adverbs and adjectives to emphasize opinions.

This chapter introduces the patterns and functional uses of the complement of degree and related adverbs and adjectives. It also pinpoints some differences between Chinese and English in terms of the usage of adverbs and adjectives.

教学重点 Content of Teaching and Learning

程度补语	Complement of Degree

教学难点 Difficulties

程度补语句型	Structure of the Complement of Degree
程度补语功用	Function of the Complement of Degree
“一点” vs. “有一点”	
动词组 vs. 双音节动词	Verbal Phrases vs. Two-word Verbs
汉语的副词与英语的副词	Chinese Adverbs vs. English Adverbs
难以翻译的形容词	Adjectives Difficult to Translate

词汇表 Glossary

常用副词表	List of Commonly Used Adverbs
常用简易形容词表	List of Commonly Used Simple Adjectives

教学重点

Content of Teaching and Learning

程度补语 Complement of Degree

功用 Function：评论、评估、判断行为事件。

Give a subjective view of an action, and evaluate, judge, comment on an action.

句型 Sentence Pattern：

Subject + VO	+	V + de（Adverb）	+ Adjective
我 看书		看 得	快。
我，书		看 得	快。
书，我		看 得	快。

Complement of Degrees Shown with Adverbs：

kuài jí le
快 极 了

tèbié kuài
特别 快

fēicháng kuài
非常 快

zhēn kuài
真 快

tài kuài le
太 快 了

hěn kuài
很 快

yǒudiǎnr kuài
有点儿 快

我看书看得

bú tài kuài
不 太 快

hěn màn
很 慢

tài màn le
太 慢 了

zhēn màn
真 慢

fēicháng màn
非常 慢

tèbié màn
特别 慢

màn jí le
慢 极 了

教学难点

Difficulties

难点一 程度补语句型 Structure of the Complement of Degree

In structure, the action verb must be followed by "de" immediately. For two-word verbal phrases, the verb must be repeated.

wrong	correct
我看书 得快。	我看书 看得 很快。 我 看得 特别快。

难点二 程度补语功能 Function of the Complement of Degree

"He plays hard." 这句话有两个可能的意思，翻译时酌情用不同的句型表达。

一个是说话人对当事人行为的评论和看法。(主观)

一个是说话人描述当事人的行为。(尽量客观)

In English, if you want to say "He plays hard". It could mean two things:

1) You are commenting on/judging his attitude about his playing. (Subjective)

2) You are describing his action/effort. (Objective)

Since different perspectives are reflected, different sentence patterns must be used.

比较对比 Contrast

(Opinion/comment: subject view)

Wǒ juéde tā dǎ pīngpāngqiú dǎ de fēicháng rènzhēn
我 觉得 他 打 乒乓球 打 得 非常 认真 。

In my opinion, he plays ping-pong with great seriousness.

(Manner of action: objective description)

他总是非常认真地打球。

He always plays ball very seriously.

难点三 "(一)点" vs. "有(一)点"

"A little bit"可以是"一点"或"有一点",对学生来说是一个大问题。参看例句,对比不同和用法。简单地说:"(一)点"是量。"有(一)点"是程度。

In English, "a little bit" can be translated into "一点" or "有一点". In other words, "一点" and "有一点" are the same in English. But they are not the same in Chinese. Thus these "little" expressions often pose "big" difficulties to learners. To make it simple: "(一)点" refers to quantity. "有(一)点" refers to a degree or an extent.

"(一)点": After a verb/Before a noun (quantify nouns: some)

Wǒ xiǎng hē (yì) diǎn shuǐ
我 想 喝(一) 点 水。
I want to drink some (a little amount of) water.

Tā zhǐ huì shuō yìdiǎn Zhōngwén
他 只 会 说 一点 中文 。

He can only speak some (a little) Chinese.

"（一）点"：After an adjective (quantify description)

Tā bǐ nǐ gāo yìdiǎn
他 比 你 高 一点。
He is taller than you by a little (he is a little bit taller than you.)

"（一）点"：After an adjective/Before a verb (quantify the speed)

Kuài (yì) diǎn zǒu
快 （一） 点 走。
Walk a little faster (hurry up).

Màn diǎn pǎo
慢 点 跑。
Run a little slower (slow down).

"有（一）点"：Before an adjective to modify a description

wrong	correct
我一点渴。	Wǒ yǒu yìdiǎn kě 我 有 一点 渴。 I am a little thirsty.
今天的天气一点冷。	Jīntiān de tiānqì yǒu diǎn lěng 今天 的 天气 有 点 冷。 Today's weather is a little bit cold.

难点四　动词组 vs. 双音节动词

Verbal Phrases vs. Two-word Verbs

Many simple daily life action verbs in English are verbal phrases (verb-noun) in Chinese.

English **(verb)**	**Chinese** **(verb + noun)**
eat	吃饭

drink	喝水
sleep	睡觉
get up	起床
swim	游泳
sing	唱歌
dance	跳舞

When in sentence patterns showing complements, such as 程度补语 or 时量补语, only the verb should be repeated.

Some Chinese verbs are two-word verbs, e. g. :

study	学习	rest	休息
participate	参加	prepare	准备

When in sentence patterns showing complements such as 程度补语 or 时量补语, no part of the two word (two syllables) verb needs to be repeated.

Learners tend to, when translate from English to Chinese, make mistakes.

1) Not to repeat the verb when must: (in patterns for complements)

wrong	correct
我游泳得好。	我游泳游得好。
我跳舞了一个钟头。	我跳舞跳了一个钟头。

2) Repeat word when not necessary:

wrong	correct
我学习得很好。	我学习学得很好。

难点五　汉语的副词与英语的副词

Chinese Adverbs vs. English Adverbs

汉语的副词与英语的副词的概念和用法不同。见例句。

In English, many adjectives can become adverbs when describing actions, simply by adding "ly," e. g. "beautiful-beautifully."

A. She is beautiful. 她真漂亮。

B. She did it beautifully. 她干得真漂亮。

In Chinese, adverbs are adverbs and adjectives are adjectives. They don't change. "漂亮" in Sentence A is an adjective used to describe (as predicate of the sentence) and in Sentence B it is still an adjective but used as a complement of the sentence.

难点六 难以翻译的形容词 Adjectives Difficult to Translate

1) Age

"大" and "小": are used to refer to age, not size, when used to describe people.

"老" and "小/少 shào young": are also used for age.

年轻 niánqīng young (of people, often of teenagers) is another word used for "young".

However, for most K-12 learners, when they want to say: "when I was young ...", they really should say:

"我小时候"。(They are too young to say "我年轻的时候".)

2) Old

Both "旧" and "老" are translated as "old" in English, but:

"新旧" is used for objects.

"新老" is used for people.

3) Short:

"矮", "低", and "短" are all translated as "short" in English, but:

Though "高矮" and "高低" are all used for height, "高矮" is for the height people and objects. "高低" is used for temperature or height in a more abstract sense. "长短" is used for length.

4) Cheap and mean:

In English, youngsters like to use the expression "cheap" and "mean" to describe people.

"便宜 piányi cheap" is only used to describe price of an object, it cannot be used to describe people. The correct expression for describing a person being cheap is "小气/小器 xiǎoqi stingy". While "小气" can also be translated into "mean", it refers to being "stingy/thrifty", not being cruel to others. What exactly is being "mean-cruel" in Chinese? This is a good question.

5) Smartness and stupidity

"聪明，灵巧，机灵" all mean smart, but:

(of intelligence)	聪明	cōngming	intelligent, bright
(of bodily function)	灵巧	língqiǎo	nimble, clever, graceful
(of street smartness)	机灵	jīling	clever, smart

"笨，傻，糊涂" are all used for stupidness, but:

(of slow mindedness)

笨 bèn awkward, clumsy, cumbersome

(of simple mindedness)

傻 shǎ silly, simple-minded, naive, foolhardy, unimaginative

(of muddle-headedness)

糊涂 hútu confused, chaotic, in a mess, blurred, indistinct

6) Thinness

"瘦，薄，稀，淡，细" can all be translated as "thin" in English. But there are differences in use:

(of body shape)	胖	pàng	fat, stout
	瘦	shòu	thin
(of volume)	厚	hòu	thick
	薄	báo	thin
(of solutions, population)	稠	chóu	dense, thick
	稀	xī	sparse; thin
(of liquids, taste, color)	浓	nóng	thick, dense

淡	dàn	thin
(of particles, voice, quality) 粗	cū	thick, coarse
细	xì	thin, fine

词汇表

Glossary

常用副词表 List of Commonly Used Adverbs (by intensity)

Adverb as prefix

有（一）点 yǒu（yì）diǎn a bit, a little

有一点饿 a bit hungry

不太 bú tài not too, not very; without much

不太高 not too tall

很 hěn very

(Though meaning "very", "很" is not as strong as "very" in English.

It is often used as a rhetorical prefix to an adjective, especially a one syllable adjective with little or no intensification of the adjective's meaning.)

很好 pretty good

很多 a lot

太……了 tài……le too, excessively

(With positive adjectives, it emphasizes greatness. However, with negative ones, it takes the tone of complaining.)

太棒了 wonderful

太贵了 too expensive

真 zhēn really

真便宜 really cheap

非常 fēicháng extraordinarily, unusually

非常好看 awfully good looking

特别	tèbié	especially, particularly, specially 特别好吃 extraordinarily tasty

Adverb as suffix

……极了	jí le	extremely (adjectival or adverbial suffix) 好极了 extremely well
……死了	sǐ le	to death (adjectival or adverbial suffix; colloquial: usually for expressions negative in meaning) 渴死了 thirsty to death

常用简易形容词表 List of Commonly Used Simple Adjectives

分类便于记忆：Categorized for Easy Memorization

形容词（1） Pairs/Anonyms

大	dà	big	小	xiǎo	small, little
多	duō	many, much	少	shǎo	few, little, less
早	zǎo	early	晚	wǎn	late
快	kuài	fast	慢	màn	slow
好	hǎo	good, well	坏	huài	bad (差 chà poorly)
容易	róngyì	simple, easy	难	nán	difficult
贵	guì	expensive	便宜	piányi	cheap
新	xīn	new	旧	jiù	old
长	cháng	long	短	duǎn	short (of length; duration)
高	gāo	high	矮	ǎi	short (of height)
轻	qīng	light	重	zhòng	heavy, serious
胖	pàng	fat, stout	瘦	shòu	thin (of body shape)
厚	hòu	thick	薄	báo	thin (of volume)

远	yuǎn	far	近	jìn	near
对	duì	correct	错	cuò	wrong
冷	lěng	cold	热	rè	hot
深	shēn	deep, dark	浅	qiǎn	shallow, light
聪明	cōngming	intelligent, smart	笨	bèn	clumsy, slow in wit
大方	dàfang	generous	小气	xiǎoqi	stingy, narrow-minded
干净	gānjìng	clean, neat	脏	zāng	dirty, filthy
香	xiāng	fragrant, delicious	臭	chòu	stinky, disgusting odor

形容词（2） Paired Adjectives Used Together as Nouns

大小	dàxiǎo	big or small (size)
多少	duōshǎo	number, amount, more or less (quantity)
早晚	zǎowǎn	sooner or later (time)
快慢	kuàimàn	(rate of) speed
好坏	hǎohuài	good and bad (quality)
难易	nányì	degree of difficulty
贵贱	guìjiàn	noble and base
长短	chángduǎn	length, accident, mishap
高矮	gāo'ǎi	height (high, low)
轻重	qīngzhòng	weight, seriousness, importance, propriety
胖瘦	pàngshòu	stout or thin, degree of stoutness (of body shape)
厚薄	hòubáo	(degree of) thickness, (degree of) generosity, favor
远近	yuǎnjìn	far and near (distance)
对错	duìcuò	correct or wrong
深浅	shēnqiǎn	depth, sense of propriety, shade (of color)
香臭	xiāngchòu	sweet-smelling and foul-smelling, good and bad

形容词（3） Simple Verbs Used to Form Adjectives

看	kàn	look
吃	chī	eat
喝	hē	drink
听	tīng	hear
玩	wán	play；have fun
唱	chàng	sing
写	xiě	write
用	yòng	use

好（good）	不好（not good）	难（bad）
好看	不好看	难看
好吃	不好吃	难吃
好喝	不好喝	难喝
好听	不好听	难听
好玩	不好玩	

or

好（easy）	不好（not easy）	难（difficult）
好唱	不好唱	难唱
好写	不好写	难写
好用	不好用	难用

有	没（有）
有意思 yǒu yìsi interesting 有用 yǒuyòng be useful 有钱 yǒuqián rich，wealthy 有名 yǒumíng famous，well-known	没意思 méi yìsi boring 没用 méiyòng useless

形容词（4）Physical Conditions

饿 è be hungry
饱 bǎo be full（after eating）
渴 kě thirsty
忙 máng busy
累 lèi tired
懒 lǎn lazy，sluggish

Sensory Comfort：

漂亮 piàoliang good-looking，pretty
可爱 kě'ài lovable，likeable，charming
方便 fāngbiàn convenient
舒服 shūfu comfortable
痛快 tòngkuai happy，delighted；to one's heart's content
高兴 gāoxìng happy，glad；be happy to，be glad to
满意 mǎnyì satisfied，pleased；determined，resolved
合适 héshì be suitable，fit
自然 zìrán natural，at ease
正常 zhèngcháng normal
难过 nánguò have a difficult life；feel bad（about something）
兴奋 xīngfèn be excited
紧张 jǐnzhāng anxious，nervous

Colloquial:

棒	bàng	fine, strong, excellent
酷	kù	"cool" (borrowed from English)
帅	shuài	handsome; elegant
丑	chǒu	ugly
讨厌	tǎoyàn	annoying, bothersome
恶心	ěxin	disgusting

10

颜色 Color

谈颜色是学习词汇。可颜色也可用来形容/描绘和确认。把颜色另立一节一是强调颜色本身的重要语用功能，二是为了方便教与学时可以和其他内容有多种的组合。例如、衣服、水果、用具、动物等。

Discussing colors is good for learning vocabulary. But colors can also be used to describe and identify objects. The purpose of making color a topic is two-fold. First, it emphasizes the function of color in language use; second it is convenient to combine color with other topics. Colors can be used to describe and identify clothing, food, animals and many other objects.

教学重点 Content of Teaching and Learning

颜色	Color
基本颜色	Basic Colors
颜色的深浅	Description of Shades of Color
颜色形容颜色	Color on Color
彩色的/花的	Multicolors/Mixed Colors
描述性的颜色	Descriptive Colors (Nature and Color)
"是……的"结构	"是……的" Structure

教学难点 Difficulties

颜色作为形容词	Colors as Adjectives
颜色的使用	Description vs. Identification
形状和颜色	Shape and Color

教学重点

Content of Teaching and Learning

颜色 yánsè Color

基本颜色 Basic Colors

红	hóng	red
黄	huáng	yellow
蓝	lán	blue
绿	lǜ	green
棕	zōng	brown（褐 hè brown；咖啡 kāfēi coffee）
黑	hēi	black
白	bái	white
灰	huī	gray
紫	zǐ	purple，violet
粉	fěn	pink
金	jīn	golden
银	yín	silver

颜色的深浅 Description of Shades of Color

Add 深 or 浅 before the color.

深	shēn	dark (of colour), deep
	深蓝/深绿/深灰	
浅	qiǎn	light (of color), shallow
	浅红/浅绿/浅粉	

颜色形容颜色 Color on Color

金黄	jīnhuáng	golden yellow，golden
银灰	yínhuī	silver gray

银白	yínbái	silver white
粉红	fěnhóng	pink
紫红	zǐhóng	purplish red, maroon
灰白	huībái	grayish white, pale
黑灰	hēihuī	blackish gray

彩色的/花的 MultiColors/Mixed Colors

彩色	cǎisè	multicolored; colored (e. g. television, film)
花的	huāde	floral, colorful

Transparent:

透明	tòumíng	transparent
无色	wúsè	colorless

描述性的颜色 Descriptive Colors (Nature and Color)

红

橘红	júhóng	tangerine red
血红	xuèhóng	blood red
火红	huǒhóng	fiery red
海棠红	hǎitánghóng	light pink (crabapple red)

黄

杏黄	xìnghuáng	apricot yellow
橘黄	júhuáng	orange yellow
土黄	tǔhuáng	yellowish brown, khaki
鹅黄	éhuáng	light-soft yellow (as a goose)

蓝

天蓝	tiānlán	azure, sky blue
碧蓝	bìlán	blue green (green jade blue)
海蓝	hǎilán	dark blue (deep sea blue)
海军蓝	hǎijūnlán	navy blue

绿

草绿	cǎolǜ	grass-green
墨绿	mòlǜ	blackish green, forest green
军绿	jūnlǜ	army green
祖母绿	zǔmǔlǜ	deep blue-green

白

雪白	xuěbái	snow white
乳白	rǔbái	milky white, cream

黑

墨黑	mòhēi	jet black

"是……的"结构 "是……的" Structure

功用 Function:

The "是……的" pattern is used to identify some characteristic of an object.

句型 Structure:

Subject 是 characteristic 的(object).

(color)

Wǒ de máoyī shì hóng de Hóng de shì wǒ de fěn de bú shì wǒ de
我 的 毛衣 是 红 的。红 的 是 我 的,粉 的 不 是 我 的。
My sweater is a red one. The red is mine; the pink is not mine.

Wǒ de máoyī shì hóng yánsè de
我 的 毛衣 是 红 颜色 的。
My sweater is the red one.

(condition)

Tā de máoyī shì xīn de bú shì jiù de
他 的 毛衣 是 新 的,不 是 旧 的。
His sweater is a new one, not an old one.

(possession)

Xīn de shì tā de jiù de shì wǒ de
新 的 是 他 的,旧 的 是 我 的。
The new one is his, the old one is mine.

(nature)

Zhè běn shū shì Yīngwén de bú shì Zhōngwén de
这 本 书 是 英文 的,不 是 中文 的。
This book is an English book, not a Chinese book.

问答 Questions and Answers

Zhè yǒu yí jiàn shàngyī shì bu shì nǐ de
这 有 一 件 上衣 ,是 不 是 你 的?
There is a jacket here; is it yours?

Wǒ de shàngyī shì xīn de (shàngyī) bú shì jiù de
我 的 上衣 是 新 的 (上衣) ,不 是 旧 的。
My jacket is a new one, not an old one.

Nà jiàn huáng yùndòngyī shì tā de ma
那 件 黄 运动衣 是 他 的 吗?
Is that yellow sports shirt his?

Bù nà bú shì tā de shì wǒ de
不,那 不 是 他 的,是 我 的。
No, that is not his, it is mine.

Tā de shì hóng de bú shì huáng de
他 的 是 红 的,不 是 黄 的。
His is (a) red (one), not (a) yellow (one).

Zhè shì shénme shū Yīngwén de háishi Zhōngwén de
这 是 什么 书? 英文 的 还是 中文 的?
What kind of book is this? English or Chinese?

Zhè běn shì Yīngwén de Nà běn shì Zhōngwén de
这 本 是 英文 的。那 本 是 中文 的。
This is an English book, that one is Chinese.

Zhè běn Yīngwén de shì jìsuànjī zázhì nà běn Zhōngwén de shì
这 本 英文 的 是 计算机 杂志,那 本 中文 的 是

kèběn
课本 。
The English one is a computer magazine; that Chinese one is a textbook.

教学难点

Difficulties

难点一 颜色作为形容词 Colors as Adjectives

“红”, when used by itself, is a description. When talking about a color, you say:

红色　红的/红色的　红颜色的

Adjectives have these characteristics in functional use:

1) Position: Adjective can be used to modify a noun, and the position of an adjective is before the noun it defines.

2) However, if the modifier is a one-syllable word, it does not require “的”:

红毛衣，黑笔

3) If the modifier is more than one syllable, we must use “的”:

很红的毛衣，深蓝的毛衣，粉红的毛衣，雪白的毛衣

难点二 颜色的使用 Description vs. Identification

颜色可以直接用来描述。

颜色也可以和“是……的”结构一起用来定义。请参照例句比较用法。

An adjective can be used to modify a noun as part of the object's identification. In this case, the sentence pattern to use is “是……的”. An adjective can also be used to describe an object directly without use of a verb.

毛衣很红。

See the contrast:

Description:

我的毛衣白，她的不白。

我的毛衣太白了，她的一点也不白。(with adverbs)

Identification：

我的毛衣是白的（毛衣)；她的毛衣不是白的，是红的。

Both are in a sentence：

我的红毛衣不是深红的，是浅红的。

难点三　形状与颜色 Shape and Color

When describing a piece of clothing, shapes are often used with colors, e. g. :

blue and white stripes：蓝白条的（条 tiáo string, stripe)

mixed color pattern：　花格的　（花格 huāgé checkered pattern)

11

Clothing and Study Tools

服装与学习用具

服装和学习用具都是名词。谈服装和学习用具就要用到数字和量词以及相应的动词。这一节的重点和难点就在于此。

Clothing and study tools are all nouns. Discussing clothing and study tools often requires using numbers and measure words along with verbs. This chapter's teaching and learning foci and cruxes are as such.

教学重点 Content of Teaching and Learning

量词	Measure Words
服装	Clothing
服饰	Accessories
学习用具	Study Tools

教学难点 Difficulties

量词的使用	Usage of Measure Words
"Wear" in Chinese	
动词与名词搭配	Matching Verbs with Nouns
复杂定语（名词组）	Complex Attributes (Noun Phrases)

教学重点

Content of Teaching and Learning

量词 Measure Words

(See Measure Words in Chapter 1: Numbers in Life)

Rules:

Different objects take different measure words

Measure words connect quantity/ "这" / "那" with nouns.

Quantity	measure word	noun
两	本	书

(这)	measure word	noun	(那)	measure word	noun
这	本	书	那	本	书

服装 fúzhuāng Clothing

衣服 yīfu clothes, clothing

穿 chuān wear, put on (clothing)

脱 tuō take off, remove (clothing)

一套 yí tào measure word: a set, a suit

衣服	yīfu	clothes, clothing
西服	xīfú	suit (Western-style)

一件 yí jiàn measure word: one piece (for upper body clothing)

上衣	shàngyī	upper outer garment (e. g. coat, jacket)
外衣	wàiyī	outerwear, coat, outer garment
夹克	jiākè	jacket
大衣	dàyī	overcoat
毛衣	máoyī	wool sweater

雨衣 yǔyī raincoat

游泳衣 yóuyǒng yī swimsuit, bathing suit

运动衣(衫) yùndòng yī (shān) sports shirt

衬衫 chènshān shirt

T-恤衫 T-xùshān T-shirt

背心 bèixīn sleeveless garment (waistcoat, vest)

内衣 nèiyī underwear (especially undershirt)

胸罩 xiōngzhào bra, brassiere

一条 yì tiáo measure word: a piece (for lower body clothing)

裤子 kùzi pants, trousers

长裤 chángkù long pants

短裤 duǎnkù short pants

半长裤 bànchángkù capris

运动裤 yùndòngkù sports pants

游泳裤 yóuyǒngkù swimming trunks

牛仔裤 niúzǎikù jeans

咔叽裤 kǎjīkù khaki pants

西服裤 xīfúkù formal/dressy pants

内裤 nèikù underpants

裤衩 kùchǎ underpants, shorts, briefs

裙子 qúnzi skirt, dress

长裙 chángqún long dress/skirt

短裙 duǎnqún short dress/skirt

迷你裙 mínǐqún miniskirt

西服裙 xīfúqún formal/career skirt

一双 yì shuāng measure word: a pair (for paired objects: shoes, socks, gloves, etc.)

一只 yì zhī a measure word for the single of a pair (like ears, hands, shoes, etc.)

鞋 xié shoes

皮鞋 píxié leather shoes

布鞋 bùxié shoes made of (cotton) fabric

运动鞋 yùndòngxié athletic shoes, sneakers

球鞋 qiúxié athletic shoes, sneakers

凉鞋 liángxié sandals

拖鞋 tuōxié slippers

靴子 xuēzi boots

袜子 wàzi socks, stockings

手套 shǒutào gloves, mittens, baseball glove

but:

一副 yí fù measure word: a pair, a set

眼镜 yǎnjìng eyeglasses

耳环 ěrhuán earrings

服饰 fúshì Accessories

戴 dài wear, put on (accessories)

一条 yì tiáo measure word for something long and skinny

围巾 wéijīn scarf, muffler

头巾 tóujīn kerchief; head wrap

领带 lǐngdài necktie

手链 shǒuliàn bracelet

项链 xiàngliàn necklace

皮带 pídài belt, leather belt

腰带 yāodài waistband, girdle, belt

一个 yí ge a general measure word

手表 shǒubiǎo wrist watch

	戒指	jièzhi	ring (for finger)
	手镯	shǒuzhuó	bracelet
	扣子	kòuzi	button, knot
一副	yí fù	measure word for a set of something	
	耳环	ěrhuán	earrings
	眼镜	yǎnjìng	eyeglasses
	鞋带	xiédài	shoelaces
一顶	yì dǐng	measure word for hat	
	帽子	màozi	cap, hat

学习用具 Study Tools

一支	yì zhī	measure word: for songs; for long, narrow things (e. g. rifle, candle)		
	笔	bǐ	pen	一支笔
一张	yì zhāng	measure word for flat things like a sheet of paper, a table, etc.		
	纸	zhǐ	paper	一张纸
	报纸	bàozhǐ	newspaper	一张报纸
	画	huà	painting, picture, drawing	一张画
	照片	zhàopiàn	photograph, picture, print	一张照片
一个	yí ge	a general measure word		
	计算机	jìsuànjī	computer	一个计算机
	计算器	jìsuànqì	calculator	一个计算器
	本子	běnzi	notebook	一个本子
	书包	shūbāo	school bag	一个书包
	广告	guǎnggào	advertisement	一个广告
一本	yì běn	measure word: for books		
	书	shū	book	一本书
	字典	zìdiǎn (词典 cídiǎn)	dictionary	一本字典

杂志 zázhì (news, etc.) magazine 一本杂志
课本 kèběn textbook 一本课本
漫画 mànhuà cartoon 一本(张)漫画
画报 huàbào pictorial (magazine) 一本画报

一篇 yì piān measure word: article, essay
文章 wénzhāng article, essay, literary works

(For more, see the List of Commonly Used Measure Words in Chapter 1: Numbers in Life.)

教学难点

Difficulties

难点一 量词的使用 Usage of Measure Words

学生不爱或不习惯用量词。不同的物件要用不同的量词。量词还有其他的用途。

请参阅第一章的量词表。

Learners often do not like to or are not accustomed to using measure words. Different objects require the use of different measure words.

Measure words also have other functions.

To quantify: Quantity + Measure Word + Noun

一	个	人
两	个	学生
三	本	书
四	件	上衣

To specify: “这”/“那” + Measure Word + Noun

To ask: “几”/“哪” + Measure Word + Noun

To order: 一个个地 + Verb

To emphasize: 个个（每个）Noun

(See Chapter 1: Numbers in Life – List of Commonly Used Measure Words for more information.)

难点二 "Wear" in Chinese

"Wear"这个词在英文里可以指很多活动。中文要用很多不同的词。参见例句。

In English, we use the verb "to wear" for many things:

wear clothes
wear accessories
wear makeup
wear a hairdo (certain hair style)
wear a scar
wear a disguise
wear a smile

In Chinese, in order to say all the above, different verbs are required.

wear clothes	穿衣服
wear accessories	戴帽子
wear makeup	化妆
wear a disguise	化妆/伪装
wear a hairdo (certain hair style)	梳（发型）
wear a scar	有伤疤
wear a smile	（面带）笑容

难点三 复杂定语（名词组）Complex Attributes (Noun Phrases)

(See the same topic in Chapter 18: Noun Phrases.)

12

复句——分析与争辩

Complex Sentence Patterns —Reasoning and Arguing

给理由和原因是分析和争辩的起步。本节就通过例句介绍一些与此相关的句型和用法。

Reasoning is the beginning phase of analyzing and arguing. This chapter uses examples to introduce the patterns and usages of some common complex sentences needed for this language function.

教学重点 Content of Teaching and Learning

复句句型	Complex Sentence Patterns
通过连词构成	Use Conjunction (s)
通过副词构成	Use Adverb (s)
通过疑问词构成	Use Interrogative Pronoun (s)

教学难点 Difficulties

主语与副词	Subjects and Adverbs
主语在句中的位置	Position of Subjects in the Sentences
“除了……以外” and “疑问词+都”	
“再” vs. “又”	
“不管”与疑问	Interrogative Form in “不管” Sentence
“正在” vs. “刚”	

教学重点

Content of Teaching and Learning

复句句型 Complex Sentence Patterns

通过连词构成 Use Conjunction (s)

1）因为……所以…… yīnwèi suǒyǐ because...(therefore)...

Yīnwèi wǒ xǐhuan dǎ qiú suǒyǐ cháng dǎ
因为 我 喜欢 打 球，所以 常 打。
Because I like to play a ball game, (therefore) I often play.

Yīnwèi jīntiān de tiānqì hǎo suǒyǐ wǒmen xiǎng chūqu wánr
因为 今天 的 天气 好，所以 我们 想 出去 玩儿。
Because today's weather is good, (therefore) we want to go out and play.

Note: "Therefore" can be often omitted in English, but is required in Chinese.

2）yàoshi rúguǒ jiǎrú jiǎshǐ jiǎshè jiù
要是（如果/假如/假使/假设）……就…… if... then...

Yàoshi wǒ yǒu shíjiān wǒ jiù qù kàn diànyǐng
要是 我 有 时间，我 就 去 看 电影。
If I have time, (then) I will go to see a movie.

Rúguǒ nǐ jīntiān bù néng qù jiù míngtiān qù ba
如果 你 今天 不 能 去，就 明天 去 吧。
If you cannot go today, (then) go tomorrow.

Note: "Then" can be often omitted in English, but is required in Chinese.

3）虽然 suīrán（尽管 jǐnguǎn *）……
可是 kěshì（但是 dànshì *）……
though/although... (nevertheless/still)...

Suīrán wǒ hěn máng kěshì wǒ chángcháng kàn diànshì
虽然 我 很 忙，可是 我 常常 看 电视。
Though I am busy, (still) I often watch TV.

Jǐnguǎn tā yǒu hěn duō shì dànshì háishi měitiān duànliàn
尽管 他 有 很 多 事，但是 还是 每天 锻炼。

Although he has many things to do, he (still) works out daily.

Suīrán tā huì shuō Hànyǔ kěshì tā bù cháng shuō
虽然 他 会 说 汉语，可是 他 不 常 说。
Although he knows how to speak Chinese, he (still) does not often use it.

Jǐnguǎn tā hěn gāo dànshì tā bú pàng
尽管 他 很 高，但是 他 不 胖 (fat)。
Although he is tall, he is (nevertheless) not fat.

Note："Nevertheless/still" can be often omitted in English, but is required in Chinese.

4) 不但 búdàn (不仅 bùjǐn) ……而且 érqiě……

not only... but also...

(Subject)

Bùjǐn wǒmen yǒu shì érqiě tāmen yě yǒu shì
不仅 我们 有 事，而且 他们 也 有 事。
Not only do we have things to do, but they do, too.

(VP)

Tā búdàn pǎo de kuài érqiě yóuyǒng yě yóu de hǎo
他 不但 跑 得 快，而且 游泳 也 游 得 好。
Not only does he run fast, but he also swims well.

(Model Verb)

Wǒ búdàn xǐhuan kàn shū érqiě xiǎng kàn hěn duō shū
我 不但 喜欢 看 书，而且 想 看 很 多 书。
Not only do I like to read, but I also want to read many books.

(Adjective)

Zhège dōngxi búdàn guì érqiě nánkàn
这个 东西 不但 贵，而且 难看。
These things are not only expensive, but also ugly.

5) 又 yòu……又 yòu……

(a. Same as yibianr... yibianr...; b. not only... but also...; both... and...)

Tā fēicháng máng yīnwèi tā yòu xué Hànyǔ yòu xué Fǎyǔ
a. 她 非常 忙，因为 她 又 学 汉语 又 学 法语。
She is very busy because she is studying Chinese and French at the same time.

Māma bú ràng wǒ yòu wán diànnǎo yòu dǎ diànhuà
妈妈 不 让 我 又 玩 电脑 又 打 电话 。
My mom does not want me to play computer game while talking on the phone.

Bú yào yòu chī yòu shuō
不 要 又 吃 又 说 。
Don't eat and talk at the same time.

Tā yòu cōngming yòu piāoliang
b. 她 又 聪明 又 漂亮 。
She is not only smart but also pretty.

Nàge rén yòu yǒu míng yòu yǒu qián
那个 人 又 有 名 又 有 钱 。
That person is rich and famous.

Tā yòu huì shuō Yīngyǔ yòu huì shuō Xībānyáyǔ
他 又 会 说 英语 又 会 说 西班牙语 。
He speaks both English and Spanish.

6）一边 yìbiān……一边 yìbiān……

（doing two things at the same time）

Tā chángcháng yìbiān chī fàn yìbiān kàn shū
他 常常 一边 吃 饭 一边 看 书 。
He often eats and reads at the same time.

Wǒ xǐhuan yìbiān tīng yīnyuè yìbiān zuò gōngkè
我 喜欢 一边 听 音乐 一边 做 功课 。
I like to listen to music and do homework at the same time.

Bié yìbiān chī yìbiān shuō
别 一边 吃 一边 说 。
Don't eat and talk at the same time.（Don't talk with your mouth full.）

7）不论 búlùn（不管 bùguǎn/无论 wúlùn）……都 dōu（还 hái）……

no matter, regardless, still...

（Subject）

Zhè běn shū búlùn shì dàrén háishi xiǎohái dōu xǐhuan kàn
这 本 书，不论 是 大人 还是 小孩，都 喜欢 看 。
As for this book, whether by adults or children, it is well liked.

（Time）

Búlùn shì jīntiān háishi míngtiān wǒmen dōu néng qù
不论 是 今天 还是 明天，我们 都 能 去。
No matter it is today or tomorrow, We can still go.

(Attributive)

Tā xǐhuan kàn diànyǐng bùguǎn shì nǎr de dōu xǐhuan kàn
他 喜欢 看 电影 ，不管 是 哪儿 的 都 喜欢 看。
He likes to watch movies, regardless where they come from.

(Adjective)

Wúlùn lèi bu lèi wǒ dōu hái děi zuò gōngkè
无论 累 不 累，我 都 还 得 做 功课。
No matter how tired I am, I have to do my homework.

8) 除了 chúleVP /NP 以外 yǐwài，还 hái（也 yě）……

besides... also... (inclusive)

(Subject)

Chúle tā yǐwài wǒmen yě qù
除了 他 以外，我们 也 去。
Besides him, we will also go.

(VP)

Chúle pǎobù yǐwài tā hái xǐhuan chàng gē
除了 跑步 以外，他 还 喜欢 唱 歌。
Besides running, he also likes singing.

9) 除了 chúleVP/NP 以外 yǐwài，都 dōu……

except for... all... (exclusive)

(Subject)

Chúle tā yǐwài wǒmen dōu bú qù
除了 他 以外，我们 都 不 去。
Except for him, none of us is going.

(Object)

Chúle pǎobù yǐwài shénme yùndòng tā dōu xǐhuan
除了 跑步 以外，什么 运动 他 都 喜欢。
Except for running, he likes all sports.

通过副词构成 Use Adverb (s)

1) 正在 zhèngzài……呢 ne just now (ongoing situation)

(action)

Wǒ huíjiā de shíhou wǒ māma zhèngzài zuò fàn
我 回家 的 时候，我 妈妈 正在 做 饭。
When I arrived home, my mom was cooking.

(time)

Wǒ māma zhèngzài zuò fàn de shíhou wǒ dào jiā le
我 妈妈 正在 做 饭 的 时候，我 到 家 了。
When my mom was cooking, I arrived home.

(both)

Wǒ zhèng zuò fàn de shíhou tā zhèng kàn shū ne
我 正 做 饭 的 时候，他 正 看 书 呢。
When I was cooking, he was reading.

Nǐmen (zhèngzài) wán jìsuànjī de shíhou wǒmen yě zhèngzài
你们 （正在） 玩 计算机 的 时候，我们 也 正在
wán
玩。
When you were playing computer games, we were playing, too.

2）先 xiān……再 zài……然后 ránhòu（再 zài）……

(sequence: plan) first... then... next...

Wǒmen xiān qù Běijīng zài qù Nánjīng ránhòu zài qù Shànghǎi
我们 先 去 北京，再 去 南京 然后 再 去 上海。
First, we go to Beijing, then go to Nanjing, next to Shanghai.

3）先 xiān……又 yòu……后来 hòulái（又 yòu）……

(sequence: done) first... then... finally...

Wǒmen xiān qù le Běijīng yòu qù Nánjīng hòulái yòu qùle
我们 先 去 了 北京，又 去 南京 后来 又 去了
Shànghǎi
上海。
First, we went to Beijing, then went to Nanjing, and finally to Shanghai.

通过疑问词构成 Use Interrogative Pronoun (s)

“疑问词＋都”表示强调无一例外：Interrogative Pronoun Plus “Dou” Emphasizing “No Exception”

功用 Function: Emphasizing “No Exception” 表强调

句型 Sentence Pattern：“疑问词 + 都”——宾语前置

rènhé shénme
任何：什么

Nǐ juéde nǐ shénme dōu dǒng
你觉得你什么都懂。
You think you know everything!

rènhé rén shénme rén shuí
任何人：什么人/谁

Wǒ shuí shénme rén dōu bú rènshi
我谁（什么人）都不认识。
I don't know anyone.

rènhé shì shénme shì
任何事：什么事

Tā yì tiān dào wǎn shénme shì dōu méiyǒu
他一天到晚什么事都没有。
He has nothing to do all day long.

rènhé dìdiǎn shénme dìfang nǎr
任何地点：什么地方/哪儿

Wǒ nǎr dōu xiǎng qù
我哪儿都想去。
I want to go everywhere.

rènhé shíjiān shénme shíhou jǐ diǎn nǎ tiān
任何时间：什么时候/几点/哪天

Nǐ shénme shíhou lái wǒ dōu huānyíng
你什么时候来我都欢迎。
I welcome you anytime.

rènhé zhuàngtài zěnme (yàng)
任何状态：怎么（样）

zěnme shuō dōu kěyǐ
怎么说都可以。
Say (it) however you want.

教学难点

Difficulties

难点一 主语与副词 Subjects and Adverbs

汉语与英语不同。副词都应在动词前，不能放在主语前。

All adverbs are before the verb. They are not to appear before a subject.

In English, we say:

If you cannot go, then I will. ("then " is placed before "I".)

In Chinese, we say:

Yàoshi nǐ bù néng qù wǒ jiù qù
要是 你 不 能 去，我 就 去。
If you cannot go, then I will go. ("就" is never to be placed before "我")

This is the same with words like "都", "还", and "也".

难点二 主语在句中的位置 Position of Subjects in the Sentences

在用复句时，应注意主语的位置。

1) Flexible: Most of the time, the position of the subject is flexible:

(Wǒ) yīnwèi (wǒ) xǐhuan dǎ qiú suǒyǐ cháng dǎ
(我) 因为 (我) 喜欢 打 球 所以 常 打。
Because I like to play a ballgame, therefore I often play.

2) Subject First:

Tā yìbiān kàn shū yìbiān hē kāfēi
他 一边 看 书，一边 喝 咖啡。
He reads a book and drinks coffee at the same time.

Tā yòu chī yòu hē
他 又 吃 又 喝。
He not only eats, but also drinks (at the same time.)

3) Depends on number of doer:

4) Singular Subject:

Tā búdàn pǎo de kuài érqiě yóuyǒng yě yóu de hǎo
他 不但 跑 得 快，而且 游泳 也 游 得 好。
Not only does he run fast, but he also swims well.

5) Plural Subject:

Bùjǐn wǒmen yǒu shì érqiě tāmen yě yǒu shì
不仅 我们 有 事，而且 他们 也 有 事。
Not only do we have things to do, but they do, too.

难点三 "除了……以外……" and "疑问词+都"

"除了……以外"与"疑问词+都"配用表强调。

When "除了……以外……都……" singles out exceptions, meaning "other than...," we often use "疑问词+都" to emphasize the part of the object/VP that is not the exception.

Chúle zhège yǐwài shénme (biéde) wǒ dōu xǐhuan chī
除了 这个 以外，什么 (别的) 我 都 喜欢 吃。

(positive)

Except for this one, I like all other ones.

(meaning: This one is the only one that I don't like)

Chúle Zhōngguócài yǐwài shénme biéde cài wǒ dōu bù xǐhuan
除了 中国菜 以外，什么 (别的) 菜 我 都 不 喜欢
chī
吃。(negative)

I don't like any kind of food except for Chinese.

(meaning: Chinese is the only food that I like.)

难点四 "再" vs. "又"

"再"和"又"都表示重复。但"再"计划期待重复，"又"表示重复已发生。

"再" and "又" both are adverbs meaning "again or repeat the action". "再 zài again, once more, time and again or repeatedly" indicates a repetition of a plan; "又 yòu again or also" is for action that has already occurred.

Wǒ xǐhuan zhège diànyǐng suǒyǐ xiǎng zài kàn yí biàn
我 喜欢 这个 电影 所以 想 再 看 一 遍。
I like this movie and want to see it again.
(Wanting to see it again but has not yet done so.)

Wǒ xǐhuan zhège diànyǐng suǒyǐ yòu kànle yí biàn
我 喜欢 这个 电影 所以 又 看了 一 遍。
I like this movie, so I saw it once more.
(Already repeated the action.)

难点五 "不管"与疑问 Interrogative Form in "不管" Sentences

不论（不管，无论）…… 都……no matter...

"不论（不管，无论）"句用疑问形式。

"不论（不管，无论）" sentences have an interrogative form embedded within them, e. g.:

1) Yes/No question:

Búlùn míngtiān tiānqì hǎo bu hǎo wǒmen dōu qù
不论 明天 天气 好 不 好，我们 都 去。
Regardless of the weather condition (good or bad,) we are going.

2) WH-question:

Búlùn shénme shíhou dōu kěyǐ。
不论 什么 时候 都 可以
It will be fine no matter when.

3) Choice "还是"

Búlùn shì Zhōngwén háishi Yīngwén tā dōu huì shuō
不论 是 中文 还是 英文，他 都 会 说。
No matter whether in English or Chinese, he knows how to speak.

难点六 "正在" vs. "刚"

It should be noted that "正在" can be confused with "刚" because both can be translated as "just as" in English.

1) "正在" emphasizes an "ongoing situation"

Tā lái de shíhou wǒmen zhèngzài chī fàn
他 来 的 时候，我们 正在 吃 饭。
When he came, we were just (during the process of) having a meal.

2) "刚" emphasizes the immediate situation that has happened before the actual action.

Tā lái de shíhou wǒmen gāng yào chī fàn
他 来 的 时候，我们 刚 要 吃 饭。
When he came, we were just about to have dinner.

Tā lái de shíhou wǒmen gāng (gāng) chīle fàn
他 来 的 时候，我们 刚 (刚) 吃了 饭。
When he came, we just finished eating dinner.

13

叙述与询问

Telling Stories —Narration and Inquiry

从方便叙述的角度讲，行为和事件分两类。一类是日常的活动和行为，即反复发生的习惯性行为；一类是特定的事件与行为，即一次性的行为。在叙述和询问这两类事件和行为时，使用的语言句型有所不同。这是本节介绍和讨论的重点和难点，并附疑问句表。

本节将两类行为放在一起是为了让读者有一个明确的概念和对比。教学时可分开，逐步掌握使用。同时，不要忘记，谈事件和行为总是要和事件行为发生的时间、地点和方式联系起来。

We divide narration of actions into two categories because they require different sentence patterns. The first category of action is defined as general activities. They refer to repeated, habitual, routine, or planned actions. The second category of action is defined as specific events. They refer to one-time behaviors. In this section, we list sentence patterns and illustrate functional usage. There is also a list of questions attached.

This chapter compares the concepts and uses of the above-mentioned categories. Mastery of narration and inquiry of actions can be developed gradually. It must be remembered that an event or an action always happens at a time, at a location and in a given manner or by certain means.

教学重点 Content of Teaching and Learning

日常活动行为	General Actions
特殊疑问句	WH – Questions
特定事件	Specific Events
“了” Sentences	
询问特定事件行为	Inquring of Specifil Events

教学难点 Difficulties

日常与特定	General Actions vs. Specific Events
比较否定词“不”和“没”	Comparing Negatives: “不” vs. “没”
“了”的各种用法	When/How to Use “了”

教学重点

Content of Teaching and Learning

日常活动行为 General Actions

定义 Definition of General Actions：

日常的活动和行为，即反复发生的习惯性行为。

Everyday activities, habitual actions, repeated occurrences, routine schedule and plans

句型 Sentence Patterns for General Actions

S	T	P	M	VO.
Wǒ				chī fàn
我				吃饭。
	I eat.			
Wǒ	měitiān			chī fàn
我	每天			吃饭。
	I eat everyday.			
Wǒ		zài jiā		chī zǎofàn
我		在家		吃早饭。
	I eat breakfast at home.			
Wǒ			gēn jiārén yìqǐ	chī zǎofàn
我			跟家人一起	吃早饭。
	I eat with my family.			
Wǒ	měitiān	zài jiā	gēn jiārén yìqǐ	chī zǎofàn
我	每天	在家	跟家人一起	吃早饭。
	I eat everyday at home with my family.			

特殊疑问句 WH-Questions

	Shuí	chī fàn
(subject)	谁	吃饭？

	Nǐ		chī shénme
(object)	你		吃　什么？
	Nǐ		chī shénme fàn
(definition)	你		吃　什么　饭？
	Nǐ		chī jǐ ge
(quantity)	你		吃 几 个pizza?
	Nǐ		chī duōshao
	你		吃　多少　pizza?
	Nǐ		chī shénme
(VO)	你		吃　什么？
	Nǐ	jǐ diǎn	chī zǎofàn
(time)	你	几 点	吃 早饭
	Nǐ	shénme shíhou	chī wǎnfàn
	你	什么　时候	吃　晚饭？
	Nǐ	zài nǎr	chī fàn
(place)	你	在 哪儿	吃 饭
	Nǐ	cóng nǎr	qù chī fàn
	你	从 哪儿	去 吃 饭
	Nǐ	qù nǎr	chī fàn
	你	去 哪儿	吃 饭
	Nǐ	zěnme	chī
(how)	你	怎么	吃？
	Nǐ	yòng shénme	chī
	你	用　什么	吃？
	Nǐ	gēn shuí	chī
	你	跟　谁	吃？

特定事件　Specific Events

定义　Definition of a Specific Event

特定的事件与行为，即一次性的行为。

"A Specific Event" refers to one-time behavior that has been completed at the time of narration.

“了” Sentences

强调特定的事件与行为，即一次性的行为发生或完成，在句尾用“了”。

了 at the end indicates that the whole event has occurred or been completed.

S	T	P	M	VO	了
Wǒ				chī fàn	le
我				吃 饭	了。
Wǒ	jīntiān			chī fàn	le
我	今天			吃 饭	了。
Wǒ		zài jiā		chī fàn	le
我		在 家		吃 饭	了。
Wǒ			gēn péngyou yìqǐ	chī fàn	le
我			跟 朋友 一起	吃 饭	了。
Wǒ	jīntiān	zài jiā	gēn péngyou yìqǐ	chī fàn	le
我	今天	在 家	跟 朋友 一起	吃 饭	了。

当宾语有数量或其他（复杂）定语时，“了”放在动词后。

Use right after the verb when a quantity or a complicated modification of the object is involved.

Wǒ jīntiān zài jiā gēn péngyou chīle yí piàn pīsà
我（今天 在 家 跟 朋友）吃了 一 片 匹萨。
I (today, at home with friends) ate a slice of pizza.

Wǒ jīntiān zài jiā gēn péngyou chī le māma zuò de pīsà
我（今天 在 家 跟 朋友）吃 了 妈妈 做 的 匹萨。
I (today, at home with friends) ate the pizza my mom made.

Double emphasis 强调：I have already eaten.

Wǒ yǐjing chī le
我 已经 吃 了。

Negative 否定：I have not eaten yet.

méiyǒu
没有 (when using“没有”, no need for “了”)
Wǒ méi (yǒu) chī fàn
我 没（有）吃 饭。

Wǒ hái méiyǒu chī ne
我 还 没有 吃 呢。

询问特定事件行为 Inquiry of Specific Events

问具体事件的发生 Questions for Specific Events:

Subject	+	(T P M)	+	Verb	+	Object

Nǐ	chī méi chī wǎnfàn
你	吃 没 吃 晚饭 ?
Nǐ	chīle méiyǒu
你	吃了 没有 ?

提供有关一次性事件具体发生的条件用“是……的”结构。

To further provide information on time, place, or means that are related to one specific event, use “是……的” structure.

Statement:

Wǒ měitiān dōu bù chī zǎofàn kěshì jīntiān chī zǎofàn le
我 每天 都 不 吃 早饭 ,可是 今天 吃 早饭 了。

询问以上动作具体发生的条件:

Inquiry of time/place/manner that is related to the specific actions stated above:

是	+	(T P M)	+	Verb + 的

Time:

Nǐ	shì	shénme shíhou	chī de (fàn)
你	是	什么 时候	吃 的 (饭)?
Wǒ	shì	zǎoshang bā diǎn	chī de
我	是	早上 八 点	吃 的。

Place:

Nǐ	shì	zài nǎr	chī de
你	是	在 哪儿	吃 的?
Wǒ	shì	zài jiā	chī de
我	是	在 家	吃 的。

How (means or manner):

Nǐ	shì	zěnme	chī de
你	是	怎么	吃 的?

Wǒ shì gēn péngyou yìqǐ chī de
我 是 跟 朋友 一起 吃 的。
Wǒ shì yòng kuàizi chī de
我 是 用 筷子（chopsticks）吃 的。

“是……的”结构 Function of the“是……的……”Structure

追问有关一次性事件具体发生的条件，包括时间、地点和方式。

When referring to a specific action that has been done and wishing the need to add or further inquire about the conditions (time, place, how) under which the action has occurred, we use the“shi... de...”structure.

That is to say that this structure supplies further information to a“le”sentence, e. g.:

Wǒ chī zǎofàn le Wǒ shì zǎoshang bā diǎn zài xuéxiào gēn
我 吃 早饭 了。我 是 早上 八 点 在 学校 跟
péngyou yìqǐ chī de
朋友 一起 吃 的。

教学难点

Difficulties

难点一 日常与特定 General Actions vs. Specific Events

对比 Compare

Statement of a General Action	Narration of a Specific Event
我每天都吃早饭。	我今天吃早饭了
I eat breakfast everyday.	I ate breakfast this morning.
我每天八点在家吃早饭。	我是八点在家吃的。
I eat breakfast daily at 8 o'clock.	I ate at home at 8 o'clock.
	(If we talk about the meal this morning.)
他不爱吃早饭。	他今天也没吃早饭。
He does like to eat breakfast.	He did not eat breakfast today.

(As preference.) (He skipped a meal.)

Comparing a General Situation with a Specific Action

(every breakfast)

Wǒ měitiān dōu chī zǎofàn
我 每天 都 吃 早饭 。
I eat breafast everyday.

Wǒ měitiān zǎoshang bā diǎn zài xuéxiào gēn péngyou chī
我 每天 早上 八 点 在 学校 跟 朋友 吃。
I eat every morning at 8 o'clock at school with my friends.

(today's breakfast)

Wǒ jīntiān zǎoshang chī zǎofàn le
我 今天 早上 吃 早饭 了。
I had breakfast this morning.

Wǒ shì zǎoshang bā diǎn zài xuéxiào gēn péngyou chī de
我 是 早上 八 点 在 学校 跟 朋友 吃 的。
I ate this morning at 8 o'clock with my friends at school.

难点二 比较否定词"不"和"没"

Comparing Negatives：不 vs. 没

"不"和"没"都是否定。否定行为时，"不"否定经常性的行为和意愿，"没"否定所有，也否定一次性的事件的发生。

Both "不" and "没" are both negatives. But："不" is used to deny a general situation or willingness to perform an action. "没" is used to deny possession or the completion of a specific event.

不：

1) Negative used for general situations：

a：Description/ Adjectives as Predicate

Tā bù hǎo
他 不 好 。

b：Identification/ "是" as Predicate

Nǐ bú shì lǎoshī
你 不 是 老师 。

c：Everyday, habitual, repeated, planned actions/Action Verbs as

Predicates

Wǒ měitiān dōu bù chī zǎofàn Wǒ bú ài chī zǎofàn yě bù
我 每天 都 不 吃 早饭 。我 不 爱 吃 早饭 ，也 不
xiǎng chī
想 吃。

I never eat breakfast. I don't like to eat breakfast, and I don't want to do it.

2) Negative indicating unwillingness: purposefully not do (did not do)

Zuótiān tā māma gěi tā zuòle zǎofàn kěshì tā bù chī
昨天 他 妈妈 给 他 做了 早饭 ，可是 他 不 吃。

Yesterday, his mom made breakfast for him but he did not eat it (decline/refuse).

没：

1) Negative for possession: (没有)

Wǒ méiyǒu gēge
我 没有 哥哥。

I don't have any older brother.

2) Negative for a specific action (one time occurrence)

Jīntiān wǒ méi zuò gōngkè
今天 我 没 做 功课 。

I did not do my homework today.

Examine the following sentences carefully. Note the differences:

1) Jīntiān wǒ méi zuò gōngkè yīnwèi lǎoshī méi liú zuòyè bú yòng
今 天 我 没 做 功课 ，因为 老师 没 留 作业 ，不 用
zuò
做 。

I did not do my homework today because the teacher did not give any, and I don't need to do it.

2) Zuótiān tā méi chī zǎofàn yīnwèi nà shíhou tā bú è suǒyǐ bù
昨天 他 没 吃 早饭 ，因为 （那 时候 ）他 不 饿，所以 不
xiǎng chī
想 吃。

He did not eat breakfast yesterday, because he wasn't hungry and did not want to eat.

难点三 “了”的各种用法 When/How to Use “了”

“了” at the end of the sentence

1) “了” at the end of a sentence indicates that occurrence has been completed at one time.

Wǒ měitiān dōu bù chī zǎofàn kěshì jīntiān zài xuéxiào chī
我 每天 都 不 吃 早饭，可是 今天 在 学校 吃
zǎofàn le
（早饭）了。

I don't normally eat breakfast, but I did today at school.

2) “了” at the end of a sentence with time duration indicates that the action is ongoing.

Wǒ xuéxí Hànyǔ xuéle yì nián bàn le Wǒ xuéle yì nián bàn
我 学习 汉语 学了 一 年 半 了。/ 我 学了 一 年 半
de Hànyǔ le
的 汉语 了。

I have been learning Chinese for a year and a half (now).

3) “了” at the end of a sentence indicates a change:

Note: “了” is always used with the current status of a situation, and not the previous one.

Adjective: Tāmen yǐqián hěn bèn xiànzài dōu cōngming le
他们 以前 很 笨，现在 都 聪明 了。
They used to be stupid but have become smart now.

“be”: Wǒ bú shì zhōngxuéshēng le wǒ shì dàxuéshēng le
我 不 是 中学生 了，我 是 大学生 了。
I am not a high school student anymore, I am in college now.

“have”: Bàba māma yǒu sān ge háizi le
爸爸 妈妈 有 三 个 孩子 了。
Daddy and Mumy have 3 children. (There must be a new addition.)

Noun: Tā shíliù suì le
他 十六 岁 了。
He is (turned) 16.

Plan: Zuótiān tā xiǎng qù kěshì jīntiān bù xiǎng qù le
昨天 她 想 去，可是 今天 不 想 去 了。

She wanted to go yesterday but today she no longer wants to go.

Preference: Nǐ yǐqián bù xǐhuan hē Kěkǒukělè xiànzài xǐhuan le
你 以前 不 喜欢 喝 可口可乐，现在 喜欢 了。
You did not like Coca-cola before but you like it now.

Habit: Wǒ yǐqián chángcháng chī pǐsà xiànzài bù cháng chī le
我 以前 常常 吃 匹萨，现在 不 常 吃 了。
I used to eat pizza often, but not too often now.

"了" Right after the Verb

Important Notes:

不要把“了”看做是过去时，很多用“了”的情况无法作如此解释。

It cannot be emphasized enough that "了" is not to be seen as an indicator of past tense. In many cases, "了" simply implies the completion of an action. There are situations when "了" appears directly after a verb:

1) "了" is used directly after the verb when quantity or complex modification of the object is involved.

Wǒ jīntiān zài jiā gēn péngyou chīle yí piàn pǐsà
我（今天 在 家 跟 朋友）吃了 一 片 匹萨。
I (today at home with my friends) ate a slice of pizza.

Wǒ jīntiān zài jiā gēn péngyou chīle māma zuò de pǐsà
我（今天 在 家 跟 朋友）吃了 妈妈 做 的 匹萨。
I (today at home with my freinds) ate the pizza my mom made.

2) "了" is used right after the verb when a series of actions is listd.

Xīngqītiān wǒ zuòle gōngkè kànle diànyǐng dǎle qiú hái
星期天 我 做了 功课，看了 电影，打了 球，还
wánle jìsuànjī
玩了 计算机。

Last Sunday, I did my homework, watched a movie, played a ballgame, and also played computer games.

3) "了" is used right after the first verb to emphasize the immediate connection with the second.

Wǒ xiàle kè jiù huí jiā
我 下了 课 就 回 家。

(This is a plan. The action has not happened yet.)

As soon as the class is over, I am going home.

(If the first action is completed, then the second will follow in no time.)

Compare:

Wǒ xiàle kè jiù huí jiā le
我 下了 课 就 回 家 了。
("了" at the end indicates both actions were done.)
As soon as class was over, I went home.

4) "了" is used right after a verb when a time duration is indicated.

Wǒ xuéxí Hànyǔ xuéle yì nián bàn Wǒ xuéle yì nián bàn
我 学习 汉语 学了 一 年 半。/我 学了 一 年 半
de Hànyǔ
的 汉语。
I learned Chinese for a year and half (during a certain period of my life).

"了" Patterns

1) "太 adjective 了!" is used to emphasize an extreme status of a situation, good or bad.

Tài hǎo le
太 好 了!(Great! Wonderful!)
Tài guì le
太 贵 了!(Too expensive!)

2) "快……了" or "(就)要/快……了" is used to predict that something is about to happen soon.

Qìchē kuài lái le
汽车 快 来 了。
The bus is coming!

Kuài yào kāi xué le
快 要 开 学 了。
The school is going to be in session!

14

疑问句

Questions

提问是索取信息情报的重要手段，是人际交流的重要方式。学会和掌握提问是国家外语教学标准（ACTFL Foreign Language Learning Standards，http：//www. actfl. org）规定的内容之一，也是 AP 中文考试等测试的重要内容之一。

本书各章节均就讨论的话题提供有关的疑问句型及使用，而本节就疑问形式作一简要归纳。

Asking questions is an essential way to obtain information. It is an indispensable means for interpersonal communication. According to National Foreign Language Standards (ACTFL Foreign Language Learning Standards, http://www. actfl. org), commanding inquiry is highly important as well. It is also included in any proficiency testing such as the AP Chinese Test.

Every chapter of this book provides question patterns and uses related to the topic. This chapter puts together a general summary of all discussions on questions.

教学重点 Content of Teaching and Learning

疑问句	Questions
是非/正反疑问句	Yes/No questions
特殊疑问句	Special Questions：WH-Questions
选择疑问句	Alternative Questions

教学难点 Difficulties

形容词做谓语："是"和"好"	Adjective as Predicate："是" vs. "好"
"or" 在疑问句和陈述句中	"Or" in Questions vs. "Or" in Statements
"To ask" vs. "问"	
"I don't know ..." vs. "我不知道"	
复合句	Complex Sentences

词汇表 Glossary

疑问词表	List of the Interrogatives

教学重点

Content of Teaching and Learning

疑问句 Questions

功能 Functions：Inquiring and Exchanging Information

句型 Structures：最基本的提问方式分三种

There are 3 basic groups of questions.

是非/正反疑问句 Yes/No Questions

Yes/No Questions：There are 2 basic forms of Yes/No Questions.

Ma Question：. ……吗？Add "ma" at the end of a sentence to form a Yes/No Question.

Nǐ lèi ma
你 累 吗？

Tā shì nǐ de péngyǒu ma
他 是 你 的 朋友 吗？

Nǐ yǒu jiějiě ma
你 有 姐姐 吗？

Nǐ ài wán jìsuànjī ma
你 爱 玩 计算机 吗？

Use positive or negative form of adjective or verb to form a Yes/No Question.

Positive / Negative：动词/形容词＋不/没动词/形容词

V / Adjective ＋Negative /Verb/Adjective

Nǐ máng bù máng
你 忙 不 忙 ？

Tā qù méi qù
他 去 没 去？

Nǐ shì bu shì zhōngxuéshēng
你 是 不 是 中学生 ？

Nǐ yǒu méiyǒu gēgē
你 有 没有 哥哥？
Nǐ xǐhuān bu xǐhuān kàn shū
你 喜欢 不 喜欢 看 书？
Nǐ xiǎng bu xiǎng chī Zhōngguócài
你 想 不 想 吃 中国菜 ？

特殊疑问句 Special Questions: WH-Questions

重点提示：汉语特殊疑问句的特点是提问时词序不变。

In Chinese, when asking a question, the words order remains the same as in a statement. To form a question, use a "WH-word" to replace the part that is being asked at its original position in the sentence.

WH-words

Who/whom	谁	shuí
Whose	谁的	shuíde
What	什么	shénme
Which	什么/哪（个）	shénme/nǎ（ge）
When	什么时候	shénme shíhou
At what time	几点	jǐ diǎn
Where	哪（里）	nǎ（li）
How	怎么	zěnme
With whom	跟谁（一起）	gēn shuí（yīqǐ）
How much/How many	多少/几（个）	duōshao/jǐ（ge）
How about it	怎么样	zěnmeyàng
Why	为什么	wèishénme
How long	多长时间/多久	duōcháng shǐjiān/duō jiǔ

陈述句与疑问句对比：

	Subject	+ Time	+ Place	+ Manner	+ Verb	+ Object
Statement	我	每天	在学校	跟同学一起	看	很多书。
Questions						

谁				看	书？
那				是	谁的书？
你				看	什么？
你				看	什么书？
你				看	哪本书？
你	什么时候			看	书？
你	几点			看	书？
你		在哪		看	书？
你			怎么	看？	
你			跟谁一起	看？	
你				看	多少（本）书？
你				看	几本书？
你			为什么	看	这本书？
这本书					怎么样？
你				看	书看得怎么样？
你				看	书看了多长时间？

选择疑问句 Alternative Questions

原则上，可用“还是”提供各项选择。

实际应用时，多与特殊疑问句结合使用。

Grammatically speaking, “还是” may be used to form a question.

Functionally, it is often used in combination with “WH-Questions”.

Subject +	Time +	Place +	Manner +	Verb +	Object
你还是他				看	书？
那本书				是	你的还是他的？
你				看	中文书还是英文书？
你	上午还是下午			看	书？
你		在家还是在学校		看	书？
你		自己看还是跟我一起看？			

你　　　　　　　　　　　　　　　　　　　　　　　　看一本还是两本书？

谁看书，你还是他？

那是谁的书，是你的还是他的？

你看哪本书，这本还是那本？

你几点看书，八点还是九点？

你在哪儿看书，在家还是在学校？

你跟谁一起看，我还是他？

你看几本书，一本还是两本？

难点提示 Attention：

应对学生强调：英语的"or"在汉语中分陈述形式"或者"和疑问形式"还是"，不可混淆。

"Or" in English can be used in either a statement or a question, while in Chinese, "还是" is used only in questions, and "或者" is used only in statements.

Question:　　你想看一本还是两本？

Statement:　　我想看一本或（者）两本。

教学难点

Difficulties

难点一　形容词做谓语："是"和"好"

Adjective as Predicate: "是" vs. "好"

Two key words for differentiation: Identification vs. Description.

Identification: 中文的"是"的功用一般只限于认定。

The verb "to be " has limited function in Chinese. It is used only to identify what is what and who is whom.

我是学生，不是老师。

I am a student, I am not a teacher.

这是书，不是杂志。

This is a book , it is not a magazine.

Description：中文的形容词具有动词的功用，可直接用来描述。

Adjectives can be used independently to describe situations and conditions.

我很好。 I am fine.

Therefore, when asking "Yes/No Questions" for description, use adjectives without the verb "to be".

positive adjective + negative adjective

你好不好？ How are you doing?

难点二 "or" 在疑问句和陈述句中

"Or" in Questions vs. "Or" in Statements

英语的 "or" 在汉语中分陈述形式 "或者" 和疑问形式 "还是"，二者不可混淆。

Attention: "Or" in English can be used in either a statement or a question, while in Chinese, "还是" is used only in questions, and "或者" is used only in statements.

Question： 你想看一本还是两本？

Do you want to read one or two books?

Statement： 我想看一本或（者）两本。

I want to read one or two books.

难点三 "To ask" vs. "问"

英文的 "to ask" 可以提问也可以请人做事。

The English word "to ask" can be used for two major purposes:

To ask a question

To ask someone to do something

中文的"问"只可以提问，请人做事要用兼语句。

In Chinese, these are two different expressions.

English	Chinese
He asked you a question. (A)	他问你一个问题。
He asked me, "what is this?" (B)	他问我"这是什么?"
He asked me where the bathroom was. (C)	他问我厕所在哪儿?
He asked you to have some tea. (D)	他请（让，叫）你喝茶。

"问" can be followed by direct or indirect objects as shown in A, B and C.

"问" must be followed by a question word or a question form as in A, B and C.

The sentence used "问" can be a direct quote or an indirect quote as in B and C.

When asking someone to do something, we cannot use "问" as shown in D.

难点四 "I don't know ..." vs. "我不知道"

"我不知道 "后要用疑问形式。

In English "I don't know..." is followed by "if ..." or "whether or not..." or some other "wh... + statement":

I don't know if he is coming.

I don't know whether or not he has a sister.

I don't know where he lives.

In Chinese, "我不知道" must be followed by a question form:

我不知道他来不来。

我不知道他有没有姐姐嘛。

我不知道他住在哪儿。

It is easy for students to make the mistakes by saying:

(×) 我不知道要是他来。

难点五　复合句 Complex Sentences

不论（不管，无论）……都…… no matter what...

“不论（不管，无论）”包含疑问形式。

“不论（不管，无论）” sentences have a question form embedded within them.

Yes/No question form:

Búlùn míngtiān tiānqì hǎo bu hǎo wǒmen dōu qù
不论 明天 天气 好 不 好，我们 都 去。
We are going tomorrow regardless of the weather.

WH-question form:

Búlùn shénme shíhou dōu kěyǐ
不论 什么 时候 都 可以。
Any time is fine.

“还是”(Or/Whether)

Búlùn shì Zhōngwén háishi Yīngwén tā dōu huì shuō
不论 是 中文 还是 英文，他 都 会 说。
No matter whether in English or Chinese, he speaks well.

15

方位

Direction and Position

谈方位是人际交流的一个重要话题。这一节为这个话题的展开提供所需的词汇和句型，并解释可能出现的教学难点。因为这个话题可谈国家、地区、社区，甚至学校、家庭、室内外，我们在本节还包括了相关的词汇表和其他语法，供教学使用。

Direction and position is an important communication topic and may include country, region, even community, school and family, inside and outside. This chapter provides the necessary vocabulary and sentence patterns for this topic. It also pinpoints some of the possible difficulties for English-speaking learners.

教学重点 Content of Teaching and Learning

方位词	Words Indicating Position/Location
方位词尾	Suffixes Indicating Position/Location
方位词组	Phrases Indicating Position/Location
有用句型	Sentence Patterns for Describing Position/Location

教学难点 Difficulties

"Northeast" vs. "东北"

复杂名词组 Complex Noun Phrases

"部""边""面""方"的用法 Use of "部", "边", "面" and "方"

文化联系 Cultural Relations

说汉语的国家与地区 Chinese-Speaking Countries and Regions

词汇表 Glossary

建筑	Structure
居家	Home
学校	School

教学重点

Content of Teaching and Learning

方位词 Words Indicating Position/Location

方向 fāngxiàng direction, orientation

东	dōng	east	南	nán	south
西	xī	west	北	běi	north

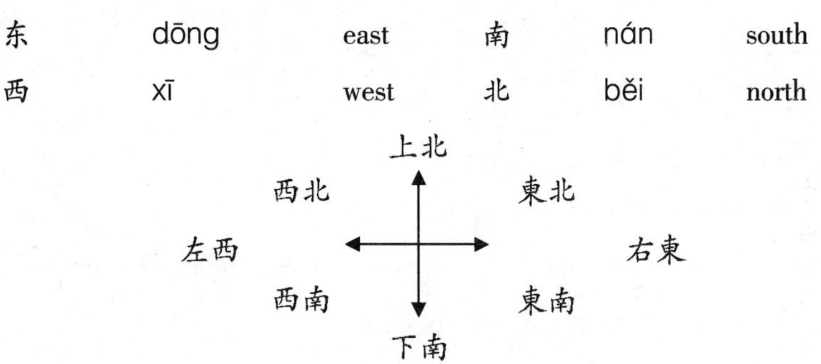

方位词尾 Suffixes Indicating Position/Location

部	bù	part, section
边	biān	side, border, edge, fringe
面	miàn	face (toward), surface, a whole area
方	fāng	direction, side, party, place, region

dōngbù	xībù	zhōngbù	zhōngxībù
东部	西部	中部	中西部
dōngfāng	xīfāng	nánfāng	běifāng
东方	西方	南方	北方

dōngbian mian	xībian mian	nánbian mian	běibian mian
东边（面）	西边（面）	南边（面）	北边（面）

方位词组 Phrases Indicating Position/Location:

前（边/面）	qián	in front, front
后（边/面）	hòu	after, behind
左（边/面）	zuǒ	left
右（边/面）	yòu	right
上（边/面）	shàng	on, on top of ...
下（边/面）	xià	under, below
里（边/面）	lǐ	in, inside
外（边/面）	wài	outside
对面	duìmiàn	opposite; across from, face to face
旁边	pángbiān	beside, next to
中间	zhōngjiān	between, in the middle
两边	liǎngbiān	both sides
附近	fùjìn	adjacent, in the vicinity
周围	zhōuwéi	around, surrounding
四周	sìzhōu	all around

A Complex Noun Phrase:

Modifier always goes before the noun.

1) Description of a location using an object as definition:

xuéxiào de yòubian
学校 的 右边

the right side of the school, to the right of the school

2) Description of an object using a position as definition:

yòubian de xuéxiào
右边 的 学校 the school on the right

有用句型 Sentence Patterns for Describing Position/Location:

以下句型是描述方位地理必不可少的。

Here are three sentence patterns needed to describe position and direction.

陈述 Statements

1）在 Something 在 somewhere

Zhījiāgē zài Měiguó de zhōngxībù
芝加哥 在 美国 的 中西部 。
Chicago is (located) in the midwest (area) of the U. S.

2）是 Somewhere 是 something (specific)

Xuéxiào hé shāngdiàn de zhōngjiān shì Zhījiāgē Túshūguǎn
学校 和 商店 的 中间 是 芝加哥 图书馆 。
In between the school and the store is the Chicago Library.

3）有 Somewhere 有 something

(a non specific place or a list of places/things)

Xuéxiào hé shāngdiàn de zhōngjiān shì yí ge túshūguǎn
学校 和 商店 的 中间 是 一 个 图书馆 。
In between the school and the store, there is a library.

Zhījiāgē túshūguǎn de pángbiān yǒu xuéxiào shāngdiàn hé
芝加哥 图书馆 的 旁边 有 学校 、 商店 和

yínháng
银行 。
Next to the Chicago Library, there are schools, stores, and banks.

问句 Questions

1）在 Something 在 somewhere

Zhījiāgē zài nǎr
芝加哥 在 哪儿?
Where Chicago is (located)?

2）是 Somewhere 是 something (specific)

Xuéxiào hé shāngdiàn de zhōngjiān shì shénme
学校 和 商店 的 中间 是 什么 ?

What is in between the school and the store?

3）有 Somewhere 有（list of things）

Zhījiāgē Túshūguǎn de pángbiān yǒu shénme
芝加哥 图书馆 的 旁边 有 什么？
What (institutions) are there next to the Chicago Library?

教学难点

Difficulties

难点一 "Northeast" vs. "东北"

对比中英的不同说法。

In English, locations and directions start with "North" and "South".

Northeast Northwest Southeast Southwest

In Chinese, locations and directions start with "东" and "西".

东北 东南 西北 西南

难点二 复杂名词组 Complex Noun Phrases

(Please also see Chapter 18: Noun Phrases)

复杂名词组 Compound/Complex Noun Phrases 对学生来说比较难。英文的名词的构成有几种方式，而汉语的定语要放在名词前。不然意思就会错了。请看下列例句对比。

复杂名词组 Compound/Complex Noun Phrases can be confusing to English speakers.

In English: There are three ways to form a noun phrase:

(noun with 's)	David's left
(of)	the left side of David
(that/which clause)	the side that is on the left of David

In Chinese: There is only one way to form a noun phrase:

the modification/definition goes before the noun：大卫的左边

If the positions of the modifier and the noun are switched, meaning changes：

A. 大卫的左边 David's left

(Uses a person to define a location)

B. 左边的大卫 David who is on the left

(Uses a location to identify a person)

(There must be another person who is on the right.)

Compare：

我们的老师在大卫的左边。

Our teacher is on David's left side.

大卫的左边是我们的老师。

The person to David's left is our teacher.

左边的大卫是我的朋友，右边的我不认识。

David who is on the left is my friend. I don't know who the one on the right is.

难点三 "部""边""面""方"的用法

Use of "部", "边", "面" and "方"

"部" indicates part of a whole area

Huáshèngdùn zài Měiguó de dōngbù Jiāzhōu zài xībù

华盛顿 在 美国 的 东部，加州 在 西部。

Washington D. C. is located in the East of the U. S., while California is in the West.

Zhījiāgē shì Měiguó zhōngxībù de yí ge dà chéngshì

芝加哥 是 美国 中西部 的 一 个 大 城市。

Chicago is a large city in the Midwest of the U. S.

"边" and "面" are interchangeable

1) Northern dialects usually use "边", while Southern dialects often use

“面”.

东边（面） 西边（面） 南边（面） 北边（面）

2）“边” and “面” may refer to an area within a region or outside the region but usually in the vicinity.

Huáshèngdùn zài Měiguó de dōngbiān Jiāzhōu zài xībiān
华盛顿 在 美国 的 东边，加州 在 西边。
Washington D. C. is on the east coast of the U. S., and California is on the west coast.

Jiānádà zài Měiguó de běibiān
加拿大 在 美国 的 北边。
Canada is located in the north of the U. S..

“方” points out direction. However, its usage is a little tricky

1）“南方” and “北方” are usually related to climatic regions or zones, such as “the South” and “the North” of a country.

Běijīng shì Zhōngguó běifāng de yí ge chéngshì Nánjīng shì
北京 是 中国 北方 的 一 个 城市，南京 是
Zhōngguó nánfāng de yí ge chéngshì
中国 南方 的 一 个 城市。
Beijing is a city in the north of China, while Nanjing is a city in the south of China.

2）In contrast, “东方” and “西方” almost exclusively refer to the “Eastern Hemisphere” and the “Western Hemisphere” of the globe rather than within a country.

Zhōngguó shì yí ge dōngfāng guójiā Měiguó shì xīfāng guójiā
中国 是 一 个 东方 国家，美国 是 西方 国家。
China is a country in the East, while the U. S. is a country in the West.

3）In order to refer to the east and west part of the country, we use “东部” and “西部”.

Huáshèngdùn zài Měiguó de dōngbù Jiāzhōu zài xībù
华盛顿 在 美国 的 东部，加州 在 西部。
Washington D. C. is on the east coast of the U. S., and California is on the west coast.

文化联系

Cultural Relations

说汉语的国家与地区 Chinese-Speaking Countries and Regions

中国（大陆、台湾、香港、澳门），新加坡，美国的中国城等

词汇表

Glossary

建筑 jiànzhù construct, build; building, structure, architecture

房子	fángzi	house, building, room (of a house, etc.)	
	楼房	lóufáng	multi-storied building
	大楼	dàlóu	multi-storied building
	高楼	gāolóu	tall building
	摩天大楼	mótiān dàlóu	skyscraper
	大厦	dàshà	mansion, large building (often used in names of such buildings)
家	jiā	family, household, home, residence	
	院子	yuànzi	courtyard, yard
	花园	huāyuán	flower garden
	菜园	càiyuán	vegetable garden, vegetable plot
	庭院	tíngyuàn	front courtyard of a Chinese-style house
	阳台	yángtái	balcony, veranda
	平台	píngtái	platform, terrace

大门	dàmén	front door, front gate, main gate
栅栏	zhàlan	railings, fence

居家 jūjiā Related Home

房间 fángjiān room (within a house, etc.)

门	mén	door, gate
窗户	chuānghu	window
墙	qiáng	wall
墙角	qiángjiǎo	corner of a wall
楼上	lóushàng	upper floor, upstairs
楼下	lóuxià	lower floor, downstairs
楼梯	lóutī	stairs, staircase, ladder
台阶	táijiē	steps, staircase
地下室	dìxiàshì	basement
阁楼	gélóu	attic, garret
走廊	zǒuláng	corridor, porch, passage
门庭	méntíng	entrance and courtyard
门厅	méntīng	vestibule, entrance hall
客厅	kètīng	drawing room, parlor
餐厅	cāntīng	dining room, restaurant
厨房	chúfáng	kitchen
书房	shūfáng	study, studio
卧室	wòshì	bedroom
工作间	gōngzuòjiān	workshop, shop (production division of a factory)
游戏室	yóuxìshì	recreation room, game room
厕所	cèsuǒ	bathroom, lavatory
洗澡间	xǐzǎojiān	bathroom

壁炉 bìlú fireplace

家具 jiājù furniture

桌子 zhuōzi table, desk

书桌 shūzhuō desk

办公桌 bàngōngzhuō desk (especially in an office)

饭桌 fànzhuō dining table

咖啡桌 kāfēi zhuō coffee table

茶几 chájī tea table

椅子 yǐzi chair

沙发 shāfā sofa

床 chuáng bed

柜子 guìzi cabinet, cupboard

衣柜 yīguì wardrobe, chest of drawers

柜橱 guìchú cupboard, sideboard

床头柜 chuángtóuguì bedside cupboard

书架 shūjià bookshelf

设施用具 shèshī yòngjù facilities, installation, utensil, appliance

家用电器 jiāyòng diànqì Facilities/Household Appliances

照片 zhàopiàn photo (graph), picture, print

画像 huàxiàng paint a portrait; portrait

挂图 guàtú wall map, wall chart

黑板 hēibǎn blackboard

镜子 jìngzi mirror, eyeglasses, plate glass

投影机 tóuyǐngjī projector

录放机 lùfàngjī VCR/DVD

电脑 diànnǎo computer

电视 diànshì television, TV

灯	dēng	lantern, lamp, light
电灯	diàndēng	electric lamp, electric light
台灯	táidēng	table lamp, desk lamp
洗衣机	xǐyījī	washing machine
烘干机	hōnggānjī	drier
洗碗机	xǐwǎnjī	dishwasher
冰箱	bīngxiāng	icebox, refrigerator, freezer
烤箱	kǎoxiāng	oven
微波炉	wēibōlú	microwave oven
空调	kōngtiáo	air conditioning

学校 School

设施	shèshī	facilities	
	教室	jiàoshì	classroom
	办公室	bàngōngshì	office (the room itself)
		校长办公室	Principal's Office
	图书馆	túshūguǎn	library
	体育馆	tǐyùguǎn	gym
	礼堂	lǐtáng	auditorium, assembly hall
	实验室	shíyànshì	laboratory
		语言实验室	language lab
	会议室	huìyìshì	conference room, meeting room
	停车场	tíngchēchǎng	parking lot, parking area
	操场	cāochǎng	drill ground, sports ground
	游泳池	yóuyǒngchí	swimming pool
	洗手间	xǐshǒujiān	bathroom, washroom
	餐厅	cāntīng	dining room
	警卫	jǐngwèi	security guard

课程设置与服务	Curricula and Academic Services	
系	xì	department
年级	niánjí	grade, year (in school)
英文	Yīngwén	English, the English language (especially written)
外文	wàiwén	foreign language (written or spoken)
数学	shùxué	mathematics (as a subject)
社会科学	shèhuì kēxué	social sciences
科学	kēxué	science
体育	tǐyù	physical education, physical culture; sports
音乐艺术	yīnyuè yìshù	music and art
计算机	jìsuànjī	computer, calculating machine
特殊教育	tèshū jiàoyù	special education
咨询	zīxún	counseling
课外活动	kèwài huódòng	extracurricular activities

16 地点表

List of Places

地点是事件行为发生的所在。地点表为扩展学习提供方便。

本表的排列一是按词尾拼音的前后顺序，二是分类。

Places are locations where actions occur. This list provides the convenience of expanded learning. The arrangement of vocabulary by suffix in alphabetical order and by category.

按词尾拼音的前后顺序　By Suffix in Alphabetical Order

吧	bā	bar	
	酒吧	jiǔbā	bar (especially Western-style)
	网吧	wǎngbā	Internet cafe
场	chǎng	open space, field, market	
	操场	cāochǎng	drill ground, sport ground
	广场	guǎngchǎng	(public) square
	机场	jīchǎng	airport
	篮球场	lánqiúchǎng	basketball court
	商场	shāngchǎng	market, marketplace, department store
	市场	shìchǎng	market, marketplace
	停车场	tíngchēchǎng	parking lot, parking area
	体育场	tǐyùchǎng	stadium
	网球场	wǎngqiúchǎng	tennis court
	足球场	zúqiúchǎng	football (soccer) field
店	diàn	shop, store, inn	
	饭店	fàndiàn	hotel, restaurant
	商店	shāngdiàn	shop, store
	书店	shūdiàn	bookstore
	小吃店	xiǎochīdiàn	snack shop, snack bar
	专卖店	zhuānmàidiàn	store exclusively for goods of a name

brand

馆	guǎn	mansion, building	
	博物馆	bówùguǎn	museum
	茶馆	cháguǎn	teahouse
	饭馆	fànguǎn	restaurant
	咖啡馆	kāfēiguǎn	coffee shop
	理发馆	lǐfàguǎn	barber shop, hairdresser's
	美发馆	měifàguǎn	beauty salon
	美术馆	měishùguǎn	art gallery
	体育馆	tǐyùguǎn	gym
	天文馆	tiānwénguǎn	planetarium
	图书馆	túshūguǎn	library
局	jú	office, bureau, department, classifier for sports events	
	警察局	jǐngchájú	police station
	邮局	yóujú	post office
所	suǒ	place, location; a suffix indicating an office, institute, etc.	
	厕所	cèsuǒ	bathroom, lavatory
	派出所	pàichūsuǒ	local police station
堂	táng	main room, main hall	
	教堂	jiàotáng	church, chapel, cathedral, abbey
	礼堂	lǐtáng	auditorium, assembly hall
厅	tīng	hall	
	餐厅	cāntīng	dining room, restaurant
	大厅	dàtīng	hall (often used for gatherings)
	客厅	kètīng	drawing room, parlor
	门厅	méntīng	vestibule, entrance hall
	市政厅	shìzhèngtīng	municipal administration hall, city hall

	舞厅	wǔtīng	ballroom, dance hall
	音乐厅	yīnyuètīng	concert hall, music hall
园	yuán	garden, park, orchard	
	菜园	càiyuán	vegetable garden, vegetable plot
	动物园	dòngwùyuán	zoo
	公园	gōngyuán	public park, public garden
	花园	huāyuán	flower garden
	游乐园	yóulèyuán	amusement park; pleasure ground (or garden)
	植物园	zhíwùyuán	botanical garden
院	yuàn	courtyard, yard	
	电影院	diànyǐngyuàn	movie theater
	剧院	jùyuàn	theater
	老人院	lǎorényuàn	nursing home for the elderly
	学院	xuéyuàn	academy, college, institute, school
	医院	yīyuàn	hospital
	院子	yuànzi	courtyard, yard
站	zhàn	stop, station, service center, service station	
	车站	chēzhàn	station, depot, stop (for bus, train, etc.)
	火车站	huǒchēzhàn	train station
	加油站	jiāyóuzhàn	gas station, service station
	汽车站	qìchēzhàn	(automobile) service station
	网站	wǎngzhàn	website

分类地点 By Category

买东西		Shopping	
	商店	shāngdiàn	shop, store

	商场	shāngchǎng	market, marketplace, department store
	超市	chāoshì	supermarket
	书店	shūdiàn	bookstore
外出旅游		Outing/Travel	
	饭店	fàndiàn	hotel, restaurant
	酒店	jiǔdiàn	wineshop
	旅馆	lǚguǎn	hotel
	旅店	lǚdiàn	inn, hotel
	饭馆	fànguǎn	restaurant
	茶馆	cháguǎn	teahouse
	咖啡馆	kāfēiguǎn	coffee shop
	餐厅	cāntīng	dining room, restaurant
	酒吧	jiǔbā	bar (especially Western-style)
	小吃店	xiǎochīdiàn	snack shop, snack bar
	车站	chēzhàn	station, depot, stop (for bus, train, etc.)
	火车站	huǒchēzhàn	train station
	加油站	jiāyóuzhàn	gas station, service station
	飞机场	fēijīchǎng	airport, airfield
	停车场	tíngchēchǎng	parking lot, parking area
服务		Service	
	市政厅	shìzhèngtīng	municipal administration hall, city hall
	警察局	jǐngchájú	police station
	派出所	pàichūsuǒ	local police station
	消防队	xiāofángduì	fire brigade
	图书馆	túshūguǎn	library
	天文馆	tiānwénguǎn	planetarium

	博物馆	bówùguǎn	museum
	体育馆	tǐyùguǎn	gym
	公园	gōngyuán	public park, public garden
	银行	yínháng	bank
	邮局	yóujú	post office
	医院	yīyuàn	hospital
	教堂	jiàotáng	church, chapel, cathedral, abbey
娱乐	yúlè	Recreation, amusement, entertainment	
	电影院	diànyǐngyuàn	movie theater
	剧院	jùyuàn	theater
	舞厅	wǔtīng	ballroom, dance hall
	游乐场	yóulèchǎng	amusement park, recreation groud

17

怎么做?

How Is It Done?
—Methods,
Manners,
Means of Action

谈论事件和行为往往与行为发生的方式和途径分不开。这一节列举出五类这样的方式和途径供教与学使用。

Events and actions are associated with methods, manners and means. This chapter lists five categories of such ways and means of action.

教学重点 Content of Teaching and Learning

行为方式与工具表	List of Methods, Manners and Means
与人	With People
工具	Tools
交通工具	Means of Transportation
描述性状态	Descriptive Manners
伴随状态	Companion Action

教学难点 Difficulties

状语在句中的位置	Positions of Adverbial Phrases in the Sentences
描述性状态 vs. 伴随状态	Descriptive Manners vs. Companion Action

词汇表 Glossary

方式状语表	List of Adverbial Phrases by Category

教学重点

Content of Teaching and Learning

行为方式与工具表 List of Methods, Manners and Means

与人 With People

跟 gēn/和 hé（一起 yìqǐ） together with someone

Wǒ gēn péngyou yìqǐ wán
我 跟 朋友 一起 玩 。
I play with my friends.

自己 zìjǐ oneself; on one's own; alone
一个人 yí ge rén by oneself; alone

Wǒ zìjǐ yí ge rén wán
我 自己（一 个 人）玩 。
I play alone.

To people 给 gěi ... give; to, toward someone

Wǒ gěi péngyou dǎ diànhuà
我 给 朋友 打 电话 。
I give my friend a phone call.

For people/purpose 为 wèi ... for someone

Wèi biéren zuò shì
为 别人 做 事。
Do things for others.

Replace, substitute for; in place of 替 tì for someone (replace, substitute)

Qǐng tì wǒ bǎ zhège gěi tā
请 替 我 把 这个 给 他。
Please give this to him for me.

工具 Tools

Use tools 用 yòng 笔 bǐ use a pen

yòng diànnǎo jìsuànjī
用 电脑 （计算机） use a computer

yòng Hànyǔ
Use language 用 汉语 use Chinese language

qǐng yòng Hànyǔ shuō
请 用 汉语 说。 Please speak in Chinese.

交通工具 Means of Transportation

Take：坐 zuò sit，travel by，go by（a vehicle）

Wǒ měitiān zuò chē qù shàng xué
我 每天 坐 车 去 上 学。
I go to school everyday by bus.

On foot：走 zǒu walk，travel on foot

Tā zǒu lù lái shàng xué
他 走 路 来 上 学。
He walks to school.

描写性状态 Descriptive Manners

"－地" is like "-ly" suffix in English.

Tā gāoxìng de pǎo lái pǎo qù
她 高兴 地 跑 来 跑 去。
She runs around happily.

In order

Qǐng nǐ yì bǐ yì bǐ de xiě
请 你 一 笔 一 笔 地 写。
Please write one stroke after another.

伴随状态 Companion Action

Active manners：

Tā xiàozhe shuō
他 笑着 说。
He said with a smile.

教学难点

Difficulties

难点一 状语在句中的位置

Positions of Adverbial Phrases in the Sentences

英文的状语的位置灵活，可在动词前，可在动词后。汉语在动词前。

In English, the position of adverbial phrases (phrases of methods, manners, means) in a sentence is flexible. Adverbial phrases may go before or after verbal phrases. In Chinese, there is no such flexibility. All phrases, as listed in this chapter, must go before the verbs. This cannot be emphasized enough.

难点二 描述性状态 vs. 伴随状态

Descriptive Manners vs. Companion Action

请看例句的对比。

This is an area where mistakes often occur in use. A comparative demonstration may explain more clearly for learners.

Comparison One:

V 着 V: companion action to show manner

A. 他笑着说。 He said with a smile/while smiling.

(Adverb) Adjective + V to show manner

B. 我们高兴地说："太好了。" We said "Great!" happily.

As we see, in (A), "with a smile" is a companion action. In (B), "happily" is a description of the action. "With a smile" does not necessarily mean "happily". "Happily" does not necessarily mean with a smile.

Comparison Two:

V 着 V: companion action to show manner

A. 他笑着说。 He said with a smile.

Use the "一边……一边……" pattern to show two actions happening at the same time.

B. 他一边说一边笑。 He is talking and laughing.

Comparison Three: Subtleness of Emphasis

"V 着" Manner of being Function: vivid description of scenes

桌子上放着一本书。 There is a book on the table.

"V 了" Completion of an Action

我在桌子上放了一本书。 I put a book on the table.

"V 在" Location of the result of an action

书放在桌子上了。 The book was put on the table.

词汇表

Glossary

方式状语表 List of Adverbial Phrases by Category

与人 With people

跟 gēn/和 hé …… (一起 yìqǐ) together with somone

Wǒ gēn péngyou yìqǐ wán

我 跟 朋友 一起 玩 。 I play with my friends.

自己 zìjǐ oneself; one's own; alone

一个人 yí ge rén by oneself; alone

Wǒ zìjǐ yí ge rén wán

我 自己(一 个 人)玩 。 I play alone.

To people

给 gěi …… give; to, toward someone

Wǒ gěi péngyou dǎ diànhuà

我 给 朋友 打 电话 。 I give my friend a phone call.

For people/purpose

为 wèi …… for someone

Wèi biérén zuò shì
为 别人 做 事。 Do things for others.

Replace, substitute for; in place of

替 tì for someone (replace, substitute)

Qǐng tì wǒ bǎ zhège gěi tā
请 替 我 把 这个 给 他。 Please give this to him for me.

工具 Tools

用 yòng use, employ, apply

Tools

yòng bǐ
用 笔 use a pen

yòng diànnǎo jìsuànjī
用 电脑（计算机） use a computer

Language

yòng Hànyǔ
用 汉语 use Chinese language

Qǐng yòng Hànyǔ shuō
请 用 汉语 说。 Please speak in Chinese.

交通工具 Means of Transportation

Verb

开	kāi	operate/drive (a vehicle)
驾驶	jiàshǐ	operate (a vehicle, plane, boat, etc.)
坐	zuò	sit, travel by, go by (a vehicle)
乘	chéng	ride on/take a vehicle
打	dǎ	take (get, hire) (e. g. a taxi)

Noun

车	chē	vehicle
汽车	qìchē	motor vehicle, automobile, car
小汽车	xiǎoqìchē	small automobile

公共汽车	gōnggòng qìchē	bus
出租车	chūzūchē	taxicab
计程车	jìchéngchē	taxicab
面包车	miànbāochē	minibus, van (so called for its oblong shape)
面的	miàndí	minibus, taxicab
救护车	jiùhùchē	ambulance
救火车	jiùhuǒchē	fire engine
校车	xiàochē	school bus
旅游车	lǚyóuchē	tourist coach, sightseeing bus
卡车	kǎchē	truck
火车	huǒchē	train
地铁	dìtiě	subway
飞机	fēijī	airplane
船	chuán	boat, ship, vessel
马车	mǎchē	horse-drawn carriage, mule (or horse) cart
牛车	niúchē	ox cart

Wǒ měitiān zuò chē qù shàng xué
我 每天 坐 车 去 上 学。
I go to school everyday by bus.

Wǒ bàba kāi chē qù shàng bān
我 爸爸 开 车 去 上 班。
My dad drives to work.

骑 qí ride (astride, like on a bicycle, horse)

马	mǎ	horse
摩托车	mótuōchē	motorbike, motorcycle
自行车	zìxíngchē	bicycle
脚踏车	jiǎotàchē	bicycle

Wǒ qí chē qù shàng xué
我 骑 车 去 上 学。
I ride a bike to school.

走 zǒu walk, travel on foot

走路 zǒu lù walk, travel on foot

Tā zǒu lù lái shàng xué
他 走 路 来 上 学 。
He walks to school.

跑 pǎo run, walk

跑步 pǎo bù run; jogging (a form of physical exercise)

Tā pǎo bù lái shàng xué
她 跑 步 来 上 学 。
She runs to school.

描述性状语 Descriptive Manner

1) adjective + "地" Use of "地": "-地" is like "-ly" suffix in English

高兴地 gāoxìng de happily

着急地 zháojí de anxiously, hurriedly

紧张地 jǐnzhāng de nervously

兴奋地 xīngfèn de excitedly

努力地 nǔlì de with extra effort; earnestly

Tā gāoxìng de pǎo lái pǎo qù
她 高兴 地 跑 来 跑 去。 She runs around happily.

2) duplicative adjective + "地"

好好地 hǎohāo de properly, thoroughly; to one's heart's content

快快地 kuàikuài de in a big hurry

慢慢地 mànmān de slowly

高高兴兴地 gāogāoxìngxìng de gladly, with great joy

Qǐng mànmān de shuō
请 慢慢 地 说 。 Please speak slowly.

Exception: A one-word (mono-syllablic) adjective can modify a verb directly:

Màn zǒu
慢 走 ! Walk slowly! (Watch your steps!)

3) Order: Duplicated Number + Measure Word + 地

一个一个地 one by one

一笔一笔地 one stroke after another

Qǐng nǐ yì bǐ yì bǐ de xiě
请 你 一 笔 一 笔 地 写。
Please write one stroke after another.

伴随状语 Companion Actions: Active Manner

1) Use of "着": Manner of Action

笑 xiào smile, laugh

Tā xiàozhe shuō Nà tài hǎo le
他 笑着 说:"那 太 好 了!"
He smiled while saying, "Great!"

哭 kū cry, weep

Tā kūzhe shuō Wǒ tài nánguò le
他 哭着 说:"我 太 难过 了."
He cried while saying, "I'm so sad."

站 zhàn stand

坐 zuò sit

Lǎoshī zhànzhe jiǎng kè wǒmen zuòzhe tīng
老师 站着 讲 课,我们 坐着 听。

Our teacher is standing while giving instructions, and we are sitting while listening.

Other verbs: commonly used with "着": 唱 chàng sing, 跑 pǎo run, 跳 tiào jump, etl.

2) Other Uses of "V 着"

Used like the "-ly" suffix or "is done" in English

Manner of Being: We may also use this pattern to indicate the manner of being of an object.

On people:

带 dài carry, bring, take to

Tā shēnshang dàizhe yìxiē qián
他 身上 带着 一些 钱。
He is carrying money on his person.

Tā cháng dàizhe péngyou qù nàr
他 常 带着 朋友 去 那儿。
He is often found taking his friends there.

拿 ná hold, grasp, take, capture

Tā shǒuli názhe yì zhī bǐ
他 手里 拿着 一 支 笔。
He is holding a pen in his hand.

穿 chuān put on (clothing)

Tā chuānzhe yí jiàn chángxiù de chènshān
他 穿着 一 件 长袖 的 衬衫 。
He is wearing a long sleeve shirt.

戴 dài wear, put on (like hat, eyeglasses, etc.)

Wǒ dàizhe yí fù mòjìng
我 戴着 一副 墨镜 。
I am wearing a pair of sunglasses.

About an object:

放 fàng release, set free, put

Shūjià shang fàngzhe hěn duō shū
书架 上 放着 很 多 书。
There are some books (put) on the table.

摆 bǎi arrange with care, placed as decoration

Chájī shang bǎizhe zhàopiàn
茶几 上 摆着 照片 。
There are picture photos (put) on the tea stand.

装 zhuāng pack, load, assemble, install

Shūbāo li zhuāngzhe hěn duō shū
书包 里 装着 很 多 书。
There are many books (packed) in the bag.

挂 guà hang, suspend

Qiángshang guàzhe liǎng zhāng huà
墙上 挂着 两 张 画。
There are two paintings hanging on the wall.

Compare the following two sentences:

"V着" is a more descriptive way to indicate there is something is some place.

Qiángshang yǒu liǎng zhāng huà
墙上 有 两 张 画。
The wall (on it) has two paintings.

Qiángshang guàzhe liǎng zhāng huà
墙上 挂着 两 张 画。
There are two paintings hanging on the wall.

18

名词组

Noun Phrases

汉语的名词的构成与英语有不同处。本节就此展开例举汉语名词组的构成及其在句中的位置。

The structures of the Chinese noun phrases are different in many ways from English. This chapter is devoted to list Chinese noun phrases, their structures and positions in sentences compared with English.

教学重点 Content of Teaching and Learning

名词组的构成	Formation of Noun Phrases
“的”的使用	“的” and Noun Phrases
其他定语	Other Modifiers
复杂定语	Compound Modifiers
复合名词组在句中	Complex Noun Phrases in the Sentences

教学难点 Difficulties

名词组	Noun Phrases
形容词修饰名词	Adjective as Modification
定语（修饰词）的顺序	Order of Modifiers

教学重点

Content of Teaching and Learning

名词组的构成 Formation of Noun Phrases

所有的修饰成分都放在被修饰的名词前。

All definitions go before the noun that is being modified/defined.

"的" 的使用 "的" and Noun Phrases

"的" 的作用是连接修饰成分和名词。

Usually, a Chinese noun phrase is formed with the help "的". "的" connects a definition to a noun.

代词修饰名词 Pronoun + Noun

(singular pronoun)	tā de chē 他 的 车	his car
(plural pronoun)	wǒmen de péngyou 我们 的 朋友	our friend

名词修饰名词 Noun + Noun

(general noun)	xuéxiào de diànnǎo 学校 的 电脑	the school's computer
(proper noun)	Wáng Míng de diànnǎo 王 明 的 电脑	Wang Ming's computer
(abstract noun)	Rìběn chē 日本 车	Japanese car

形容词修饰名词 Adjective + Noun

(one-word/charcter adjective)

	hǎo shū 好 书	a good book

(two-word/charcter adjective)

	hǎokàn de shū 好看 的 书	a very interesting book

(adverb + adjective)

hěn guì de shū
很 贵 的 书 an expensive book

动词修饰名词 Verb + Noun

wǒ mǎi de shū
(verb) (我) 买 的 书 the book I bought

主谓结构修饰名词 Subject-predicate + Noun

(subject + verb) + Noun

wǒ mǎi de shū
我 买 的 书 the book I bought

(subject + time + verb) + Noun

wǒ zuótiān mǎi de shū
我 昨天 买 的 书 the book I bought yesterday

(subject + place + verb) + Noun

wǒ zài shūdiàn mǎi de shū
我 在 书店 买 的 书 the book I bought at bookstore

(subject + manner + verb) + Noun

wǒ gēn péngyou yìqǐ mǎi de shū
我 跟 朋友 一起 买 的 书
the book I bought with my friend

wǒ zuò chē qù mǎi de shū
我 坐 车 去 买 的 书 the book I bought going by bus

wǒ yòng wǒ zìjǐ de qián mǎi de shū
我 用 我 自己 的 钱 买 的 书
the book I bought with my own money

例外 Exceptions:

三种不用"的"的情况 There are 3 exceptions without "的"

1) 单数人称代词修饰家庭成员时 A singular personal pronoun modifies a family member:

wǒ māma nǐ bàba
我 妈妈 my mom 你 爸爸 your dad

Compare:

wǒ de chē
我 的 车 my car ("Car" is not a family member.)

wǒmen de māma
我们 的 妈妈 our mom ("Our" is a plural pronoun.)

2）单音节形容词修饰名词

A one-word/character adjective modifies a noun：

hǎo shū　　　　huàirén
好　书　a good book　　坏人　a bad person

Compare：

hǎokàn de shū
好看　的　书　　a very interesting book

hěn huài de rén
很　坏　的　人　　a very bad person

3）抽象名词 The definitive noun is an abstract one：

Zhōngguórén
中国人　　Chinese（a person of Chinese origin）

Zhījiāgē Dàxué
芝加哥　大学
（the）University of Chicago（the one particular school）

Compare

Zhōngguó de chéngshì
中国　的　城市　a city in China

Zhījiāgē de dàxué
芝加哥　的　大学
a university in Chicago（one of the universities in Chicago）

其他定语　Other Modifiers

数量＋量词　　Number ＋ Measure Word

yí ge péngyou
一　个　朋友　　a friend

liǎng ge xuésheng
两　个　学生　　two students

"这"与"那"＋量词　　"This/That" ＋ Measure Word

zhège péngyou
这个　朋友　　this friend

nàge xuésheng
那个　学生　　that student

复杂定语 Compound Modifiers

wǒ de nàge péngyou
我 的 那个 朋友

that friend of mine

wǒ de nà sān ge péngyou
我 的 那 三 个 朋友

those three friends of mine

wǒ de nàge Zhōngguó péngyou
我 的 那个 中国 朋友

that Chinese friend of mine

wǒ de nà sān ge Zhōngguó péngyou
我 的 那 三 个 中国 朋友

those three Chinese friends of mine

复合名词组在句中 Complex Noun Phrases in the Sentences

Verbal Phrase (Subject (Time, Place, Manner) Verb) as Compound Noun Phrase:

Wǒ mǎi shū
我 买 书。 S V O

Wǒ mǎi de shū hěn guì
我 买 的 书 很 贵。
The book I bought is very expensive.

Nà běn shū shì wǒ mǎi de
那 本 书 是 我 买 的。
That book is the one I bought.

Tā měitiān kàn shū
他 每天 看 书。 S (T) VO

Tā měitiān kàn de shū dōu shì Yīngwén shū
他 每天 看 的 书 都 是 英文 书。
The books that he reads everyday are all English books.

Zhè běn shū shì tā měitiān dōu yào kàn de
这 本 书 是 他 每天 都 要 看 的。
This book is the one he has been reading everyday.

Nǐ zài Zhōngguó mǎi shū
你 在 中国 买 书。 S (P) VO

Nǐ zài Zhōngguó mǎi de shū shì Zhōngwén de
你 在 中国 买 的 书 是 中文 的。
The book that you bought in China is Chinese.

Nǐ jiějie kàn de shū shì bu shì nǐ zài Zhōngguó mǎi de
你 姐姐 看 的 书 是 不 是 你 在 中国 买 的？
Is the book that your sister is reading the one you bought in China?

Tāmen yòng jìsuànjī xiě wénzhāng
他们 用 计算机 写 文章。 S（M）VO

Tāmen yòng jìsuànjī xiě de wénzhāng zhēn cháng
他们 用 计算机 写 的 文章 真 长。
The article they are writing on the computer is really long.

Bào shang de wénzhāng shì tāmen yòng xuéxiào de jìsuànjī
报 上 的 文章 是 他们 用 学校 的 计算机
xiě de ma
写 的 吗？
Is the article in the paper the one they wrote on the school computer?

Dàmíng zuótiān zài jiā gēn péngyou wánr jìsuànjī le
大明 昨天 在 家 跟 朋友 玩儿 计算机 了。

S（T, P, M）VO

Dàmíng zuótiān zài jiā wánr de jìsuànjī bú shì xīn de
大明 昨天 在 家 玩儿 的 计算机 不 是 新 的。
The computer Daming played at home yesterday is not new.

Zhège jìsuànjī jiù shì zuótiān Dàmíng zài jiā gēn péngyou wánr
这个 计算机 就 是 昨天 大明 在 家 跟 朋友 玩儿
de nàge
的 那个。
This is the computer that Daming played yesterday at home with his friends.

Complex Noun Phrase as Subject：

Zuótiān lái wǒmen xuéxiào de rén shì cóng Zhōngguó lái de
昨天 来 我们 学校 的 人 是 从 中国 来 的。
The person who visited our school yesterday came from China.

Tā bú huì xiě de zì tài duō le
他 不 会 写 的 字 太 多 了。
The wordx he can't write are too many.

Comples Noun Phrase as Object:

Nǐ rènshi nàge chuān hóng shàngyī de rén ma
你 认识 那个 穿 红 上衣 的 人 吗?
Do you know that person wearing a red jacket?

Tā xǐhuan wǒ zuótiān zài shāngdiàn mǎi de zázhì
他 喜欢 我 昨天 在 商店 买 的 杂志。
He likes the magazine I bought at the store yesterday.

教学难点

Difficulties

难点一 名词组 Noun Phrases

英文名词与中文名词的构成不同，对初学者是难点。特别是复合词，尤其需要不断地练习和强调。

Noun phrases are difficult for English speakers who are beginning learners.

In Chinese, all noun modifiers, no matter how long or how complex, go before the noun.

In English, the noun is often said before the modifier. Therefore translating or using a noun phrase correctly in Chinese often requires some thinking for English speakers.

与英文对比 Compare with English:

In English, there are 3 ways of forming a noun phrase:

1) with "'s" (possession): my car, my mom's car

2) with "of": that car of mine

3) with a "that/which, who, etc." clause:

the car that I bought yesterday

In Chinese, there is only one way:

All modifications go before the noun to be defined.

English: Chinese:

1) with "'s" (possession):

my car： 我的车

2） with “of”：

that car of mine： 我的车

3） with a “that/which， who， etc.” clause：

the car that I bought yesterday： 我昨天买的车

难点二 形容词修饰名词 Adjective as Modification

并非所有的单音节形容词都能直接修饰名词，“多”“少”“贵”就是这样的例外。

In theory， when a one-word/character adjective modifies a noun，“的” can be omitted. But it is not always so. Some one-word adjectives cannot be used alone without an adverb when modifying a noun， and therefore require “的”， for example：

	wrong	**correct**
多	多书	很多的书；特别多的书
少	少书	很少的书；非常少的书
贵	贵书	很贵的书；非常贵的书

难点三 定语（修饰词）的顺序 Order of Modifiers

When using multiple modifiers， the order of the modification is decided by their closeness to the nature of the object.

The closer to the nature of the noun， the closer the modifier is placed to the noun. See below and compare with the English translations：

wǒ de péngyou
我 的 朋友 friend of mine/my friend

nàge péngyou
那个 朋友 that friend

sān ge péngyou
三 个 朋友 three friends

Zhōngguó péngyou
中国 朋友 a Chinese friend

but, when combined:

wǒ de nàge péngyou
我 的 那个 朋友 that friend of mine

wǒ de nà sān ge péngyou
我 的 那 三 个 朋友 those three friends of mine

wǒ de nàge Zhōngguó péngyou
我 的 那个 中国 朋友 that Chinese friend of mine

wǒ de nà sān ge Zhōngguó péngyou
我 的 那 三 个 中国 朋友
those three Chinese friends of mine

19

度量衡

Measurements

长度 chángdù	**Length**	
(Decimal System)		
公里	gōnglǐ	kilometer
米	mǐ	meter (linear measurement)
厘米	límǐ	centimeter
毫米	háomǐ	millimeter
(English System)		
英里	yīnglǐ	mile
英尺	yīngchǐ	foot (twelve inches)
英寸	yīngcùn	inch
重量 zhòngliàng	**Weight**	
(Decimal System)		
公斤	gōngjīn	kilogram
克	kè	gram
(English System)		
磅	bàng	pound (unit of weight)
盎司	àngsī	ounce
面积 miànjī	**Area, surface area**	
(Decimal System)		
平方(米)	píngfāng (mǐ)	square (meter)
(English System)		
平方(英尺)	píngfāng (yīngchǐ)	square (foot)
容积 róngjī	**Volume, bulk, content**	
(Decimal System)		
升	shēng	liter
(English System)		
加仑	jiālún	gallon

钱 qián Cash, money

人民币	rénmínbì	Renminbi (unit of currency in the PRC)
美元	měiyuán	United States dollar, American dollar
元	yuán	*yuan* (unit of Chinese currency)
(块)	kuài	colloquial expression: same as "*yuan*" (unit of Chinese currency)
角	jiǎo	unit of Chinese currency, one-tenth of a *yuan*
(毛)	máo	colloquial expression: same as "*jiao*", one-tenth of a *yuan*)
分	fēn	unit of Chinese currency, one-tenth of a *jiao*

句型 jùxíng Sentence Patterns

……等于……

……一共是……

等于 děngyú be equal to, be equivalent to, be tantamount to……

一共 yígòng altogether

20

Comparison

比较

比较是高级思考的一个方面。可以比人、比东西、比行为事件。比较可以与其他话题交叉教学。本节按照语法的特点把比较分为五种。

Comparison is a higher level of thinking. In daily life, we can compare people, objects and behavior/activity. Comparison can be used with other topics in teaching and learning, such as number, object, activity, weather, etc. This chapter can be placed into five categories according to grammatical characteristics.

教学重点 Content of Teaching and Learning

三级比较	Three-levels of Comparison
比较不同	Comparing Difference
比较相同	Comparing Similarity
比较所有	Comparing Possession
比较喜好	Comparing Preferences

教学难点 Difficulties

“很”和“much”在比较句中	“很” vs. “Much” in Comparison
比较句中数量的位置	Position of Quantity in Comparative Sentences
中英文比较所有的不同	“有” vs. “to Have” in Comparison
喜好的比较	Preferences in Comparison
比较句的否定式	Negatives in Comparison
“比” vs. “跟”	

教学重点

Content of Teaching and Learning

三级比较 Three-levels of Comparison

功用 Function：用形容词把比较分成比较级、更高级和最高级。

句型 Structures：

Level I： Use an adjective itself to establish the difference

Level II： Use “更/还” before an adjective

Level III： Use “最” before an adjective

比人 Comparing People

Wǒ		gāo
我		高。

I am tall.

Tā	gèng hái	gāo
他	更（还）	高。

He is (even) taller.

Nǐ	zuì	gāo
你	最	高。

You are the tallest.

比东西 Comparing Objects

Zhège diànnǎo hǎoyòng

这个 电脑 好用。

This computer is easy to use.

Wǒ de	gèng	hǎoyòng
我 的	更	好用。

Mine is easier to use.

Nǐ de	zuì	hǎoyòng
你 的	最	好用。

Yours is the easiest to use.

比行为 Comparing Actions

Wǒ yóuyǒng yóu de		kuài
我 游泳 游 得		快 。
I swim fast.		
Nǐ yóuyǒng yóu de	gèng	kuài
你 游泳 游 得	更	快 。
You swim faster.		
Tā yóuyǒng yóu de	zuì	kuài
她 游泳 游 得	最	快 。
She swims the fastest.		

比较不同 Comparing Difference

功用 Function：找出人、物、行为的不同

句型 Structure：

A 比 B	Adjective	（Quantity）

比人 Comparing People

I, compared to you, am	taller	by this much.
Wǒ bǐ nǐ	gāo	
我 比 你	高 。	
Wǒ bǐ nǐ	gāo	yì diǎn
我 比 你	高	一 点 。
Wǒ bǐ nǐ	gāo	hěn duō
我 比 你	高	很 多 。
Wǒ bǐ nǐ	gāo	de duō de duō
我 比 你	高	得 多（得 多）。

比东西 Comparing Objects

This/My computer, compared to that one, is easier to use by this much.

Zhège diànnǎo	bǐ nàge	hǎoyòng	
这个 电脑	比 那个	好用 。	
Wǒ de	bǐ nàge	gèng	hǎoyòng
我 的	比 那个	更	好用 。

Wǒ de bǐ nàge hǎoyòng yì diǎn
我 的 比 那个 好用 一 点 。

Wǒ de bǐ nàge hǎoyòng hěn duō de duō
我 的 比 那个 好用 很 多（得 多）。

比行为 Comparing Actions

I swim, compared to you, faster by this much.

Wǒ yóuyǒng bǐ nǐ yóuyǒng yóu de kuài
我 游泳 比 你 游泳 游 得 快 。

Wǒ bǐ nǐ yóuyǒng yóu de kuài
我 比 你 游泳 游 得 快 。

Wǒ yóuyǒng bǐ nǐ yóu de kuài
我 游泳 比 你 游 得 快 。

Wǒ yóuyǒng bǐ nǐ yóu de kuài yìdiǎn
我 游泳 比 你 游 得 快 一点 。

Wǒ yóuyǒng bǐ nǐ yóu de kuài de duō
我 游泳 比 你 游 得 快 得 多 。

否定 Negatives

没有：(True negative)

Wǒ méiyǒu nǐ dà Wǒ bǐ nǐ xiǎo
我 没有 你 大，我 比 你 小 。
I am not as old as you are. I am younger than you.

Wǒ de diànnǎo méiyǒu nǐ de hǎoyòng
我 的 电脑 没有 你 的 好用 。
My computer is not as useful as yours/ Yours is better than mine.

Wǒ méiyǒu nǐ yóuyǒng yóu de kuài
我 没有 你 游泳 游 得 快 。
I don't swim as fast as you do/You swim faster than I do.

不比：(not necessarily negative, could mean the same)

Wǒ shíliù suì nǐ yě shíliù suì nǐ bù bǐ wǒ dà
我 十六 岁，你 也 十六 岁，你 不 比 我 大。
I am 16, you are also 16. You are not older than I.

Wǒ de diànnǎo bù bǐ nǐ de hǎoyòng
我 的 电脑 不 比 你 的 好用 。
My computer is no better than yours.

Wǒ bù bǐ nǐ yóuyǒng yóu de kuài
我 不 比 你 游泳 游 得 快 。
I don't swim faster than you do.

问句 Questions

Yes/No Question：e. g.

Nǐ bǐ tā yóu de kuài ma
你 比 他 游 得 快 吗？
Do you swim faster than he does?

WH-Question：e. g.

Shuí bǐ nǐ yóu de kuài
谁 比 你 游 得 快 ？
Who swims faster than you do?

Choices：e. g.

Nǐ bǐ tā yóu de kuài háishi màn
你 比 他 游 得 快 还是 慢 ？
Do you swim faster or slower than he does?

比较相同 Comparing Similarity

功用 Function：认同相似处。

句型 Structure：

A 跟 B	+	一样	+	Adjective (specify similarity).

比人 Comparing People

Positive

Wǒ gēn nǐ yíyàng
我 跟 你 一样 。
I am the same as you are.

Wǒ gēn nǐ yíyàng dà
我 跟 你 一样 大 。
I am as old as you are.

Negative：

Wǒ gēn nǐ bù yíyàng dà
我 跟 你 不 一样 (大)。
I am no of the same (age) as you are.

Wǒ bù gēn nǐ yíyàng
我 不 跟 你 一样 。
I am not the same as you are.

比东西 Comparing Objects

Positive
Nàge diànyǐng gēn zhège yíyàng
那个 电影 跟 这个 一样 。
That movie is the same as this one.

Negative
Nàge diànyǐng gēn zhège bù yíyàng
那个 电影 跟 这个 不 一样 。
That movie is not the same as this one.

Positive
Nàge diànyǐng gēn zhège yíyàng yǒu yìsi
那个 电影 跟 这个 一样 有 意思。
That movie is as interesting as this one.

Negative
Nàge diànyǐng bù gēn zhège yíyàng yǒu yìsi
那个 电影 不 跟 这个 一样 有 意思。
That movie is not as interesting as this one.

比行为 Comparing Actions

Positive
Wǒ pǎobù pǎo de gēn nǐ yíyàng kuài
我 跑步 跑 得 跟 你 一样 快 。
Wǒ pǎobù gēn nǐ pǎobù pǎo de yíyàng kuài
我（跑步）跟 你（跑步）跑 得 一样 快 。
I run as fast as you do.

Negative
Wǒ pǎobù bù gēn nǐ pǎo de yíyàng kuài
我 跑步 不 跟 你 跑 得 一样 快 。
Wǒ pǎobù gēn nǐ pǎo de bù yíyàng kuài
我 跑步 跟 你 跑 得 不 一样 快 。
I don't run as fast as you do.

问句 Questions

Yes/No Question:.

Nǐ gēn tā yíyàng dà ma
你 跟 他 一样 大 吗 ?
Are you and he the same age?

Zhège gēn nàge yíyàng ma
这个 跟 那个 一样 吗 ?
Are this one and that one the same ?

Nǐ gēn tā yóu de yíyàng kuài ma
你 跟 他 游 得 一样 快 吗 ?
Do you swim as fast as he does?

WH-Question:

Nǎge gēn zhège yíyàng dà
哪个 跟 这个 一样 大？
Which one is as big as this one?

Shénme gēn zhège yíyàng
什么 跟 这个 一样 ？
What is the same as this?

Shuí gēn nǐ yóu de yíyàng kuài
谁 跟 你 游 得 一样 快 ？
Who swims as fast as you do ?

Choices：

Nǐ gēn wǒ yíyàng dà háishi gēn tā yíyàng dà
你 跟 我 一样 大 还是 跟 他 一样 大？
Are you the same age as I am or as he is?

Zhège gēn nàge yíyàng dà háishi yíyàng guì
这个 跟 那个 一样 大 还是 一样 贵 ？
Is this one as big or as expensive as that one?

Nǐ gēn tā yóu de yíyàng kuài háishi pǎo de yíyàng kuài
你 跟 他 游 得 一样 快 还是 跑 得 一样 快 ？
Do you swim as fast or run as fast as he does?

(which one?)

比较所有 Comparing Possession

与英文不同，中文不能用动词“有”比较所有，只能比较所有的数量。

In English, we say, “I have more sisters than you do.” In Chinese, never use the verb “有” when comparing the number of things two parties have. Compare the number/of objects only.

比不同 Comparing Difference

Structure: A's possession 比 B's possession 多/少 quantity.

I have (two) more sisters than you do.

	Wǒ de mèimei	bǐ nǐ (de mèimei)	duō
Positive	我 的 妹妹	比 你(的 妹妹)	多 。
	Wǒ	bǐ nǐ de mèimei	duō
	我	比 你 的 妹妹	多 。

Wǒ de mèimei bǐ nǐ(de) duō liǎng ge
我的妹妹比你(的)多两个。

比相同 Comparing Similarity

Structure: A's possession 跟/和 B's possession 一样多/少.

I have (don't) the same number of sisters as you do.

Wǒ de mèimei gēn nǐ de mèimei yíyàng duō
Positive 我的妹妹跟你(的妹妹)一样多。

Wǒ de mèimei gēn nǐ bù yíyàng duō
Negative 我的妹妹跟你不一样多。

问句 Questions

Do you have more (fewer) sisters than he does?
Nǐ de mèimei bǐ tā de duō shǎo ma
你的妹妹比他的多(少)吗?

Do you have the same number of sisters as he does?
Nǐ de mèimei gēn tā de yíyàng duō(shǎo)ma
你的妹妹跟他的一样多(少)吗?

Who has more (fewer) sisters?
Shuí de mèimei duō(shǎo)
谁的妹妹多(少)?

比较喜好 Comparing Preferences

喜欢/爱是一个特别的动词，比较喜好的用法与其他动词不同。

In Chinese, 喜欢/爱 "like" is a special verb. It is not an action but indicates a preference.

比不同 Comparing Difference

Wǒ bǐ tā xǐhuan chàng gē
Positive 我比他喜欢唱歌。
I like singing more than he does.

Nǐ bǐ wǒ gèng hái xǐhuan chàng gē
你比我更(还)喜欢唱歌。
You like singing more than I do.

Wǒ méiyǒu tā nàme xǐhuan chàng gē
Negative 我 没有 他（那么） 喜欢 唱 歌。
I don't like singing as much as he does.

Wǒ bù bǐ tā xǐhuan chàng gē
我 不 比 他 喜欢 唱 歌。
I don't like singing as much as he does.

比相同 Comparing Similarity

Wǒ gēn nǐ yíyàng xǐhuan chàng gē
Positive 我 跟 你 一样 喜欢 唱 歌。
I like singing as much as you do.

Wǒ gēn tā yíyàng bù xǐhuan chàng gē
Negative 我 跟 他 一样 不 喜欢 唱 歌。
I dislike singing as much as he does.

问句 Questions

Nǐ bǐ tā xǐhuan chàng gē ma
你 比 他 喜欢 唱 歌 吗？
Do you like singing more than he does?

Nǐ yǒu tā（nàme）xǐhuan chàng gē ma
你 有 他（那么）喜欢 唱 歌 吗？
Do you like singing as much as he does?

Nǐ gēn tā yíyàng（nàme）xǐhuan chàng gē ma
你 跟 他 一样（那么）喜欢 唱 歌 吗？
Do you like singing as much as he does?

教学难点

Difficulties

难点一 “很”和“Much”在比较句中

“很” vs. “Much” in Comparison

“很”跟英语的“much”，“a lot”用法不同。在比较句中，“很”只能跟“多”在一起作为比较的数量补语，不能在形容词前修饰形容词。

In English, "much/a lot" appears before an adjective to show a difference:

I am much (a lot) taller than you are.

In Chinese, "很" is part of the quantity. It must appear after adjective. 我比你高很多。This cannot be emphasized enough.

wrong	correct
我比你很高。	我比你高很多。

难点二 比较句中数量的位置

Position of Quantity in Comparative Sentences

在比较句中，形容词指示差别，数量补语得放在形容词的后边用来指明差别的多少。

In English, a difference of quantity goes before the adjective:

I am a little bit (two inches) taller than you are.

In Chinese, a difference of quantity must appear after the adjective that it refers to.

我比你高一点（两寸）。

难点三 中英文比较所有的不同

"有" vs. "to Have" in Comparison

与英文不同，中文不能用动词"有"比较所有。要比只能比要比的人与物，只能比所有的数量。

In English, when comparing possession, we use the verb "to have":

I have more sisters than you do.

In Chinese, never use the verb "有" to compare the number of objects being possessed.

我的书比你（的）多三本。

难点四　喜好的比较 Preferences in Comparison

喜欢/爱是一个特别的动词，比较喜好的用法与其他动词不同。

In Chinese, the verb “喜欢/爱” “to like” is a special word. It is different from other action verbs.

难点五　比较句的否定式 Negatives in Comparison

Negative:

没有：(true negative)

我没有你大，我比你小。

I am not as old as you are, I am younger.

不比：(not necessarily negative. It could mean “the same” .)

我不比你大。

I am not as old as you are. (I may be younger or the same age.)

我十六岁，你也十六岁，你不比我大。

I am16, you are also 16, you are not older than Iam. (We are the same age.)

难点六　“比” vs. “跟”

“比”用来表示不同，“跟”表示相同。

“比” is used to compare differences. “跟/和/与/同” are used to identify similarties.

21

指路

Asking and Giving Directions

问路和指路在我们的日常生活中经常发生，本章介绍了结果补语、可能补语、相关句型、有用词汇及可能的指示顺序。最后附有有关交通词汇表。

Asking and giving directions are done daily. This chapter supports that topic with introductions to resultant complements and potential complements, related sentence patterns, useful vocabularies, and a recommended sequence of coherent direction giving. Vocabulary lists of road signs and expressions related to traffic are also provided.

教学重点 Content of Teaching and Learning

认识路标	Identifying Landmarks
结果补语	Resultant Complement
计划路线和预测时间	Plan the Route and Predict the Time
可能补语	Potential Complement
指方向	Giving Directions
往……	Toward . . .
指路——有用的句型	Giving Directions—Useful Sentence Patterns

教学难点 Difficulties

结果补语	Resultant Complement
“在”作为结果	“在” as A Result
可能补语 vs. 结果补语	Potential Complements vs. Resultant Complement
“能”与“可能”	Potentials and Abilities
可能补语 vs. 程度补语	Potential Complement vs. Complement of Degree

词汇表 Glossary

常用结果补语	Frequently Used Resultant Complements
常用可能补语	Frequently Used Potential Complements

路标	Road Signs
交通用语	Related Traffic Expressions

补充语法点 Supplementary Notes

趋向补语	Directional Complement

教学重点

Content of Teaching and Learning

指路最常用到的句型有以下的3个：

1）认证路标要用结果补语。

2）计划、预测路线和时间要用可能补语。

3）指方向要用"往……"等。

Asking and Giving Directions is an essential life task. The most useful patterns to carry out this task are:

1）Identify landmarks by using "看见（when you see ...）" and "走到 when you walk to..."；

2）Identify possibilities in time, accessibility, etc. by using "到得了/到不了"；

3）Identify direction by using "往 go toward ..." or "turn to this or that way".

认识路标 Identifying Landmarks

In order to identify landmarks, we use a pattern like:

Kànjian lùkǒu de shāngdiàn yǐhòu wǎng yòu guǎi
看见 路口 的 商店 以后 往 右 拐。
When you see the store at the corner, turn right.

Zǒudào dì èr ge hónglǜdēng wǎng dōng kāi
走到 第 二 个 红绿灯 往 东 开。
Drive up to the second traffic lights and turn towards the east.

The patterns used here are called "结果补语 Resultant Complement".

结果补语 Resultant Complement

1）功用 Function：

英文的动词自身指企图的有些包括结果，例如："I looked and I saw."（我看了，并看见了。）可以说"looked"是努力，"saw"是结果。中文的"看"差不多包括眼的所有功能，相当于英文的"look/see/watch/observe/

read”至更多，可并不暗示动作的程度或结果。需要其他的成分，比如补语，补充需要说明的情况。结果补语是用动词或形容词来说明动作达到或取得什么成果。

In English, when we say “I looked and I saw”, we mean that we took the action of “look” and we received the sight with our eyes: “looked” implies the effort while “saw” implies the result.

In Chinese, “看” is to look/see/watch/observe/read, covering almost everything you do with your eyes. But the verb itself gives no implication as to how far the action is carried and what result is achieved. We need another verb or an adjective to be attached directly to the verb to indicate the result.

2）句型 Sentence Pattern:

Wǒ kàn
我 看。(Action)
I look/see/watch/read.

But to show result of an action, we use:

Subject	Verb + Verb/Adjective

动词做结果：A verb indicates the result of the action:

Wǒ kàndǒng le
我 看懂 了。
I comprehended (through observing).

形容词做结果：An adjective indicates the result of the action:

Wǒ kàncuò le
我 看错 了。
I saw it wrong.

3）否定 Negative: “没” denies the result not the action.

（我看了，可是……）

Wǒ méi kàndǒng
我 没 看懂。
I did not understand (through observing.)

Wǒ méi kàncuò
我 没 看错。
I did not see it wrong.

4）宾语在句中的位置 Position of object in sentence:

结果必须紧挨着动作。宾语次之，除非将宾语前置。

The result must follow the action immediately. The object of the sentence usually has to go after the action and result. Unless the object is put before the verb for emphasize:

Wǒ kànjiàn tā le
我 看见 他 了。
I saw him.

Wǒ hái méi kànwán nà běn shū
我 还 没 看完 那 本 书。
I have not yet finished reading that book.

5）带结果补语的副词 Adverbs with resultative complement:

已经……了 yǐjing……le already

还没有……呢 hái méiyǒu……ne not yet

Wǒ yǐjing kànwán liǎng běn shū le
我 已经 看完 两 本 书 了。
I have already finished reading two books.

Wǒ yì běn hái méi kànwán ne
我 一 本 还 没 看完 呢。
I have not yet finished even one.

6）问句 Questions:

Nǐ kànjian wǒ gēge le ma
你 看见 我 哥哥 了 吗？
Have you seen my brother?

Nǐ kànjiàn méi kànjian wǒ gēge
你 看见 没 看见 我 哥哥？
Have you seen my brother?

Nǐ kànjian wǒ gēge méiyǒu
你 看见 我 哥哥 没有？
Have you seem my brother?

7）常用结果补语 Frequently Used Result ant Complements

形容词 Adjectives (To the extend)

好 hǎo well, properly

做好 zuòhǎo finished, did nicely and thoroughly

坐好 zuòhǎo sat still, sat well

对 duì correct

	看对	kànduì	saw correctly, saw through to the point
错	cuò	wrong	
	说错	shuōcuò	spoke incorrectly
清楚	qīngchǔ		clear, distinct
	看清楚	kàn qīngchǔ	saw clearly, saw distinctly

动词 Verbs (Pay attention: you may achieve the same result through different actions.)

见	jiàn	perceive through senses	
	看见	kànjian	saw
	听见	tīngjian	heard
	闻见	wénjian	smelled
	遇见	yùjian	came across, encountered
会	huì	know how	
	看会	kànhuì	mastered (know how) through observing
	听会	tīnghuì	mastered (know how) through listening
	学会	xuéhuì	mastered (know how) through learning
懂	dǒng	comprehend	
	看懂	kàndǒng	comprehended through watching/reading
	听懂	tīngdǒng	comprehended through listening
完	wán	finish	
	看完	kànwán	finished reading/watching
	听完	tīngwán	finished listening
	学完	xuéwán	finished studying
到	dào	arrive	
	看到	kàndào	saw
	听到	tīngdào	heard
	学到	xuédào	learned up to
	走到	zǒudào	arrived at
走	zǒu	depart, walk	

开走 kāizǒu drove away

拿走 názǒu took away

带走 dàizǒu carried off

计划路线和预测时间 Plan the Route and Predict the Time

可能补语 Potential Complement

功用 Function：Potential complement is used to predict the potential result of an action. It is intended to be more objective than subjective in perspective.

句型 Sentence Pattern：

Subject	Verb	+得	Verb/Adjective

Wǒ kàn de jiàn

我 看 得 见。

I can see it. (I will achieve seeing (it).)

A verb indicates the potential result of the action：

Wǒ kàn de dǒng

我 看 得 懂。

I can comprehend through observing/reading.

(It is a possibility that I can achieve comprehension.)

An adjective indicates the potential result of the action：

Wǒ kàn de qīngchu

我 看 得 清楚。

I can see it clearly.

(I will achieve seeing (it) with clarity.)

否定 Negative："不" denies the potential result not the action.

（要是我看，可能……）

Wǒ kàn bu dǒng

我 看 不 懂。

I cannot understand.

Wǒ kàn bu qīngchu

我 看 不 清楚。

I cannot see clearly.

宾语在句中的位置 Position of object in sentence:

The result must follow the action immediately. The object of the sentence usually has to go after the action and result.

Wǒ kàn de jiàn tā
我 看 得 见 他。
I can see him (I can receive the sight of him)

Wǒ kàn bu wán nà běn shū
我 看 不 完 那 本 书。
I cannot finish reading that book.

鉴别、预测可能性 Identify Possibilities:

若对旅行的时间、路面的情况作鉴定和推测，需要用可能补语。

In order to predict possibilities, such as traveling time, accessibility of the road or transportation, etc., we use "可能补语 Potential Complement."

Jīntiān de tiānqì bù hǎo, tā kěnéng lái bu liǎo le
今天 的 天气 不 好，他 可能 来 不 了 了。
Today's weather is not good, I don't think he can make it here.

Qù nàr de lù bú tài yuǎn, shí fēnzhōng kāi de dào dào de liǎo
去 那儿 的 路 不 太 远，十 分钟 开 得 到/到 得 了。
It is not far, we will get there in 10 minutes.

其他的可能 Other Possibilities:

lái de liǎo lái bu liǎo
来 得 了/来 不 了

qù de liǎo qù bu liǎo
去 得 了/去 不 了

zǒu de liǎo zǒu bu liǎo
走 得 了/走 不 了

dào de liǎo dào bu liǎo
到 得 了/到 不 了

huí de liǎo huí bu liǎo
回 得 了/回 不 了

问句 Questions:

Nǐ kàn de jiàn tā ma
你 看 得 见 他 吗？
Can you see him?

Nǐ kàn de jiàn kàn bu jiàn tā
你 看 得 见 看 不 见 他？
Can you see him, or not?

常用可能补语 Frequently Used Potential Complements

形容词 Adjectives

好 hǎo well, properly

 做得好 zuò de hǎo can finish, do nicely and thoroughly

清楚 qīngchu clear, distinct

 看得清楚 kàn de qīngchu can see clearly/distinctly

 说得清楚 shuō de qīngchu can communicate/explain clearly

动词 Verbs (Pay attention: you may achieve the same result through different actions.)

见 jiàn perceive through senses

 看得见 kàn de jiàn can see

 听得见 tīng de jiàn can hear

会 huì know how

 看得会 kàn de huì can master (know how) through observing/reading

 学得会 xué de huì can master (know how) through learning

懂 dǒng comprehend

 看得懂 kàn de dǒng can comprehend through watching/reading

 听得懂 tīng de dǒng can comprehend through listening

完 wán finish

 看得完 kàn de wán can finish reading/watching

 听得完 tīng de wán can finish listening

到 dào arrive

 看得到 kàn de dào can see

	听得到	tīng de dào	can hear
	走得到	zǒu de dào	can arrive at
走	zǒu	depart, walk	
	开得走	kāi de zǒu	can drive away
	拿得走	ná de zǒu	can take away

指方向 Giving Directions

往…… Toward...

"往……V" 可能是用得最多的一个句子

In order to identify a direction to travel, we use the pattern "往... V". In English, when giving directions, we simply say, "go south, turn left." In Chinese, we usually specify the direction first, then the action:

Go south: wǎng nán zǒu 往 南 走

Turn left: wǎng zuǒ guǎi 往 左 拐

1) 其他相似的介词 Other Prepositions Similar to "往..." to Show Directions:

往	wǎng	toward; go to
朝	cháo	towards; facing ...
向	xiàng	face; turn toward
冲	chòng	towards; in the direction of

2) 方向 Possible Directions:

east/west/south/north: dōng xī nán běi 东 / 西 / 南 / 北

up/down/left/right: shàng xià zuǒ yòu 上 / 下 / 左 / 右

front/back/in/out: qián hòu lǐ wài 前 / 后 / 里 / 外

3) 可能用的动词 Possible Action Verbs Used to Show Directions:

拐	guǎi	turn, change direction

走 zǒu walk, travel on foot

开 kāi drive

跑 pǎo run

Note

有人说“拐左”，但不是标准说法。汉语的介词结构/状语应置于动词前。

Some people say “拐左,” but, this is not a standard (grammatically correct) expression. In Chinese, habitually, all prepositional phrases go before verbs. “往” is such a phrase.

指路——有用的句型 Giving Directions — Useful Sentence Patterns

问路 wènlù Asking the way

Qǐngwèn qù zěnme zǒu
请问， 去 ××× 怎么 走？
Excuse me, how do I get to xxx (place)?

回答 huídá Reply, answer

1) 从 cóng……到 dào…… from... to...

Cóng zhèr zǒu dào nàr
从 这儿 走 到 那儿。
Go from here to there.

2) 从 cóng……往 wǎng…… from ... towards ...

Cóng nàr wǎng yòu guǎi
从 那儿 往 右 拐
From there turn right.

3) 过…… guò Cross, pass; across; over

Zài nàr guò mǎlù
在 那儿 过 马路。
Cross the street there.

Guò liǎng tiáo jiē
过 两 条 街。
Over two blocks.

4) 走 zǒu (period of time) go/walk (a period of time)

Zǒu wǔ fēnzhōng
走 五 分钟
Walk for 5 minutes

5）沿着 yánzhe……（一直 yìzhí）往 wǎng……

... along ...（go straight）towards ...

yánzhe zhè tiáo jiē yìzhí wǎng qián zǒu
沿着 这 条 街 一直 往 前 走。
Go straight ahead along this road.

6）走 zǒu 到 dào（看见 kànjian）……往 wǎng

……until you get to（see）...

Zǒudào lùkǒu kànjian hónglǜdēng wǎng yòu guǎi
走到 路口 看见 红绿灯 往 右 拐。
Walk to the corner, after seeing the traffic lights, turn right.

7）先 xiān……然后 ránhòu（再 zài）…… first ... then ...

Nǐ xiān yánzhe zhè tiáo jiē yìzhí wǎng qián zǒu zǒudào lùkǒu
你 先 沿着 这 条 街 一直 往 前 走，走到 路口
wǎng yòu guǎi kànjian hónglǜdēng ránhòu zài wǎng yòu guǎi
往 右 拐，看见 红绿灯 然后 再 往 右 拐，
jiù dào le
就 到 了。
First go straight ahead along this road, come to the corner and turn right, then when you see the traffic lights, make another right turn. Then you will be there.

教学难点

Difficulties

难点一　结果补语 Resultant Complement

结果补语比较难。有的容易掌握，有的相对难懂。常出错的有几个。

Resultant Complement itself is a difficult learning point. Some results of actions are easier for learners, some are more difficult to understand. Here we list a few that are easy to misuse.

看见 kànjiàn see/saw

“看见”用得最多也最难掌握。“看 kàn look”是做的事，“见 jiàn perceive”是做到的事。“看”不一定“见”，“见”不一定在“看”。相似的还有“听见、闻见、遇见”。

This is perhaps the most frequently used but the most confusing for learners. But once understood, it may be helpful in understanding other resultant complements.

“看 kàn look” is the effort while “见 jiàn perceive” is to receive the sight. The logic here is that you may try to look, but you may or may not see anything. Also you may accidentally see something even though you have not actively looked. The same applies to “听见，闻见，遇见”. e. g. :

看见　　kànjiàn　　saw

Nǐmen kàn kànjian shénme le
你们 看，看见 什么 了？
(Look, what did you see?)

听见　　tīngjiàn　　heard

Wǒ zhùyì tīng le kěshì shénme dōu méi tīngjiàn
我 注意 听 了，可是 什么 都 没 听见 。
(I listened carefully but did not hear anything.)

闻见　　wénjiàn　　smelled

Tā wénjian le yì gǔ xiāngwèi
他 闻见 了 一 股 香味 。
(He smelled some delicious aroma.)

遇见　　yùjiàn　　come across, encounter

Wǒ zài lùshang yùjian le tā
我 在 路上 遇见 了 他。
I met with (bumped into) him on the way.

做完 zuòwán finish doing

英文说“finish doing”，中文说“做完 zuòwán finish doing”。“做”是行为，“完”是结果。

In English, we say “finished doing” something when it is completed.

In Chinese, “做” or other verbs are actions; “完” is one of the results you achieve through actions, thus “完” appears after the action verb, e. g. :

Wǒ chīwán le
我 吃完 了。
I have finished eating.

拿走 názǒu take away

学生一般先学了“走 zǒu walk”，不太习惯用“走”做补语。若把“走”当做“move away，leave”就容易了。教学中，创造使用的情景很重要。

For most learners who have learned “走 zǒu ” “to walk” it is a little difficult for them to understand it as a result of an action. But once they know “走 zǒu ” also means “to move” and “to leave”, it will be easier for them to get accustomed to use “走 zǒu” to indicate the result, e. g. :

Tā bǎ nà běn shū názǒu le
他 把 那 本 书 拿走 了。
He took the book (away.)

Huǒchē kāizǒu le
火车 开走 了。
The train took off (drove away).

难点二 “在”作为结果 “在” as a Result

做补语常会与“在 a place”做状语混淆；做状语出现在动词前；做补语放在动词后。

“在 a place” as a result also causes confusion at times. Most learners learned “在” as the location of an action and it has to be put before the action verbs in a sentence:

Wǒ bàba zài zhōngxué gōngzuò
我 爸爸 在 中学 工作 。
My dad works in a high school.

However, “在 a place” can also be the result as an action and be used after the verb.

Wǒ bàba zhàn zài nàr
我 爸爸 站 在 那儿。
My dad stood there.

Don't panic! Please note: the emphases are not the same.

If the "在 a place" phrase is needed before the verb, it refers to the location where the action is/has been conducted.

Wǒ jiā zài Zhījiāgē zhù
我 家 在 芝加哥 住 。
My family lives in Chicago.

Emphasis: It is at Chicago where my family lives.

Wǒ zài zhuōzi shang fàngle yì běn shū
我 在 桌子 上 放了 一 本 书 。
I put a book on the table.

Emphasis: The table is the location where I put a book.

If the "在" is needed after the verb, it refers to where the object is ended up as a result of the action.

我家住在芝加哥。 My family lives in Chicago.

Emphasis: My family is at Chicago because we live there.

Wǒ bǎ nà běn shū fàng zài zhuōzi shang le
我 把 那 本 书 放 在 桌子 上 了 。
I put the book on the table.

Emphasis: What happened to the book? It ended up on the table.

难点三 可能补语 vs. 结果补语

Potential Complement vs. Resultant Complement

可能补语与结果补语的不同：顾名思义，一个是可能，一个是结果。

Both "可能补语" and "结果补语" are intended to be objective in perspective. While "结果补语" is meant to show result of an action, how far an action is planned or has been carried out; "可能补语" is to predict or estimate a possible result.

"结果补语" is used to show result.

"看见 kànjiàn see/saw"

"可能补语" is used to predict potential/possibility.

"看得见 kàn de jiàn can be seen"

难点四　“能”与“可能” Potentials and Abilities

“能”与“可能”的不同在看问题的角度。“能”指的是做事者的能力，“可能”指的是事情。同时使用，“能”在句中可以加强“可能”。

What is the difference? The difference is the perspective! “能 néng can ...; be possible” expresses a more subjective view. It emphasizes capability. “可能 kěnéng possibility, likelihood” expresses a more objective view and it meant to predict a possibility. “能” can be used to enhance “可能” in a sentence:

Wǒ néng jīntiān kànwán zhè běn shū
我　能　今天　看完　这　本　书　。
I can finish reading this book today.

(I have the capacity to finish this book today.)

Wǒ jīntiān kàn de wán zhè běn shū
我　今天　看　得　完　这　本　书　。
I can finish reading this book today.

(It is possible that I will finish reading this today.)

Wǒ jīntiān néng kàn de wán zhè běn shū
我　今天　能　看　得　完　这　本　书　。
I can finish reading this book today.

(Double emphasis: it can be and will be done!)

难点五　可能补语 vs. 程度补语

Potential Complement vs. Complement of Degree

“可能补语” and “程度补语” obviously have different grammatical functions. However, they can be confused because they seem to be similar in structure since both use “Verb 得 Adjective”. Note: they are not as similar as one may believe.

对比不同: Note the differences:

When using 程度补语, you may add adverbs to modify adjectives:

Tā tiàowǔ tiào de fēicháng hǎo
他 跳舞 跳 得 非常 好 。
He dances very well.

When using 可能补语 , you cannot add an adverb before adjective:

Tā tiào de hǎo tiào bu hǎo Tā tiào de hǎo
他 跳 得 好 跳 不 好 ？他 跳 得 好 。
Can he dance well? Yes, he can.
(Can he possibly deliver a quality performance?)

词汇表

Glossary

路标 Road Signs

停	tíng	stop
慢行	màn xíng	move (act, progress) slowly
出口	chūkǒu	exit
入口	rùkǒu	enter; entrance
请绕行	qǐng ràoxíng	detour
禁止通行	jìnzhǐ tōngxíng	no thoroughfare (as a posted prohibition), road blocked
安全行驶	ānquán xíngshǐ	drive safely

交通用语 Related Traffic Expressions

交通	jiāotōng	traffic	
	交通工具	jiāotōng gōngjù	means of transportation
	交通警	jiāotōngjǐng	traffic police
路	lù	road, path	
	公路	gōnglù	highway, public road
	高速公路	gāosù gōnglù	expressway
	马路	mǎlù	street (the part for vehicular traffic)

	路口	lùkǒu	intersection, street cornor
	十字路口	shízì lùkǒu	intersection (of two roads in an x – shape)
街	jiē	street, road	
	大街	dàjiē	main street
	街道	jiēdào	street, road, neighborhood
红绿灯	hónglǜdēng	traffic lights	
堵车	dǔ chē	traffic jam	
塞车	sāi chē	traffic jam	

补充语法点

Supplementary Notes

趋向补语 Directional Complements

简单趋向补语 Simple Directional Complement

功用 Function:

"来" or "去" goes after a verb to indicate the direction of the action.

"来" indicates that the action is towards the speaker;

"去" indicates that the action is away from the speaker.

句型 Sentence Patterns:

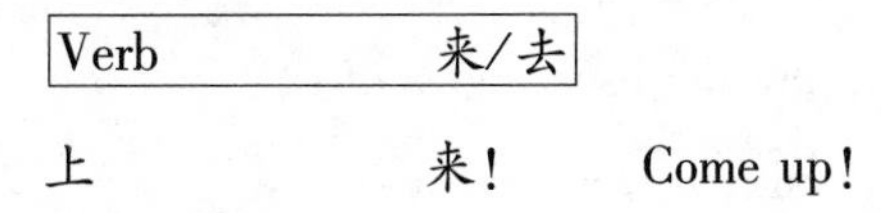

Verb	来/去

上 来! Come up!

If there is a destination for the action, then it goes in between the verb and 来/去.

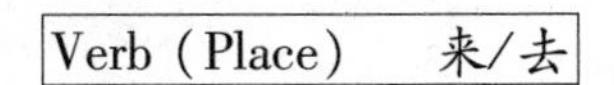

Verb (Place)	来/去

上 这儿 来。 Come up here.

If there is a starting location for the action, then it goes before the verb.

从（place）Verb 来/去

从 家 带 来 一本书。 Bring a book from home.

有关动词 Related Verbs

The basic group of verbs that implies directional movements of the body

上	shàng	get on, go up
下	xià	get off, go down
进	jìn	enter
出	chū	go out, exit
过	guò	pass by, come across, go over
回	huí	return, go back
到	dào	arrive, go to
起	qǐ	rise, stand up

Toward speaker	away from speaker
上来	上去
下来	下去
进来	进去
出来	出去
过来	过去
回来	回去
到（Place）来	到（Place）去
起来	

Other verbs that indicate moving back and forth:

走	zǒu	walk, travel on foot
跑	pǎo	run, run away
爬	pá	crawl, creep, climb
滚	gǔn	roll

开	kāi	drive, operate (a machine, etc.)
骑	qí	ride (astride, like on a bicycle, horse, etc.)

Common verbs that refer to moving objects:

搬	bān	move, take away (mostly heavy or large objects)
带	dài	carry, bring, take to
买	mǎi	buy, purchase
拿	ná	hole, grasp, take, capture
扔	rēng	throw, toss
运	yùn	transport
装	zhuāng	pack, load

复合趋向补语

功用 Function:

Combine a verb with a simple directional complement to enrich an expression.

句型 Sentence Pattern:

Combine a verb with a simple directional complement.

Verb	simple directional complement
跑	上来

toward speaker	**away from speaker**
走上来	走上去
走下来	走下去
走进来	走进去
走出来	走出去
走过来	走过去
走回来	走回去
走到(Place)来	走到(Place)去
走上(Place)来	走上(Place)去

趋向补语的引申用法

Some simple directional complement phrases have extended meanings. They serve as suffixes.

Extended Use:

出来 chūlái achievement or completion of a task

想出来 xiǎng chūlai come up with an idea

看出来 kàn chūlai see through, understand

起来 qǐlái arising, beginning to do, accomplishing

唱起来 chàng qǐlai sing out, start singing

想起来 xiǎng qǐlai remember, recall

下去 xiàqù indicating continuation or completion

吃下去 chī xiàqu eat (sth.)

22

指令

Giving Instructions (Orders, Directions)

给指令是经常发生的事。在公共场所和服务设施等会遇到，紧急情况和日常活动都需要。在中小学课堂上就会不断出现。

但指令所用的语法点有可能是比较复杂的。本节着重介绍下指令时必用的一些语法点和可能的学习难点。

后附的词汇表是与食物等有关的。教与学做饭、看病、买东西等话题时，可参考。

Giving instructions (orders, directions) is a daily occurrence. It happens in public places and at home, for service and emergencies. We do it in classroom instruction all the time.

The grammatical structures used for giving instructions can vary. This chapter introduces some necessary sentence patterns and explains some common difficulties.

The attached vocabulary lists relates mostly to food. Cooking, doctor's visits, shopping and similar activities often use instruction. Use whenever necessary.

教学重点 Content of Teaching and Learning

指令	Giving Instructions (Orders, Directions)
动词句	Verb as Action
兼语句	Pivotal Sentence
“把”字句	“把” Sentence
常用的指令	Commonly Used Instructions

教学难点 Difficulties

“问” vs. “请”	Asking a Question vs. Asking Someone
“想” vs. “想让”	Wanting Someone to Do Something
听什么？	Listening to “What”?
“把”字句的使用	Use of “把” Sentence
“把”字句与“被”字句的比较与使用	“把” Sentence vs. “被” Sentence

词汇表 Glossary

食物	Food
用餐	Having a Meal
饮料	Drinks/Beverages
蔬菜	Vegetables
水果	Fruits
动物	Animals
植物	Plants

文化联系 Cultural Relations

中国食品	Chinese Food
中国珍宝	Chinese Treasures

教学重点

Content of Teaching and Learning

指令 Giving Instructions (Orders, Directions)

给指令时可用以下三类句子。

In order to give instructions, orders or directions, we may use three kinds of sentence patterns.

动词句 Verb as Action

功用 Function: To give an order or instruction.

句型 Sentence Pattern:

	Guòlai
Come over here.	过来 ！
	Gěi wǒ
Give it to me.	给 我 ！
	Chī ba
Eat (it)!	吃 吧 ！

否定形式 Negative: 不要

	Búyào guòlái
Don't come over here.	不要 过来 ！
	Búyào gěi wǒ
Don't give it to me.	不要 给 我 ！
	Búyào chī ba
Don't eat it.	不要 吃 吧 ！

客气起见请用“请”。

For the sake of politeness, we may add 请—meaning “please” —at the beginning of the sentence:

	Qǐng guòlai
Please come over here.	请 过来！
	Qǐng gěi wǒ
Please give it to me.	请 给 我！

Please eat it.　　Qǐng chī ba
请　吃　吧！

Note

“吧”在句末有建议的意思。“吧” usually indicates a tone of suggestion.

兼语句　Pivotal Sentence

Use “请”,“让”, or “叫” to invite, make or allow someone to do something:

功用　Function: Give an invitation, order or permission for an action.

句型　Sentence Pattern:

请/让/叫	Someone	Verb (Object)

Wǒ qǐng nǐ hē kāfēi
我　请　你　喝　咖啡　。
I will take you out for some coffee.

Wǒ māma ràng wǒ xiànzài jiù zuò gōngkè
我　妈妈　让　我　现在　就　做　功课　。
My mom wants me to do homework now.

Tā jiào wǒmen kuàidiǎn zǒu
他　叫　我们　快点　走　。
He asked us to hurry up.

否定形式　Negative Form:　不 or 不想

Wǒ bù qǐng tā hē kāfēi wǒ qǐng nǐ
我　不　请　他　喝　咖啡，我　请　你　。
I am not inviting him for coffee, I am inviting you.

Wǒ bù xiǎng qǐng nǐ hē kāfēi
or 我　不　想　请　你　喝　咖啡　。
I don't feel like taking you out for coffee.

Wǒ māma bú ràng wǒ xiànzài jiù zuò gōngkè
我　妈妈　不　让　我　现在　就　做　功课　。
My mom won't allow me to do my homework now.

Wǒ māma bù xiǎng ràng wǒ xiànzài jiù zuò gōngkè
or 我　妈妈　不　想　让　我　现在　就　做　功课　。
My mom does not want me to do my homework now.

Tā bú jiào wǒmen nàme kuài de zǒu
他　不　叫　我们　那么　快　地　走　。
He won't let us walk that fast.

Tā bù xiǎng jiào wǒmen nàme kuài de zǒu
or 他不想叫我们那么快地走。
He does not want us to walk that fast.

“把”字句 “把”Sentence

Give instructions by focusing on the object of the action

功用 Function：Emphasize how the object of the action should be manipulated.

句型 Sentence Pattern：

把	Object	Verb	Extent of the Action

Qǐng nǐ bǎ nà běn shū gěi wǒ
请你把那本书给我。
Please pass that book to me.

Bǎ tā sòng dào yīyuàn qù
把他送到医院去。
Take him to the hostipal.

Bǎ yīfu chuānshang
把衣服穿上。
Put on your jacket.

比较 Compare：

Give me that book.
Gěi wǒ nà běn shū
给我那本书。(A)
Bǎ nà běn shū gěi wǒ
把那本书给我。(B)

显然（A）和（B）都对。（A）和（B）会起同样结果。

不同的是：（A）和（B）的注意点不同。（A）的注意点是“给我”；（B）的注意点是“那本书”。

Obviously,（A）and（B）are both perfectly correct sentences. （A）and（B）may cause the same action, producing the same result.

A simple way to explain：（A）and（B）differ in emphasis：（A）The emphasis is on “to me” — “给我”； （B）The emphasis is on “the book” — “那本书”.

常用的指令 Commonly used Instructions

课堂用语 Language Used in the Classroom

Qǐng ānjìng
请 安静！
Be quiet!

Qǐng zhùyì tīng
请 注意 听 。
Please pay attention.

Qǐng jǔ shǒu
请 举 手 。
Raise your hand!

Bié pǎo
别 跑 ！
Stop running!

Qǐng gēn wǒ shuō
请 跟 我 说 。
Please say it after me.

Kuài diǎn
快 点 ！
Hurry up!

Qǐng dào qiánmian lái qǐng dào nàbian qù
请 到 前面 来/请 到 那边 去 。
Please come to the front/go over there.

Shàng kè de shíhou búyào chī dōngxi
上 课 的 时候 不要 吃 东西 。
No food in class.

Bǎ diànnǎo dǎkāi
把 电脑 打开 。
Turn on your computer.

Qǐng bǎ běnzi cóng shūbāo li ná chūlai
请 把 本子 从 书包 里 拿 出来 。
Please take out your notebook from your bag.

Qǐng bǎ shū fàng zài zhuōshang
请 把 书 放 在 桌上 。
Put the book on your desk.

在医院里 In Hospital

Qǐng bǎ yīfu xiézi tuō xiàlai
请 把 衣服/鞋子 脱 下来 。
Please take off your clothes/shoes.

Qǐng bǎ zhège sòng dào nàr qù
请 把 这个 送 到 那儿 去 。
Please take this over there.

做饭 Cooking

Bǎ cài xǐ gānjìng
把 菜 洗 干净 。
Clean the greens.

Bǎ cài qiēchéng xiǎo kuài
把 菜 切成 小 块 。
Cut the vegetables into small pieces.

Bǎ róuhǎo de miàntuán fàngjìn kǎoxiāng kǎo sìshí fēnzhōng
把 揉好 的 面团 放进 烤箱 烤 四十 分钟 。
Put the dough in the oven and bake for 40 minutes.

教学难点

Difficulties

难点一 "问" vs. "请" Asking a Question vs. Asking Someone

英文的"ask"有两个功能：问问题和请人做事。

在汉语里，这两个功能是用不同动词句子表示的。"问"只能问问题，请人做事要用兼语句。

The word "ask" is commonly used. It must be used with care.

In English, the word "ask" can be used for two different functions:

1) To ask a question.

2) To ask someone to do something.

In Chinese,

1) To ask a question is "问/问题"

2) To ask someone to do something is "请/让/叫"某人做事.

"问"：

Wǒ wèn tā yí ge wèntí
我 问 他 一 个 问题。
I am asking him a question.

Wǒ wèn tā nǐ máng bu máng
我 问 他"你 忙 不 忙 ？"

I asked him, "Are you busy?"

Wǒ wèn tā máng bu máng
我 问 他 忙 不 忙 ?
I asked him if he was busy.

"请/让/叫":

Wǒ qǐng tā gěi wǒ jiǎng yí ge gùshi
我 请 他 给 我 讲 一 个 故事。
I asked him to tell me a story.

Tā ràng wǒ tīng tā shuō
他 让 我 听 他 说 。
He asked me to listen to him.

Qǐng nǐ jiào tā lái hǎo ma
请 你 叫 她 来, 好 吗?
Would you please ask her to come here?

对比 Compare:

Wǒ qǐng tā wèn wǒ yí ge wèntí
我 请 他 问 我 一 个 问题。
I asked (invited) him to ask me a question.

难点二 "想" vs. "想让" Wanting Someone to Do Something

在英文里,可以说:"I want you to do this." 这句话中的 "want" 不能直接译成汉语的"想"。

"想"和"想让"在汉语里的意思是不一样的。

In English, when we say, "I want you to do this," the word "want" refers to your desire to have someone to get something done. That is to say, you ask someone to carry out an action according to your instructions.

Therefore, in Chinese, this "want" must be translated as "(想) 请/让/叫" not just "想".

Wǒ bà bù xiǎng ràng wǒ gēn péngyou chūqu
我 爸 不(想) 让 我 跟 朋友 出去 。
My dad does not want me to go out with my friends.

Tā bú jiào wǒ gàosu nǐ
她 不 叫 我 告诉 你 。
She does not want me to tell you.

难点三 听什么？Listening to "What"?

英语的"listen"后可跟人："listen to me/you/him/her..."

汉语的"听"后只能跟物不能跟人。

In English, we may say "listen to me/you/him/her...". One listens to "a person".

In Chinese, we don't listen to a person. We listen to "what a person says" or "a person's words".

Tā ràng wǒ tīng tā shuō
他 让 我 听 他 说 。
He asked me to listen to him.

Bié tīng tā de huà
别 听 他 的（话）。
Don't listen to him.

同样 The same applies to:

	tīng bù tīng lǎoshī de
listen/not listen to your teacher	听/不 听 老师 的
	tīng bù tīng fùmǔ de
listen/not listen to your parents	听/不 听 父母 的
	tīng bù tīng péngyou de
listen/not listen to your friends	听/不 听 朋友 的

难点四 "把"字句的使用 Use of "把" Sentence

"把"字句的功用是强调动作的对象宾语。

在句子的结构上有两个值得注意的地方。

Functionally, the emphasis of the action is on the object of 把 sentence.

In terms of sentence structure, there are two things worth noting:

1）"把"将宾语提到动词之前以示强调，这个宾语应是已知的。

We use "把" to move the object in front of the verb to reflect this emphasis on the object. Thus the object must be a known or designated one.

bǎ shū fàng zhuō shang
Put the book on the table：把 书 放 桌上 。

"The book 书" is not a random one. It is the particular book that we are talking about.

2）"把"字句动词的后边必须有附加成分，如补语等，以示动作的程度。不可与"把"字句同用的只有可能补语。

There has to be an element after the verb. This element indicates to what extent the action is going to be/has been done.

In other words, it is incorrect to end a "把" sentence with a verb alone.

bǎ shū fàng
(×) 把 书 放 。

The only linguistic element that is not suitable to go with a "把" sentence is a "potential complement." In this case, you can only use "能不能" instead.

Would you be able to finish reading the book today?

Nǐ jīntiān bǎ zhè běn shū kàn de wán kàn bu wán
(×) 你 今天 把 这 本 书 看 得 完 看 不 完 ?(A)

Nǐ jīntiān néng bu néng bǎ zhè běn shū kànwán
(√) 你 今天 能 不 能 把 这 本 书 看完 ?(B)

（A）错。因为完成的可能性不是可以实际测量的行为本身。

（B）对。因为谈的是行为者的能力而不是书。

If you think about it, (A) does not make sense because the potential of finishing is not a tangible result of the action.

(B) is our choice because "能不能" means the doer has the capacity to achieve the goal of finishing the book. The potential is about the doer, not the action itself.

同样，情态动词都应该放在"把"之前。

Similarly, all modal verbs must be put before the "把" phrase.

Tā yīnggāi bǎ shū huán gěi nǐ
他 应该 把 书 还 给 你 。
He should return the book to you.

The following is a list of the linguistic elements indicating the result or extention of the action in a "把" sentence:

What will you do with your homework?

(Adjective as Result) Get it done properly.

Bǎ nǐ de gōngkè zuò hǎo
把 你 的 功课 做 好 。

(Direction of Action) Take it home.

Bǎ nǐ de gōngkè dàihuí jiā qù
把 你 的 功课 带回 家 去 。

(Duplication of Verb) Have a look!

Bǎ nǐ de gōngkè kàn yi kàn
把 你 的 功课 看 一 看 。

(Evaluation of Action) Must do it very well!

Yídìng yào bǎ nǐ de gōngkè zuò de tèbié hǎo
一定 要 把 你 的 功课 做 得 特别 好。

(Frequency of Action) Should get it checked twice.

Yīnggāi bǎ gōngkè jiǎnchá liǎng biàn
应该 把 功课 检查 两 遍 。

(Place as Result) Put it on the table.

Bǎ nǐ de gōngkè fàng zài zhuōzi shang
把 你 的 功课 放 在 桌子 上 。

(Quantity) Did half.

Bǎ gōngkè zuòle yíbàn
把 功课 做了 一半 。

(To Indicate Completion) Get it done!

Bǎ nǐ de gōngkè zuò le
把 你 的 功课 做 了 。

(Time Duration) Only did half a hour.

Zhǐ bǎ gōngkè zuòle bàn ge zhōngtóu
只 把 功课 做了 半 个 钟头 。

(To a Person as Result) Hand it to the teacher.

Bǎ nǐ de gōngkè jiāo gěi lǎoshī
把 你 的 功课 交 给 老师 。

(Verb as Result) Finish it.

Bǎ gōngkè zuòwán
把 功课 做完 。

难点五 “把”字句与“被”字句的比较与使用

“把”Sentence vs.“被”Sentence

比较 Comparison

Zuòyè zuòwán le
作业 做完 了。 Homework is done!

这个句子可以是“把”字句也可能是“被”字句。

To be more specific, this sentence could also be expressed as:

Wǒ bǎ zuòyè zuòwán le
A. 我 把 作业 做完 了。 I got my homework done!

Zuòyè ràng tā zuòwán le
B. 作业 让 他 做完 了！ The homework was done by him!

“把”字句与“被”字句的相同点 Similarities:

功用上都强调行为的对象。句型上都要动词后的附加成分以示动作完成的程度。

In function, both sentences focus on the object. In structure, both sentence patterns require the same kind of elements after verbs.

“把”字句与“被”字句的不同点 Differences:

简单地说，在功用上，“把”字句是主动的被动。行为者的动作是主动的，动作的目标是被强调的，行为的情景是受限定的。“被”字句是真的被动。

In function, “把 Sentence” is “actively passive” in nature: The doer of the action is in an active mode but the action itself is in a given situation and the focus of the action is on the object. 被字句 is truly “passive.”

从结构上说，区别见以下例句。

Structure of “把 Sentence”:

Subject	“把”	Object	Verb	Complement
Wǒ 我	bǎ 把	zuòyè 作业	zuò 做	wán le 完 了。

I finished my homework.

Structure of “被 Sentence”:

Object	“被/让/叫”	Doer	Verb	Complement

Zuòyè ràng tā zuò wán le
作业 让 他 做 完 了。
Homework was done by him.

“被”字句 “被” Sentence

功用 Function: An action is/was done to an object.

句型 Sentence Pattern:

Object	“被/让/叫”	(Doer)	Verb	Extent of the Action

Zuòyè ràng tā zuò wán le
作业 让 他 做 完 了。
The homework has been completed by him.

Note

1）“被”字句的重点在宾语和行为本身，行为者是谁不重要。

In the “被” sentence the focus is on the object and the action. Who carries out the action is much less significant. Thus doers are not frequently mentioned in Chinese sentences.

Zuòyè yǐjing zuòwán le
作业 已经 做完 了。
The homework is already done.

2）引出行为者的词

Words that introduce the “doers” of an action in the “被” sentence:

被 bèi by
让 ràng by (less formal)
叫 jiào by (least informal)

3）用“被”时，人称也可省略。

If “被” is used, the doer may be omitted:

Zuòyè bèi tā zuòwán le
作业 被 他 做完 了。

Homework was done by him.
Zuòyè bèi zuòwán le
作业　被　做完　了。
Homewrok was done.

词汇表

Glossary

食物 shíwù Food

(食品 shípǐn food, foodstuffs, provisions)

吃 chī eat

- 饿 è be hungry
- 饱 bǎo be full (after eating)

中餐(中国饭) Zhōngcān Chinese food, Chinese cuisine

西餐 xīcān Western-style food (meal)

米 mǐ hulled rice

- 米饭 mǐfàn cooked rice

面 miàn wheat flour

- 面条 miàntiáo noodles
- 面包 miànbāo bread
- 点心 diǎnxin snacks, refreshments, dim sum
- 蛋糕 dàngāo cake
- 饼干 bǐnggān cracker, biscuit

肉类 ròulèi meats

- 肉食 ròushí meat

家禽 jiāqín domesticated fowl, poultry

水产 shuǐchǎn aquatic product

- 海鲜 hǎixiān seafood

素食 sùshí vegetarian diet

菜 cài vegetables, dishes

豆类 dòulèi legumes

豆子 dòuzi beans, peas, legumes

豆制品 dòuzhìpǐn bean products (beancurd, dried beancurd, etc.)

豆腐 dòufu beancurd

豆浆 dòujiāng soybean milk

奶制品 nǎizhìpǐn diary products

奶酪 nǎilào cheese

冰激凌 bīngjīlíng icecream

营养 yíngyǎng nutrition, nourishment

维生素 wéishēngsù vitamin

纤维 xiānwéi fiber

用餐 yòngcān dine, have a meal

饭馆 fànguǎn restaurant

餐厅 cāntīng dining room, restaurant

酒店 jiǔdiàn wineshop

饭店 fàndiàn hotel, restaurant

服务 fúwù service, serve

服务员 fúwùyuán attendant, service person

菜谱 càipǔ menu, cookbook

菜单 càidān menu

账单 zhàngdān invoice, bill, check

付钱 fù qián pay

饮料 yǐnliào drink, beverage

喝 hē drink

渴 kě thirsty

醉	zuì	drunk, intoxicated
果汁 guǒzhī fruit juice, syrup		
橘汁	júzhī	orange juice
苹果汁	píngguǒzhī	apple juice
汽水 qìshuǐ sofe drink, soda water		
可口可乐	Kěkǒukělè	Coca-Cola
百事可乐	Bǎishìkělè	Pepsi
雪碧	Xuěbì	Sprite
七喜	Qīxǐ	7-up
酒 jiǔ alcoholic beverage, wine, liquor		
白酒	báijiǔ	white liquor
葡萄酒	pútaojiǔ	grape wine
米酒	mǐjiǔ	rice wine (made of glutinous rice)
料酒	liàojiǔ	cooking wine
其他 qítā others		
茶	chá	tea
咖啡	kāfēi	coffee
牛奶	niúnǎi	milk (from a cow)

蔬菜 shūcài vegetables, greens

白菜	báicài	Chinese cabbage, celery cabbage, bok choy
扁豆	biǎndòu	hyacinth bean, green bean
葱	cōng	scallions, leeks, green onion
胡萝卜	húluóbo	carrot
黄瓜	huángguā	cucumber
姜	jiāng	ginger
韭菜	jiǔcài	Chinese chives

辣椒	làjiāo	hot pepper
萝卜	luóbo	radish, turnip
蘑菇	mógu	mushroom
南瓜	nánguā	pumpkin
茄子	qiézi	eggplant
芹菜	qíncài	celery
青椒	qīngjiāo	green pepper
生菜	shēngcài	(romaine) lettuce
蒜	suàn	garlic
土豆	tǔdòu	potato
西红柿/番茄	xīhóngshì/fānqié	tomato
香菜	xiāngcài	coriander

水果 shuǐguǒ Fruit (s)

菠萝	bōluó	pineapple
草莓	cǎoméi	strawberry
橙子	chéngzi	orange
橘子	júzi	tangerine
梨	lí	pear
李子	lǐzi	plum
荔枝	lìzhī	litchi
苹果	píngguǒ	apple
葡萄	pútao	grape
桃子	táozi	peach
甜瓜	tiánguā	muskmelon
西瓜	xīguā	watermelon
香蕉	xiāngjiāo	banana
杏	xìng	apricot
樱桃	yīngtáo	cherry

椰子	yēzi	coconut

动物 dòngwù animals

公	gōng	male (animal)
母	mǔ	female (animal)
大象	dàxiàng	elephant
长颈鹿	chángjǐnglù	giraffe
刺猬	cìwei	hedgehog
狗	gǒu	dog
猴子	hóuzi	monkey
狐狸	húli	fox
老虎	lǎohǔ	tiger
老鼠	lǎoshǔ	rat, mouse
狼	láng	wolf
鹿	lù	deer
马	mǎ	horse
猫	māo	cat
牛	niú	ox
蛇	shé	snake
狮子	shīzi	lion
松鼠	sōngshǔ	squirrel
兔子	tùzi	rabbit, hare
熊猫	xióngmāo	panda
羊	yáng	sheep, goat
猪	zhū	pig, hog

禽 qín birds

鸡	jī	chicken
鸭	yā	duck (the bird)
鸟	niǎo	bird

火鸡	huǒjī	turkey

海洋动物 hǎiyáng dòngwù marine animals

鱼	yú	fish
虾	xiā	shrimp
龙虾	lóngxiā	lobster
螃蟹	pángxie	（river） crab
乌龟	wūguī	tortoise
青蛙	qīngwā	frog

植物 zhíwù plants，flora；vegetables

树	shù	tree，plant
草	cǎo	grass，herbs
花	huā	flower

文化联系

Cultural Relations

中国食品 Zhōngguó shípǐn Chinese Food

饺子 jiǎozi "jiaozi"，boiled stuffed dumplings（traditional food at Chinese New Year；when the boiled stuffed dumplings are fried，they are called 锅贴 guōtiē "pot-stickers"）

长寿面 chángshòumiàn long-life noodles（eaten at weddings and birthdays）

年糕 niángāo lunar New Year's cake（made with glutinous rice flour）

元宵 yuánxiāo sweet glutinous rice flour dumpling（prepared for the Lantern Festival）

月饼 yuèbing moon cake（eaten during Mid-autumn Festival）

粽子 zòngzi "zongzi"（pyramid-shaped glutinous rice dumpling

with various fllings, special food at the Dragon Boat Festival)

中国珍宝 Zhōngguó zhēnbǎo Chinese Treasures

珍奇动物 zhēnqí dòngwù (precious) rare animals

熊猫	xióngmāo	panda
金丝猴	jīnsīhóu	golden monkey
丹顶鹤	dāndǐnghè	red-crowned crane
东北虎	dōngběihǔ	Manchurian tiger
雪豹	xuěbào	snow leopard

吉祥物 jíxiángwù lucky charms, mascots (for sports teams)

松柏	sōngbǎi	pine and cypress (as a symbol of fidelity)
寿桃	shòutáo	long-life peach (as a symbol of immortality)
鲤鱼	lǐyú	carp (as a symbol of prosperity)
牡丹	mǔdan	peony (as a national flower)
福娃	fúwá	blessed baby (as a symbol of happiness/hope)
红包	hóngbāo	red wrapping (gift of money wrapped in red paper)

23

季节与天气

Seasons and Weather

季节与天气是个经久不衰的话题。本节集中介绍跟此话题密切相关的词汇和句型。不同的年级和不同水平的学生都可以根据学习的要求加减学习的内容。

Seasons and weather is a classic topic. This chapter concentrates on vocabulary and sentence patterns related to this topic. Learners of all ages and levels may choose from the content according to the needs.

教学重点 Content of Teaching and Learning

季节	Seasons
四季	Four seasons
季节变化	Changing Seasons
天气	Weather
描述天气	Describing Weather
天气预报	Weather Fore cast
温度	Temperature
描述温度	Describing Tenperature

教学难点 Difficulties

一年四季	Seasons in the Year
描述天气	Describing Weather
温度	Temperature

词汇表 Glossary

季节	Seasons
天气	Weather
温度	Temperature

教学重点

Content of Teaching and Learning

季节 Seasons

四季 sìjì four seasons

Yì nián yǒu sì ge jìjié
一 年 有 四 个 季节。
In some places, there are four seasons in a year.

春季（春天）	chūnjì	spring, springtime
夏季（夏天）	xiàjì	summer
秋季（秋天）	qiūjì	fall, autumn
冬季（冬天）	dōngjì	winter

Yì nián zhǐyǒu liǎng jì
一 年 只有 两 季。
In other places, there are only two seasons in a year.

旱季	hànjì	dry season
雨季	yǔjì	rainy season

季节变化 Changing Seasons

1）表季节或时间的变化在句末用“了”。请参看第13章关于“了”的用法部分。

To indicate the time/season changes, we use “了” at the end of the sentence. For more details on use of “le” and “le” indicating change, please refer to “When/How to use ‘了’” in Chapter 13.

Dōngtiān guòqu le chūntiān dàolái le
冬天 过去 了，春天 到来 了。
Winter passes, spring arrives.

Shù lǜ le huā kāi le xiǎocǎo zhǎng chulai le
树 绿 了，花 开 了，小草 长 出来 了。
Trees are turning green, flowers are blossoming, and the grass is growing.

2）表季节变化还可以用比较。请参看第20章：比较。

To indicate change, we may also use comparison. For more details on comparisons, please refer to the Chapter 20: Comparison.

Chūntiān tiānqì yì tiān bǐ yì tiān nuǎnhuo le
春天 天气 一 天 比 一 天 暖和 了。
In spring, the weather gets warmer day by day.

Jīnnián dōngtiān méiyǒu qùnián nàme lěng
今年 冬天 没有 去年 那么 冷。
This winter is not as cold as last year.

Zhījiāgē de dōngtiān gēn Běijīng chàbuduō yíyàng
芝加哥 的 冬天 跟 北京 差不多 一样。
The winter in Chicago is almost the same as that in Beijing.

3）表季节的时间长短，还可以用时间段。请参看第一章：时间。

To indicate duration of a season, we may use time duration. For more details on time duration, please refer to Chapter 1: Time.

Zhījiāgē de chūntiān hěn duǎn shì cóng sān yuè dào wǔ yuè
芝加哥 的 春天 很 短，是 从 三 月 到 五 月，
zhǐyǒu liǎng ge yuè
只有 两 个 月。
In Chicago, spring is short. It lasts from March to May, only for two months.

天气 tiānqì Weather

描述天气 Describing Weather

句型 Sentence Patterns:

1）又……又…… not only... but also...

Chūntiān chángcháng yòu guā fēng yòu xià yǔ
春天 常常 又 刮 风 又 下 雨。
It is windy and also rainy in spring.

2）不……不…… neither... nor...

Qiūtiān bù lěng yě bú rè
秋天 不 冷 也 不 热。
It is not cold nor hot in the fall.

3）有时候……有时候…… sometimes... sometimes...

Dōngtiān yǒu shíhou guā dà fēng yǒu shíhou xià dà xuě
冬天 有 时候 刮 大 风，有 时候 下 大 雪。

In winter, sometimes it has strong wind, sometimes it has heavy snow.

两个不同的中文句子表达同一个英文的意思：

There are two ways to say the same thing:

A. 有（刮） noun

Jīntiān yǒu(guā) dà fēng
今天 有（刮）大 风 。
It has strong wind today.（It is very windy today.）

B. verb 得 怎么样（adjective）

Jīntiān guā fēng guā de hěn dà
今天 刮 风 刮 得 很 大 。
Today's wind is blowing hard.（It is very windy today.）

问句 Question

问天气情况

The typical way to inquire about weather is by using "怎么样".

Zuìjìn de tiānqì zěnmeyàng
最近 的 天气 怎么样 ？
How has the weather been lately?

有关词汇 Expressions to Describe Weather

1）形容词（Adjectives:）

冷	lěng	cold
热	rè	hot
暖和	nuǎnhuo	nice and warm
凉快	liángkuai	pleasantly cool
潮湿	cháoshī	moist, damp
闷热	mēnrè	hot and stuffy
晴	qíng	sunny, clear, fine
阴	yīn	cloudy
多云	duōyún	partially cloudy

2）名词（Nouns:）

晴天	qíngtiān	fine day, clear weather

阴天 yīntiān cloudy day, overcast sky

3）成语（Idioms, Set Phrases:） 理想的天气 Ideal Weather

四季分明 sìjì fēnmíng four seasons are distinct

四季如春 sìjì rú chūn like spring all year round

冬暖夏凉 dōng nuǎn xià liáng winter is warm and summer is cool

天高气爽 tiān gāo qì shuǎng high sky and refreshing air of autumn

北京的四季 Four Seasons in Beijing:

Běijīng yì nián sìjì fēnmíng
北京 一 年 四季 分明 。
Beijing has four distinctive seasons.

Chūntiān tiānqì nuǎnhuo
春天 天气 暖和 。
The weather in spring is warm.

Xiàtiān yòu mēn yòu rè
夏天 又 闷 又 热 。
Summer is hot and suffocating.

Qiūtiān liángkuai tiān gāo qì shuǎng bù lěng yě bú rè
秋天 凉快 ，天 高 气 爽 不 冷 也 不 热 。
Fall is cool. The sky is high and the air is fresh. It is neither too hot nor too cold.

Dōngtiān lěng yǒu shíhou guā dàfēng yǒu shíhou xià dàxuě
冬天 冷 ，有 时候 刮 大风 ，有 时候 下 大雪 。
Winter is cold. Sometimes, it is windy, sometimes, it is snowy.

天气预报 tiānqì yùbào Weather Report, Weather Forecast

What do we have today? Actions:

下 xià (of rain, snow, etc.) fall

下雨 xià yǔ rain

大雨	dàyǔ	heavy rain
小雨	xiǎoyǔ	light rain
毛毛雨	máomaoyǔ	drizzle
暴雨	bàoyǔ	rainstorm
暴风雨	bàofēngyǔ	storm

	下雪	xià xuě	snow	
		大雪	dàxuě	heavy snow
		小雪	xiǎoxuě	light snow
		暴风雪	bàofēngxuě	snowstorm，blizzard
		雨夹雪	yǔjiāxuě	sleet
	下雾	xià wù	mist，fog	
	下霜	xià shuāng	be covered with frost	
	下雹子	xià báozi	hailstone	
刮	guā	（of the wind）blow		
	刮风	guā fēng	（of the wind）blow	
		大风	dàfēng	strong wind
		小风	xiǎofēng	light breeze，slight wind
		轻风	qīngfēng	light breeze
		台风	táifēng	typhoon
		暴风	bàofēng	storm wind
		龙卷风	lóngjuǎnfēng	tornado
打	dǎ	strike，hit		
	打雷	dǎ léi	thunder	
闪	shǎn	lightning，flash		
	闪电	shǎndiàn	lightning	
出	chū	arise，emerge，appear		
	出太阳	chū tàiyáng	sun comes out，sunshine	
	出彩虹	chū cǎihóng	rainbow appears	

温度 Temperature

温度的度量用“度”。美国用华氏，中国用摄氏。

描述温度 Describing Temperature

Measurement of Temperature：

Temperature is measured using "度 dù degree ".

Two systems of measuring temperature are in use：

a. 摄氏 shèshì Celsius or centigrade

b. 华氏 huáshì Fahrenheit

The U. S uses Fahrenheit to measure the temperature. China uses Celsius.

Description of Temperature：

The description of temperature is "高 gāo high " or "低 dī low ".

temperature is high or low：

温度高 温度低

high or low temperature：

高温 低温

有关词汇 Related Expressions

气温	qìwēn	atmospheric temperature, air temperature
体温	tǐwēn	body temperature
室温	shìwēn	indoor temperature, room temperature
摄氏	shèshì	Celsius, Centigrade
华氏	huáshì	Fahrenheit
度	dù	degree (are in temperature, angle, latitude)
最高气温	zuì gāo qìwēn	highest air temperature
最低气温	zuì dī qìwēn	lowest air temperature
平均温度	píngjūn wēndù	average temperature
零上	língshàng	above zero (temperature)
零下	língxià	below zero (temperature)
	língxià dù 零下 30 度	30 degrees below zero

教学难点

Difficulties

难点一　一年四季 Seasons in the Year

英文说“spring 2006”。中文说“2006 年春天”。

中文的季节表达有两点要强调：

1）中文的时间表达总是从大概念到小概念。

2）季节总是与当年的时间概念联系在一起。

In English, we say “spring 2006.”

In Chinese, we say “2006 年春天”. As with any time expressions, the broader concept goes before the smaller one. A year is longer than a season, therefore all seasons fall into a year's time frame.

This year's seasons	Last year's seasons
jīnnián chūntiān 今年　春天 jīnnián xiàtiān 今年　夏天 jīnnián qiūtian 今年　秋天 jīnnián dōngtiān 今年　冬天	qùnián chūntiān 去年　春天 qùnián xiàtiān 去年　夏天 qùnián qiūtian 去年　秋天 qùnián dōngtiān 去年　冬天

难点二　描述天气 Describing Weather

请注意中英文的表达的不同：

In English, we say “It is windy/rainy today”.

In Chinese, there is no literal translation. We use two patterns to say the same thing.

Jīntiān yǒu guā dà fēng
今天 有/刮 大 风。
There is (blows) a strong wind today. (It is very windy today.) or
Jīntiān de fēng guā fēng guā de hěn dà
今天(的 风)刮 风 刮 得 很 大。
Today's wind is blowing hard. (It is very windy today.)

Also, in English, we say, "It is sunny today".

In Chinese, we may express the same idea in two ways:

	Jīntiān hěn qíng	
(Description)	今天 很 晴。	It is clear today.
	Jīntiān shì qíngtiān	
(Identification)	今天 是 晴天。	Today is a clear day.

难点三 温度 Temperature

请注意中英文的表达的不同：

There are three aspects relating to describing temperature that need to be stressed.

1) Since there are two systems of measuring temperature, with the U.S. using Fahrenheit and China using celsius, it is important for the learners to be aware of the difference.

Two systems of temperatures are

摄氏	shèshì	Celsius, centigrade
华氏	huáshì	Fahrenheit

2) There are three types of commonly used temperatures:

气温	qìwēn	atmospheric temperature, air temperature
体温	tǐwēn	body temperature
室温	shìwēn	indoor temperature, room temperature

3) Reading "below zero" in Chinese:

零上	língshàng	above zero (temperature)
零下	língxià	below zero (temperature)

In English, you say: 30 below zero

In Chinese，we say： língxià sānshí dù
零下 30 度

你知道以下的常识吗？Did you know?

正常室温 zhèngcháng shìwēn normal indoor temperature（room temperature）

The normal/comfortable air temperature and room temperature is：

摄氏 20 到 22 度	20 to 22 degrees Celsius/centigrade
华氏 68 到 72 度	68 to 72 degrees Fahrenheit

正常体温 zhèngcháng tǐwēn normal body temperature

The normal body temperature is：

摄氏 36. 6 度	36. 6 degrees Celsius/centigrade
华氏 96 度	96 degrees Fahrenheit

And at one point，-40 degrees，Fahrenheit and Celsius are the same.

摄氏零下 40 度	40 below zero degrees centigrade
华氏零下 40 度	40 below zero degrees Fahrenheit

24

健康/身体/看病

Health/Body/See a Doctor

谈到健康就难免涉及目前的状况和过去的经历。这节列出所需的句型和词汇让两者顺理成章，教学的重点以词汇开始以便利与其他话题的灵活组合。

When speaking about health and sickness, we cannot avoid talking about the present situation and past experiences. This chapter aims to relate the present situation with the past by supplying sentence structures and vocabularies for health, the body and seeing a doctor. The content of teaching and learning begins with vocabulary easily combined with other possible thematic unit designs.

教学重点 Content of Teaching and Learning

身体部位	Body Parts
症状	Symptoms
去医院	Going to Hospital
谈经历	Discussing Past Experience

教学难点 Difficulties

“过” vs. “了”	
动量词“次”	Measure Word for Action—“次”
看病	Seeing a Doctor
“大夫” vs. “医生”	How to Refer to a Doctor?

词汇表 Glossary

身体部位	Body Parts
与得病有关的说法	Expressions Related to Illness
常见病名表	Names of Common Illnesses
常见病症	Common Symptoms
看病相关用语	Expressions Related to Hospital

教学重点

Content of Teaching and Learning

身体部位 Body Parts

头部	tóubù	head	
	头	tóu	head
	脸	liǎn	face，front（part）
	眼睛	yǎnjing	eye
	眉毛	méimao	eyebrow
	鼻子	bízi	nose
	耳朵	ěrduo	ear
	嘴	zuǐ	mouth
	牙	yá	tooth
	舌头	shétou	tongue
	下巴	xiàba	chin，lower jaw
	胡子	húzi	beard，goatee，moustache
	头发	tóufa	hair（on human head）
	脖子	bózi	neck
	嗓子	sǎngzi	throat，larynx
	喉咙	hóulóng	throat
肢体	zhītǐ	four limbs，body	
	胸	xiōng	chest
	后背	hòubèi	back（of the body，etc.）
	肩（膀）	jiān（bǎng）	shoulder
	胳膊	gēbo	arm
	肘	zhǒu	elbow

手	shǒu	hand
手腕	shǒuwàn	wrist （of the hand）
手掌	shǒuzhǎng	palm （of the hand）
手指	shǒuzhǐ	finger
腰	yāo	waist
屁股	pìgu	butt，behind
腿	tuǐ	leg
大腿	dàtuǐ	thigh
小腿	xiǎotuǐ	lower leg，shin，shank
膝盖	xīgài	knee
脚	jiǎo	foot
脚腕(踝)	jiǎowàn （huái）	ankle
脚趾	jiǎozhǐ	toe

脏器 zàngqì internal organs

心	xīn	heart
肺	fèi	lung
肝	gān	liver
胃	wèi	stomach
肾	shèn	kidney
脾	pí	spleen

症状 Symptoms

相关词汇 Expressions related to illness

病 bìng ill，illness，sickness，disease

become ill：

有病(yǒu bìng)/生病(shēng bìng)/得病(dé bìng)

serious illness：

重病（zhòng bìng）/大病（dà bìng）

seriously ill：

病得重（zhòng）/病得厉害（lìhai）

minor illness：

小病（xiǎo bìng）

not seriously ill

病得轻（qīng）

see a doctor

看病 kàn bìng see a doctor

去医院看病/去大夫那儿看病

病名 Names of Illnesses

感冒	gǎnmào	cold，common cold，flu
心脏病	xīnzàngbìng	heart disease
肺炎	fèiyán	pneumonia
肝炎	gānyán	hepatitis
肾炎	shènyán	nephritis
过敏	guòmǐn	allergy，hypersensitive
高血压	gāoxuèyā	high blood pressure，hypertension
低血压	dīxuèyā	low blood pressure

病症 bìngzhèng Symptoms of Illness

发烧	fāshāo	have a fever，run a temperature
咳嗽	késou	cough
流鼻涕	liú bítì	have a running nose
打喷嚏	dǎ pēntì	sneeze
拉肚子	lā dùzi	have diarrhoea
痒	yǎng	itch
难受	nánshòu	feel ill
不舒服	bù shūfu	uncomfortable，not feeling well，ill
疼	téng	ache，pain

头疼	tóu téng	headache
牙疼	yá téng	toothache
腿疼	tuǐ téng	pain in the leg
腰疼	yāo téng	backache, lumbago
嗓子疼	sǎngzi téng	sour throat
肚子疼	dùzi téng	abdomen pain

去医院 Going to Hospital

地点 Places

医院	yīyuàn	hospital
诊所	zhěnsuǒ	clinic
医务室	yīwùshì	medical clinic
药房	yàofáng	drugstore, pharmacy

医务人员 Medical Personnel

大夫	dàifu	doctor, physican
医生	yīshēng	doctor, physician
护士	hùshi	nurse (in a hospital)
药剂师	yàojìshī	pharmacist

检查 Physical Examination

检查	jiǎnchá	inspect, check, examine	
体检	tǐjiǎn	physical examination	
量	liáng	measure	
	体温	tǐwēn	body temperature
	身高	shēngāo	height(of a person)
	体重	tǐzhòng	body weight
	血压	xuèyā	blood pressure
化验	huàyàn	laboratory test	
	大便	dàbiàn	stool, feces

- 小便 xiǎobiàn urine
- 血 xiě blood
- 照 X 光 zhào X-guāng take an X-ray
- 透视 tòushì have an X-ray taken

开药 Prescribing Medicine

- 吃药 chī yào take medicine
  - 西药 xīyào Western medicine
  - 中药 zhōngyào traditional Chinese medicine
  - 药片 yàopiàn pill
  - 药水 yàoshuǐ liquid medicine
- 打针 dǎ zhēn give or receive an injection
- 药方 yàofāng prescription

服药 fúyào Taking Medicine

- 饭前 fàn qián before meals
- 饭后 fàn hòu after meals
- 睡前 shuì qián before sleep
- 服用 fúyòng take（medicine）

用法 yòngfǎ Way of Using，Usage

- 每天三次 three times per day，or
- 一天三次 three times per day
- 每次三片 three tablets per dose，or
- 一次一片 one tablet per dose

谈经历 Discussing Past Expereince

句型 Sentence Pattern：

Verb	过（动量补语）	Object

Wǒ chī guo liǎng cì Zhōngguócài
我 吃 过 两 次 中国菜 。

Wǒ céngjīng chī guo liǎng cì Zhōngguócài
我 曾经 吃 过 两 次 中国菜 。
I have had Chinese food twice before.

功能 Function：

Discussing about past experience. 谈经历。

提问 Questions：

Experience

Nǐ chī guo Zhōngguócài ma
你 吃 过 中国菜 吗？
Have you ever had Chinese food?

Frequency

Nǐ chī guo jǐ cì
你 吃 过 几 次？
How many times have you had Chinese food?

Conditions

Nǐ shì shénme shíhou chī de
你 是 什么 时候 吃 的？
When did you have it?

Nǐ shì zài shénme dìfang chī de
你 是 在 什么 地方 吃 的？
Where did you have it?

Nǐ shì zěnme qù de
你 是 怎么 去 的？
How did you go there?

(See 教学难点 for more detailed explanations)

教学难点

Difficulties

难点一 “过”vs.“了”

“过”和“了”所指不同。“过”强调过去经历，“了”强调特定事件的一次性完成。

“过” and “了” both can be put after a verb. “过” emphasizes the action as a past experience, while “了” indicates the completeness of a one-time occurrence.

我去过中国城，我吃过中国菜。(as a past experience)
I have been to Chinatown and I have had Chinese Food.

昨天我去了芝加哥的中国城，我吃了中国菜。(as a one-time action)
Yesterday I went to Chicago's Chinatown and I had some Chinese food.

难点二 动量词“次”Measure Word for Action“次”

“次”是最常用的动量词。见以下动量词表。

“次” is the most commonly used measure word for actions. There are others. See below to examine the subtle differences.

常用动量词使用比较表 Commonly Used Measure Words for Actions

遍 biàn emphasizes the process from beginning to end

这本书，我看了两遍。
I have read this book twice.

请你一个字写五遍。
Please write each character five times.

次 cì emphasizes the number of occurrences

这本书我看了五次才看完一遍。
I started this book five times before I finished the whole thing.

请你一次写五遍。
Every time you write, please write five times.

回 huí similar to “次”, but used informally

这个电影我看了五回。
I have seen this movie five times.

趟 tàng emphasizes back and forth (of a round trip)

昨天他去了一趟图书馆。
Yesterday, he went (took a trip) to the library.

下 xià emphasizes briefness of an action

请给她看一下。
Let her have a look.

Note

"一下" vs. Duplication of Verbs:

"一下" when suggesting briefness of action, is equivalent to duplication of verbs:

Have a look/had a look { 看一下 看一看 看看 / 看了一下 看了一看 看了看

动量词在句中的位置 Position in a Sentence

动量词在句中的位置有点复杂。见下例。

Where to place a measure word for action in a sentence is a little complicated. If the object of the action is a place/person, the position is more flexible:

(Place) 我们去过两次北京。
我们去过北京两次。

(Person) 我们见过两次这个人。
我们见过这个人两次。

If the object of the action is a thing, it can only be put before the object:

(Thing) 我们吃过两次中国菜。

难点三 看病 seeing a Doctor

英文说"go to see a doctor"，中文说"看病"。意思是说让医生看看你有什么病。

In English, we say "see a doctor".

In Chinese, we say "看病", meaning that one wants the doctor to examine the possible heacth problem one has.

去医院看病/去大夫那儿看病

难点四 “大夫” vs. “医生” How to Refer to a Doctor?

怎么称呼？叫“大夫”还是“医生”？这不是学生的问题，是老师的个人选择。

总的来说，北方人用“大夫”，南方人称“医生”。或说“大夫”是口语，“医生”是正式称呼。

“大夫”的发音是“dàifu a doctor”。

This is not a difficult point for learners. It is a teacher's preference.

Generally speaking, people from northern part of China call a doctor “大夫”, while people from south China call a doctor “医生”. Since the Common Speech “普通话” that we teach is based on the pronunciation of northern dialects, we generalize that “大夫” is a colloquial expression and “医生” is a formal title. Also, the pronunciation of “大夫” is “dàifu a doctor”.

Index
索引

语法教学内容 Grammatical Coverage

(Chapter Number in A Functional and Grammatical Walkthrough)

Phonetic Chart
汉语语音表
(与 bopomofo 对照)

Group One Finals

		a	o	e	er	-i	ai	an	ang	ao	ei	en	eng	ong
	b	ba	bo				bai	ban	bang	bao	bei	ben	beng	
	p	pa	po				pai	pan	pang	pao	pei	pen	peng	
	m	ma		me			mai	man	mang	mao	mei	men	meng	
	f	fa						fan	fang		fei	fen	feng	
	d	da		de			dai	dan	dang	dao	dei		deng	dong
	t	ta		te			tai	tan	tang	tao			teng	tong
	n	na		ne			nai	nan	nang	nao	nei	nen	neng	nong
	l	la		le			lai	lan	lang	lao	lei		leng	long
	g	ga		ge			gai	gan	gang	gao	gei	gen	geng	gong
	k	ka		ke			kai	kan	kang	kao		ken	keng	kong
	h	ha		he			hai	han	hang	hao	hei	hen	heng	hong
	j													
	q													
	x													
	zh	zha				zhi	zhai	zhan	zhang	zhao	zhei	zhen	zheng	zhong
	ch	cha				chi	chai	chan	chang	chao		chen	cheng	chong
	sh	sha				shi	shai	shan	shang	shao	shei	shen	sheng	
	r					ri		ran	rang	rao		ren	reng	rong
	z	za				zi	zai	zan	zang	zao	zei	zen	zeng	zong
	c	ca				ci	cai	can	cang	cao		cen	ceng	cong
	s	sa				si	sai	san	sang	sao		sen	seng	song
		a	o	e	er		ai	an	ang	ao	ei	en	eng	ong

Group Two Finals: "i" and "i" Sounds

		i	ia	ian	iang	iao	ie	in	ing	iong	iou
	b	bi		bian		biao	bie	bin	bing		
	p	pi		pian		piao		pin	ping		
	m	mi		mian		miao		min	ming		
	f										
	d	di		dian							
	t	ti		tian							
	n	ni		nian							
	l	li		lian							
	g										
	k										
	h										
	j	ji	jia	jian	jiang	jiao	jie	jin	jing	jiong	jiu
	q	qi	qia	qian	qiang	qiao	qie	qin	qing	qiong	qiu
	x	xi	xia	xian	xiang	xiao	xie	xin	xing	xiong	xiu
	zh										
	ch										
	sh										
	r										
	z										
	c										
	s										
		yi	ya	yan	yang	yao	ye	yin	ying	yong	you

Group Three Finals: "u" and "u" Sounds

		u	ua	uai	uan	uang	uei	uen	ueng	uo	uong
	b	bu									

	p	pu									
	m	mu									
	f	fu									
	d	du			duan		dui	dun		duo	
	t	tu			tuan		tui	tun		tuo	
	n	nu			nuan					nuo	
	l	lu			luan			lun		luo	
	g	gu	gua	guai	guan	guang	gui	gun		guo	
	k	ku	kua	kuai	kuan	kuang	kui	kun		kuo	
	h	hu	hua	huai	huan	huang	hui	hun		huo	
	j										
	q										
	x										
	zh	zhu	zhua	zhuai	zhuan	zhuang	zhui	zhun		zhuo	
	ch	chu		chuai	chuan	chuang	chui	chun		chuo	
	sh	shu	shua	shuai	shuan	shuang	shui	shun		shuo	
	r	ru			ruan		rui	run		ruo	
	z	zu			zuan		zui	zun		zuo	
	c	cu			chuan		cui	cun		cuo	
	s	su			suan		sui	sun		suo	
		wu	wa	wai	wan	wang	wei	wen	weng	wo	wong

Group Four Finals: “ü” and “ü” Sounds

		ü	üe	üan	üen
	b				
	p				
	m				
	f				

	d				
	t				
	n	nü	nüe		
	l	lü	lüe		
	g				
	k				
	h				
	j	ju	jue	juan	jun
	q	qu	que	quan	qun
	x	xu	xue	xuan	xun
	zh				
	ch				
	sh				
	r				
	z				
	c				
	s				
		yu	yue	yuan	yun

Reference

建议参考资料

This series focuses on concrete examples and practical tips for classroom teaching and learning. For teachers who are interested in current research, theoretical frameworks and further guidance and tools, we provide a topical list of references.

这套书主要是为初高中学汉语课堂教与学提供操作实例和具体技巧。都是经验之谈。对相关教学研究、教学理论或纲要及工具有兴趣的老师,可参阅下列书目和网址。参考资料也是按题目排列的。

Adolescent Psychology

Rice, F. Philip. *The Adolescent — Development, Relationships, and Culture.* Needham Height, MA: Allyn & Bacon, 1999.

Assessment and Rubric

Bachman, L. F. & A. S. Palmer. *Language Testing in Practice.* Oxford: Oxford University Press, 1996.

Pearson Education Development Group. *Authentic Assessment Overview.* Retrieved from http://teachervision. fen. com/teaching-methods/educational-testing/4911. html

Chicago Public Schools. *The Rubric Bank.* Retrieved from http://www. cps. k12. il. us

The Web Portal for Educators! At http://www. teach-nology. com

Oral Language Assessment — *Oral Proficiency Interview (OPI)* and Written Language Assessment — *Written Proficiency Test (WPT).* Retrieved from http://www.languagetesting.com

Hancock, Charles R. *Alternative Assessment and Second Language.* ERIC Clearinghouse on Languages and Linguistics Washington D. C., 1994.

Baker, E. L., O'Neill, H. F., Jr., & Linn, R. L. (1993). Policy and validity prospects for performance-based assessments. *American Psychologist*, *48*, 1210 – 1218.

U. S. Congress, Office of Technology Assessment. (1992, February). *Testing in American schools: Asking the right questions.* (OTA-SET-519). Washington, D. C.: U. S. Government Printing Office.

Bloom's Taxonomy

Bloom, Benjamin S. *Taxonomy of Educational Objectives.* Boston MA: Allyn & Bacon, 1984.

Differentiated Instruction

Tomlinson, C. *How to Differentiate Instruction in Mixed-ability Classrooms.* Alexandria, VA: ASCD, 1995.

Tomlinson, C. *The Differentiated Classroom: Responding to the Needs of All Learners.* Alexandria, VA: ASCD, 1999.

Wiggins, G. & McTighe, J. *Understanding by Design.* Alexandria, VA: ASCD, 1998.

Chinese Grammar

黎锦熙,刘世儒.《汉语语法十八课》. 北京:商务印书馆,1964.

李德津,程美珍.《外国人实用汉语语法》. 北京:华语教学出版社,1988.

Cooperative Learning

Silver, Strong, & Perini. *So Each May Learn, Alexandria.* VA: Association for Supervision and Curriculum Development, 2000.

David & Roger Johnson. *Learning Together and Alone.* NJ: Prentice Hall, 1999.

Foreign Language Teaching and Learning Standards

ACTFL Foreign Language Learning Standards. Retrieved from http://www.actfl.org

ACTFL Performance Guidelines for K-12 Learners. Yonkers, NY: The American Council on the Teaching of Foreign Languages, 1998.

Language Learning

Curtain, H. & Carol Ann Dahlberg. *Language and Children — Making the Match.* Boston: Pearson Education, Inc., 2004.

Learning

Sousa, David A. *How the Brain Learns.* NASSP, VA: Corwin Press, 2000.

Multiple Intelligences

Gardner, Howard. *Frames of Mind: The Theory of Multiple Intelligences.* New York: Basic, 1983.

Gardner, Howard. *Multiple Intelligences: The Theory in Practice.* New York: Basic, 1993.

Gardner, Howard. *Intelligence Reframed: Multiple Intelligences for the 21st Century.* New York: Basic, 2000

Armstrong, Thomas. *Multiple Intelligences in the Classroom.* Alexandria, VA: Association for Supervision and Curriculum Development, 1994.

Problem Solving

Stanovich, Keith E. *Progress in Understanding Reading: Scientific Foundations and New Frontiers.* New York: Gilford Press, 2000.

Woll, Stanley. *Everyday Thinking: Memory, Reasoning, and Judgment in the*

Real World. Mahwah NJ: Lawrence Erlbaum Associates, Inc. , 2001.

Reading

Koda, Keiko Koda. *Insights into Second Language Reading.* Cambridge: Cambridge University Press, 2005.

Alderson, C. *Assessing Reading.* New York: Cambridge University Press, 2000.

Day, R. R. & Bamford, J. *Extensive Reading in the Second Language Classroom.* New York: Cambridge University Press, 1998.

Grabe, W. & Stoller, F. *Teaching and Researching Reading: Applied Linguistics in Action.* New York: Longman, 2002.

Pressley, M. *Reading Instruction that Works.* New York: Guilford, 1998.

Reading Critically. Reading Guide. Retrieved from http://writing.colostate.edu/guides/reading/critread/pop4b.cfm

Student-Centered Learning

Aaronsohn, Elizabeth. *Going Against the Grain: Supporting the Student-Centered Teacher.* Thousand Oaks: Corwin Press. 1996.

Benson, P. & Voller, P. *Autonomy and Independence in Language Learning.* London: Longman, 1996.

Tudor, I. *Learner-Centeredness as Language Education.* Cambridge: Cambridge University Press, 1996.

Task-based Learning

Krashen, S. D. *Principles and Practices in Second Language Acquisition.* New York: Prentice Hall, 1987.

Willis, J. A *Framework for Tasked-Based Learning.* London: Longman, 1996.

Thematic Instruction

Bruning, R. H. , Schraw, G. J. , & Ronning, R. R. *Cognitive Psychology and Instruction.* Englewood Cliffs, NJ: Merrill, 1999.

Vogt, M. (1997). *Cross-Curricular Thematic Instruction.* Retrieved from http://www. eduplace. com/rdg/res/vogt. html

National Standards in Foreign Language Education Project. (1996). Retrieved from http://www. actfl. org

TPR

Seely & Elizabeth Kuizenga Romijn. *TPR is More Than Commands — At All Levels.* Berkeley California, 1995.

US Department of Education — Teacher to Teacher Initiative Workshops on Chinese Language Teaching. (2006). Retrieved from http://www. t2tweb. us/Workshops/Sessions. asp

Bibliography
参考书目

ACTFL Foreign Language Learning Standards. Retrieved from http://www. actfl. org

Bachman, L. F. & A. S. Palmer. *Language Testing in Practice*. Oxford: Oxford University Press, 1996.

Bloom, Benjamin S. *Taxonomy of Educational Objectives*. Boston MA: Allyn & Bacon, 1984.

Chicago Public Schools. *The Rubric Bank*. Retrieved from http://www. cps. k12. il. us

Curtain, H. & Carol Ann Dahlberg. *Language and Children — Making the Match*. Boston: Pearson Education, Inc. , 2004.

Krashen, S. D. *Principles and Practices in Second Language Acquisition*. New York: Prentice Hall, 1987.

黎锦熙,刘世儒.《汉语语法十八课》. 北京:商务印书馆,1964.

Rice, F. Philip. *The Adolescent — Development, Relationships, and Culture*. Needham Height, MA: Allyn & Bacon, 1999.

Silver , Strong, & Perini. *So Each May Learn*. Alexandria, VA: Association for Supervision and Curriculum Development, 2000.

The Web Portal for Educators! At http://www. teach-nology. com

US Department of Education — Teacher to Teacher Initiative Workshops on Chinese Language Teaching. (2006). Retrieved from http://www. t2tweb. us/ Workshops/Sessions. asp